A DIP IN THE
OCEAN

ROWING SOLO ACROSS THE INDIAN

SARAH OUTEN

Foreword by
DAME ELLEN MACARTHUR

A DIP IN THE OCEAN

Summersdale Publishers Ltd
46 West Street
Chichester
West Sussex
PO19 1RP
UK

www.summersdale.com

Printed and bound in Great Britain

ISBN: 978-1-84953-127-6

For Dad, thank you for showing me how to live

For Mum, thank you for helping me chase the dreams

For Taid, I wish I could have written this faster

Thank you for seeing me home

'It is not the goal but the way there that matters and the harder the way, the more worthwhile the journey'

SIR WILFRED THESIGER

I've received a splendid email
From a most courageous female.
Battling onward to Mauritius,
Lone among the flying fishes,
Albatrosses, giant whales,
Turning turtle in the gales.
To hell with Health and Safety rules,
She's in tune with tuna schools.
She'll dance, while others dance in bars,
With pilot fish and Pilot Stars.

I have not the faintest notion
How to brave the Indian Ocean
In anything that keeps afloat,
Let alone a rowing boat.
But Sarah takes it in her stride,
And going with her, for the ride,
A book, or audio CD
Read by Lalla and by me.
To speed her trip to its conclusion
We're reading her The God Delusion!

So fly the flags, with sirens hootin',
And raise a glass to Sarah Outen.

RICHARD DAWKINS

CONTENTS

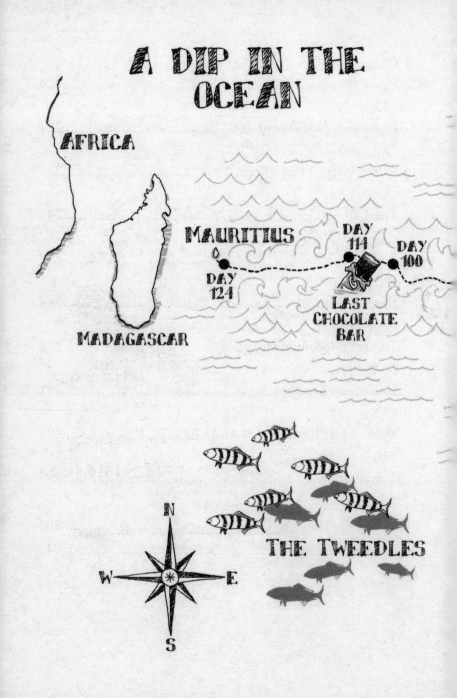

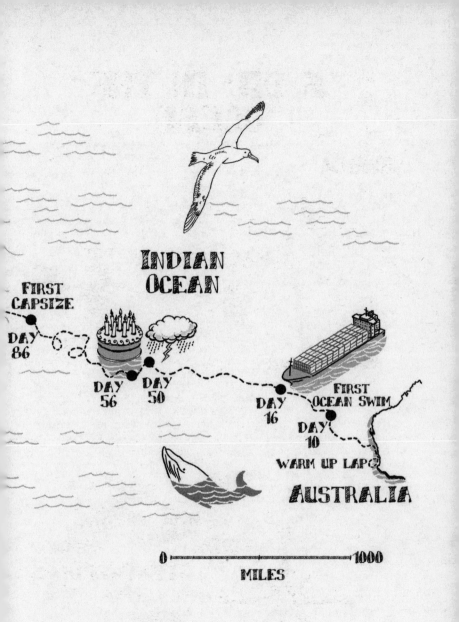

FOREWORD

by Dame Ellen MacArthur

When I first met Sarah at the London Boat Show she was full of energy, humour and adventure and I warmed to her instantly. Reading this book you will warm to her too. She is honest, open, courageous and inspiring, and taking you on her journey with her she'll have you holding your breath one minute, and then laughing out loud the next. Understanding the oceans I can just begin to comprehend what she's been through at sea, but her story on land is equally compelling. She has written this book wonderfully and has a contagious love for life which jumps right out of the pages at you! Sarah – I can't wait for your next book!

Ellen

PROLOGUE
THE SEED
IS SOWN

'Whatever you think you can do, or believe you can, begin it. Boldness has genius, power and magic in it'

GOETHE

It all started while I was at Oxford. Room 24, Main Building, St Hugh's College, December 2005. I was sitting at my desk chewing a pen, surrounded by open textbooks and piles of notes. I was trying, quite unsuccessfully, to write a proposal to study basking sharks in Scotland that summer. My degree was biology, so that wasn't unusual and neither was my procrastination; it was a rowing day after all and I was hungry for some action after too many hours indoors. I typed distractedly at my laptop, clock-watching and already thinking about my pre-training snack: a banana, a malt loaf, a Mars bar or all three? For the umpteenth time that day I opened up my inbox and read through the already-read emails, taking as much time as I possibly could. While

I was reading a new one arrived with a ping. Result; at least another two minutes of beautiful time-wasting lay ahead. I paused. And then I smiled as I read the subject line: 'Ocean Rowing Races'. This was going to be more than two minutes' grace from the proposal; it was easily the most exciting email I had ever received. I clicked and read an advert for a rowing race across the Atlantic. I had only ever rowed on the Isis and, whilst I had sailed a bit, I had never crossed an ocean. An ocean! Across a whole ocean in a rowing boat? I was speechless. I put my feet up on my desk and leant back on my chair, rocking on the two back legs in exactly the way you're always told not to as a child, thinking and spinning the pen in my fingers. I was hooked by the idea of it; oceans and rowing were two of my favourite words and I was sure that if I put the two together they would make an incredible adventure. I had always wanted to see what it was like to make a big journey in the wild under my own steam, living and breathing the raw power of the elements, at one with nature. With no specific plans for life after graduation in a year's time, I decided there and then that I would start with an ocean row. I wasn't sure which ocean, or when, or how, or who with, and I don't know why I was so sure of myself but I knew that I would do it.

In 2009 I did it, rowing solo across the Indian Ocean from Australia to Mauritius. It was a journey of more than just an ocean and it was far more than a rowing trip. It made me and it has shown me all the more clearly that life is for living, here and now, not tomorrow or some other day – because you never know what might be over the next wave or round the next corner. You have to make the most of the moment, or the adventures and opportunities might fade with the sunset and you will be forever left wondering what was over the horizon.

This is my story and I hope you enjoy it.

Sarah Outen
November 2010

CHAPTER 1
PORTRAIT OF THE ROWER AS A YOUNGSTER

'Life is either a great adventure or nothing'

HELEN KELLER

I couldn't see any clear water – it was all white behind me and more waves were breaking. I felt a cold numbing fear that I was about to be obliterated. I had just enough time to shove the phone in the cabin and lock the door before throwing myself to the deck, holding on tight to the safety rails.

As I screamed, a bomb of a wave exploded over the boat and my world went white. But it was dark somehow, beneath the water, it was loud and I could taste salt everywhere. I was a rag doll, somersaulting through the surf which was now rushing us along the reef, growing louder and louder. And then I breathed a sweet breath – we must have come back around. I had floated off *Dippers* on my line and was surrounded by fizzing water while the wave receded. I looked round and saw no one and nothing but surf. I screamed again, and even I struggled to hear it over the sound of crashing waves. *Dippers* tilted over to one side with the water on deck but I scrambled on board, heaving myself through the safety rails. An oar was broken and the throw line was tangled, but there was no time to do anything but hold on; another wave was on its way. I knew that the reef must only be metres below now and with it certain annihilation.

I remember my dad once compared me to a carthorse. I like to think that this was his way of saying that he thought I was resilient and had stamina and strength, hopefully both in mind and body. I had to be, really; I was the only girl sandwiched between my two brothers, Michael and Matthew, and our family was always on the move, professional nomads of the Royal Air Force. Dad was an officer and so change became the norm for us from very early on as we trooped all over. By my seventh birthday I had already chalked up three infant schools and lived in five different houses in three different countries. Nothing too exotic, mind; Wales is as foreign as I remember, though we lived in Europe for my first couple of years.

The lack of interesting postings was due to Dad's ill health. In my memory he always had arthritis; it was diagnosed when I was toddling about and he was just inside thirty. Unfortunately it was one of the worst forms of all – rheumatoid arthritis. This causes the immune system to go haywire, attacking itself and wreaking havoc on every joint in the body, causing inflammation, disintegration and degeneration. One of my memories is of him sitting down at the breakfast table with a mountain of tablets beside him, wearing splints on his wrists, and sometimes spending days at a time in bed, too sore to move. Too sore even for a hug. Too sore to do anything but sleep and hope and fight on for a better day. If I was a carthorse, then Dad was a superhero carthorse. When you are fighting pain twenty-four hours a day with a crumbling skeleton, stamina takes on a whole new meaning. In my mind at least, he was as strong as an ox.

Another defining period in my own evolution as a carthorse (remember, we're thinking resilience and stamina here) is my time at boarding school. When I was seven, one of my RAF friends boasted that he would be going off to boarding school the next year. I was rather in awe of the idea, and thought he must be very grown-up and that I must be missing out on some sort of grand adventure. I started a campaign of pestering to go, too, and the next school year I started at Stamford Junior School in Lincolnshire, sporting a regulation crimson corduroy beret and looking perfectly ridiculous. My older brother Michael joined the boys' version on the other side of town, with no ridiculous headwear in sight, much to my annoyance. Now, some might recoil at the thought of my cruel parents packing us off to boarding school at the sweet young age of eight and ten, but it made sense. It promised stability in our so far very unstable education; we could also make friends and keep them, settle in, and progress through school uninterrupted for the first time in our lives. My own reason for wanting to go was not at all sensible and based purely on the idea of it being a permanent sleepover, and therefore a lot of fun.

It didn't start out quite like that, and I roundly hated my first half term, writing long tear-smudged letters home to my parents warning of my bid to get myself expelled. Truth is, I had no idea about how to get myself expelled, and I don't think I had the balls to do it anyway. It was tough for my parents as well; later on, Mum said that she cried all the way home after every time she dropped us back at school at the start of term. I now see that it was a huge thing for them to do and I am grateful for it and all those useful things it taught me – independence, tolerance and friendship. Once I settled down I loved it. My favourite thing was the school grounds and the hours we spent outside playing and doing all the things inquisitive, active children love to do. Even at eight I was an adrenaline junkie, keen to test my boundaries and see how fast I could go. One day I did just that by rolling down our favourite grassy hill in a plastic barrel, emerging rather bruised and dazed at the bottom.

Thankfully, the holidays were made of real adventures; Dad knew all about these and Mum knew how to make a fine lunch, so our family was well set up for some happy times, as long as Dad wasn't too sore. At home we often pitched tents in the garden and camped out overnight, complete with hot water bottles in winter; in the summer we caravanned all over the UK and later on we had a share in a canal barge. My brothers were keen fishermen and I was quite content exploring and painting and whittling and reading, so we were easily entertained by rural campsites beneath mountains, by beaches or next to babbling rivers. As anyone who has camped in Britain knows, it was nothing flash or fancy, just freedom and encouragement to have a go at new things and enjoy our surroundings.

The Family Walk was a great tradition and we clocked some good mileage in the years before Dad's arthritis stopped them. I was nine when he first taught me about using a map and compass, which was a big step for me and very exciting. It was on a mountain walk that he and I left the rest of the family walking down the normal path, while we returned cross-country. Dad went in front with his floppy hat, big red backpack and the map around his neck and I trotted along behind, following his huge steps, and alternately singing and asking a barrage of questions as children do. We trekked through bracken, down scree slopes and skirted round bogs, Dad hauling me out when I sunk in one of the latter up to my knees.

A year later we camped under Cadair Idris, a craggy Welsh mountain, and one day went on a walk to the summit. I had actually planned what I would wear for a whole week before, such was the anticipation. As the path wound out of the campsite through the shade of the damp forest I imagined the top. Would there be a cairn? Would we see the sea? We three children played in the icy streams and scrambled on rocks the whole way up and opted for an afternoon playing in the glacier lake before the final peak rather than punching on for the summit. Dad and I went up again a few days later and this time I carried my own rucksack, full of all sorts of useless things that I was sure we couldn't do without and that of course we didn't actually use at all. The beach mat, for example – nice idea but not at all necessary. It rained all day, turning paths into streams and our boots into puddles. Mist crept over the summit ridge, alternately hiding and revealing the views as we neared the top. I was hooked – it was so mysterious and beautiful – and I found myself falling in love with the wild. After eating a stack of soggy sandwiches, while sheltering behind a rock in the whiteout, we headed back down without reaching the top. With this, I was already learning to respect the elements; formative lessons to stay with me forever. To get to the top of that mountain is still on my list of things to do, sixteen years later.

As I grew up I had more adventures and dreamed of others; I didn't know what or how or when, but I knew deep down that I wanted to make a big journey one day. I wanted to feel what I had read other people write about: excitement, fear, the unknown, the struggle, exhaustion and survival. I loved challenges, especially those where I truly didn't know if I could make it, and the satisfaction of being exhausted after a long walk or bike ride. Fear was exciting and I chased those moments where I was pushed outside my comfort zone, eager to test and show my strength. I climbed trees until branches snapped; I ran races as hard as I could until I thought I was going to faint. In my head, I was George from Enid Blyton's *Famous Five*, strong, adventurous and as stubborn as can be.

I was competitive, too, and I don't think that was entirely due to having two brothers, but more about pushing myself and testing my strength. I found it so raw, so defining to have such a narrow line between success and failure when I stepped up to the discus cage, for example, the only person in the world capable of controlling the outcome. Win or lose, it all rested on my shoulders. The more I studied and played, the more I found that perfection was untenable and always would be, which was (and still is) simultaneously motivating and frustrating. On and off the sports field, I was very driven and very busy, actively filling my time with everything I loved, mainly sport but other stuff too. People ask me what drives me, and I think part of it comes from having watched Dad suffer so horribly. It didn't take me long to work out that life is too short to wait and health too precious to waste.

I was eleven when Dad was medically discharged from the RAF in 1996. He limped more and more as his feet deteriorated, until his walk became a shuffle and his ankles were so deformed that they didn't look like ankles at all. They were swollen beyond all recognition, his toes deformed and then latterly fused solid with operations, in an attempt to stop them curling into knots. A wheelchair appeared from time to time, a walking stick at others, and then the wheelchair became the norm. Seeing my huggable giant of a dad, being beaten down like this was so sad – he had always seemed so big and strong to me, even with the arthritis. Unfortunately, his health was only ever going to get worse. The pain wasn't just physical, and with the added side effects of the drugs, he had an unthinkably rough time of it. We all did, but for him it was hideous. The drugs affected his mood, he gained weight, looked sick, felt sick and emotionally struggled with the pain and the consequences of it – the immobility, the loss of independence and freedom. In many ways I think he grew old before his time. I can't imagine how hard it must have been for Mum too, often doing the work of two parents, while also nursing him when he was at his worst. My parents' marriage is a beautiful example of unconditional, devoted and selfless love and I salute them both for showing me how to carry on through the best of times and the worst of times.

CHAPTER 2
IN THE BEGINNING WAS THE WATER

'There is nothing more enticing, disenchanting, and enslaving than the life at sea'

JOSEPH CONRAD

After Dad left the RAF we moved to Rutland so that Michael and I could carry on at Stamford as day pupils through our senior years. It is a tiny English county, nestled in the Midlands, little known and landlocked. Lots of people find it quite surprising, therefore, that I am so in love with the sea. It all started when I followed Michael to our local canoe club when I was about twelve, partly because I wanted to have a go and partly because of the need, if only in my head, to be as good as him. Sibling rivalry prevented me from admitting it at the time, but I looked up to him and still do – we are chalk and cheese in many ways, as different as black from white, but for the values and traits that we've inherited from the same gene pool. As teenagers we wound each other up so fiercely that I'm surprised Mum and Dad didn't put us up for sale but I'm happy that I followed him to the water all those years ago. I was soon hooked and found that I loved the longer journeys, especially on the coast.

So instead of revising for my exams in the summer half term of 2003, I joined a little expedition up in the Hebrides, the rugged islands off the west coast of Scotland. I was charmed by the spirit of the place, the raw untamed energy that showed itself when a storm burst out of a calm seascape and rattled through a camp in moments. At the other extreme, I also loved the still nights, and spent a couple of them under the stars, sleeping on the beach for the first time in my life. I remember one night bedding down in my sleeping bag as waves tickled the shore nearby and lulled me to sleep. Waking up to see the stars stretched right across the sky was a gorgeous, breathtaking moment, especially as it meant I could wriggle down into my bag again and sleep some more. The next morning, as the grapefruit sky roused the oystercatchers, my friend tried to do the same to me. I opened one eye and saw the sea lapping at my sleeping bag, the kayaks already floating and tugging at their lines; we were about to be stranded on an uninhabited island. I'm glad she woke me up.

As well as admiring the beauty of these places, I also came to understand that I loved being the engine that took me there, creating the force behind the speed, or at least in control of it. To use my own wit and muscle to journey from A to B was so simple and satisfying; that's why rowing captured my imagination after watching Sir Steve Redgrave and his crew on TV racing to gold at the Sydney Olympics in 2000. They were so skilful, so powerful and the whole thing so spine-tinglingly alluring that I decided that I wanted to row and race one day. I had also been inspired by seeing Dame Ellen MacArthur shaking up the sailing world with great results in the Vendée Globe in 2001 – as a young woman making a name for herself in the medal positions in this male-dominated sport, it made me think that one day I would like to go to sea too. I say one day as there was nowhere to row in Rutland. As I was already super busy with other stuff, I put these ideas on my list of things to do another day and I planned to start rowing when I headed off to university.

A teacher suggested I was capable of winning a place at Oxford and I figured that if anyone knew how to row it would be those folks in dark blue, their famous crew colours. All my university choices were based on whether I would be able to row, shortly after whether I could study biology – sadly none offered joint honours in the two. With no idea how to choose which one of the thirty-something Oxford colleges to apply to, I based my choice on the pictures in the brochure, which showed Worcester College had its own lake and a boathouse on the river. The interview at Worcester terrified and confused me – partly because one of the interviewers was Chinese and I didn't understand what she was saying and partly because I felt way out my depth. I also decided at this time that I didn't like the silly rule about not walking on the grass in the quad. Why plant grass that you can't walk on? A second interview at Hertford

College was less terrifying and actually good fun, mostly because the tutor handed me a live grasshopper and asked me to talk about it – which was much less daunting than the confusing stuff I had been challenged with at Worcester. I left Oxford 103 per cent certain that I wouldn't be going there, but feeling like I had redeemed myself with some sensible and cogent grasshopper comments. Either way, I was fully prepared for the rejection letter from Worcester which I received a little white later and not too bothered by the bit that said I had been 'pooled', which effectively meant that I might be offered a place at a different college if another had space.

I put it out of my head and thought nothing more of it until a few days later I took a call from Dr Iles, Biology Fellow of St Hugh's College, asking me if I would like to come and study there instead. Apparently Worcester had been impressed by my interview but hadn't had space for me, so the place at Hugh's was mine if I wanted it. I paused, nibbling my lip and twirling the phone cord round my thumb. Then very calmly I said I would need to consider and visit to see if I liked the college. Idiot child! Who in their right mind says they will sit and think about an offer from Oxford, one of the world's leading centres of thinking, research and, importantly, a flippin' good place to row? Muppet Outen. Anyway, I did visit and I liked what I saw. Importantly, the Hughsie gardens were there to be walked on, sat on, played on and generally enjoyed, so I accepted the offer and set about nailing the A levels I would still need. There was real danger of only scooping a B in chemistry and I needed straight A grades.

About this time I failed my driving test, twice. It was the first thing in my life which I had outright flunked and it stung, both times, but it was one of the best lessons I have ever learned. After the first time I rang Dad, angry and upset, to be told that he didn't think I had been ready for it in the first place. I was amazed and pissed off; why the hell hadn't he said anything beforehand? Quietly he said, 'Well, you wouldn't have listened anyway.' That hurt even more than failing, and mostly because it was absolutely true. So once I had dusted myself off and acknowledged that he was right, I realised that failure can be a positive thing – a chance for another shot, a clean canvas to walk out in the right direction.

Spring came and so did my third and final driving test. I passed and turned my attention to the exams as summer arrived, bringing the grades I had worked so hard for and a ticket to Oxford – I was en route to a rowing boat at last.

CHAPTER 3
AN OCEAN TO ROW

'Dream as if you'll live forever; live as if you'll die today'

JAMES DEAN

Before university I took a gap year, doing a succession of mostly unexciting jobs before heading to Mexico for three months in search of adventure and some experience in nature conservation. I got both, by volunteering on a sea turtle conservation camp and then backpacking round the country, doing all the things young travellers do.

A few months before I went off travelling I visited my doctor, because my normally compliant eczema had rumbled up with a vengeance and I had found a bald patch on the back of my head. Blood tests diagnosed autoimmune hypothyroidism. This translates to my immune system rather stupidly and very unhelpfully breaking down a very important hormone, which in turn leaves me with the metabolism (and figure) of a tired slug. It also means sporadic bouts of crazed eczema, occasionally kamikaze hair and a lifelong ticket to daily tablets ('Slug Pellets') to kick-start my metabolism. Annoyingly, it also meant that my medical rating for the army was immediately downgraded, scratching my plans to fly helicopters after university. I was an Army Scholar, being sponsored through my final years of education with a commitment to at least a three-year commission after university, so a lot of my future hopes rested on this; I would now have to think of something else – still in the army, just on the ground instead of in the air.

October 2004 heralded the start of a new era for me – Oxford exploded onto the scene and I jumped in a boat as soon as I possibly could. Unfortunately, I also made the mistake of getting back into hockey and joining the university team. If you have ever heard a ligament snap, you will know that it is generally followed by a stomach turning scream. Four weeks into my first term, I heard one of the cruciate ligaments in my knee resign with a snap during a hockey match. It was the result of nothing at all heroic or skilful, just a case of turning too quickly and sharply so that all the fibres tore with a ping, sending bone crashing into bone as my knee dislocated. Not only did it put me on crutches for the rest of term but it also took me off the water and out of the rowing boats and meant that I bowed out from my Army Scholarship – none of which had been in my original game plan. My goal had been to trial with the University Blues Rowing Squad in my second year but now that was off the cards too.

By the end of the first term in my second year, my knee was fixed and I felt truly happy. I had a lovely crowd of new friends including Alex, my boyfriend, and I found the biology course challenging and interesting. I loved everything about the rowing now that I was back in a boat: the team spirit, the training, being out on the river in the morning mist and the technical demands of learning a new sport. I was proud to be appointed captain of my college crew and had high hopes for the year ahead.

It was during that same year that I first heard about ocean rowing, with the arrival of an email while I sat at my desk procrastinating and dreaming of Mars bars and rowing training. Captivated by the idea and now with no plans for after university, I started to look into it and soon decided that I wanted to attempt an ocean one day. The question of which ocean was easily solved. The Indian was more tempting than the Atlantic, which had been rowed by a couple of hundred people and was therefore a relative motorway, mostly because there are organised biannual races across it and a comparatively nice set of trade winds offering routes into the Caribbean. The Pacific is so huge that I didn't even consider it and the Southern Ocean, being in fact part of the other oceans and such a very crazy place and not at all rowed before, didn't warrant discussing either: an unforgiving environment so close to Antarctica didn't seem like a good place to start. So I set my sights on the Indian. It had been attempted very few times with even fewer successes and only a couple of men had made successful solo crossings, no woman ever having tried it at all, in a team or alone. To me, this was not an obvious ticket for failure, as some folk tried to have me believe. I considered it pioneering and exciting. I had no experience or credentials to suggest that I could even row any ocean, but I had a belief that if other people had rowed oceans then so could I. Clearly it wasn't rocket science – you just needed to prepare well, be driven and focused and hope for a good dollop of luck and keep on rowing until you got to the other side. Given that this was a remote adventure sport in which I had no experience whatsoever, right from the start I thought I should take a team along with me. I asked family and friends, and one after another they all said 'no', apparently not very keen on the idea at all. In fact one of my very best friends, Roostie, ignored my messages completely in the hope that she could put me off by not answering. Undeterred, I looked within the university; surely Oxford had folks who wanted to row an ocean? Yes, they did. I put the idea out across various channels within the university, sending emails to different clubs and societies, standing up at various meetings to announce my plans and doing my best to sound as knowledgeable as possible in the face of questioning. At the meetings there were usually a few giggles and gasps as my call for rowers was received and digested, and one tutor sent an email which simply said 'Are you completely mad?' Nonetheless, I received a bundle of positive applicants wanting to join my crew. Meanwhile, my parents kept surprisingly silent, clearly hoping that I would lose interest. Instead, I continued to feed them nuggets about the latest ocean-rowing veteran to advise me, and within a few months it dawned on them that I was serious. I spent hours trawling the Internet and making notes, reading books of historic rows and picking the brains of veterans. Mum still tried not to mention it at all but Dad quizzed me, testing my thinking and trying to see what I could see in my head. Even I didn't know all the details at that stage but I was fixed on the goal and had my sights set on the Indian Ocean for 2009, three years away: I still had my degree to finish after all. Then there was the huge matter of a team, a lot of money, a boat, a plan and some training – all in all it would be a monster effort on all fronts, logistically, financially, emotionally and practically. But it all excited me and so I didn't mind one bit. Call me naive, but that's how it was.

Considering that I was supra-happy and not at all stressed at this point, I was surprised when my hair started to fall out. I had had little patches of alopecia at various stages before, but this time I clocked nearly 40 per cent hair loss. When my doctor had nothing very helpful to say I looked for my own solution, soon deciding to shave it all off. My reasoning was easy; I wasn't ill and I would rather have no hair at all than hair which jumped out of its own accord, leaving handfuls on my pillow or disappearing down the plughole in the shower. Dad, on the other hand, was in more pain than I could ever contemplate and I found that always helped me with perspective: this was small fry. And so one afternoon before a rowing session at the start of the summer term, a friend chopped and shaved my hair for me. After a nervous half hour before I summoned up the courage to leave the room, I embraced the Baldilocks era with enthusiasm. I was in control again, if a little chilly. If my remaining follicles abandoned me even further then it wouldn't bother me too much, though my boyfriend Alex and my parents found it harder to deal with. My only qualm was that I had to shave the fuzzy regrowth every few days to stop myself from looking like an unkempt doormat. What really surprised me was the assumption from strangers, accompanied by sympathetic noises, that I was having chemotherapy. To those who knew me, I was as healthy as ever: my shark project for the summer vacation was all lined up, Alex and I were madly in love, my rowing was going really well and I planned to trial for the Blues Squad in my final year. The energy and adrenaline of an Oxford life was exciting and addictive, meaning that I worked and played (and rowed and rowed and rowed) really hard. I was just a normal, happy student doing all the normal, happy things that students do.

In May my parents came down and took Alex and me out for lunch to celebrate my twenty-first birthday. I had a rowing test that afternoon so it wasn't ideal timing, but our schedules were tight. We met the car as it pulled up outside college and Mum got out and held me tight for one of those hugs that only mums know how to give, then got the wheelchair out of the car for Dad and helped him in. It still surprised me to see him in his chair – once a towering six foot, he was now shorter than Mum who is only a couple of inches into the five foot club. As she pushed him down the corridor, questions flying between us at one hundred miles an hour. I smiled, very pleased to see them again. Dad was on good form and full of banter, despite the brutal scaffolding round his leg which had been wired up in some major operations eight weeks earlier. Surgeons had fused his disintegrated ankle joint with a bone graft and lots of screws, in the hope that it would bring some relief from pain and allow him to walk again. I was surprised at how bouncy he seemed, although I noticed he looked older and perhaps a bit ashen. After lunch I cycled along as fast as I could pedal, grinning and singing to myself; I was at one with the world and still too stuffed to appreciate the difficulty of a 2-kilometre sprint test on three full courses and a splash or three of delicious wine.

On the first page of my new journal that week, I declared 2006 the best year of my life; these were good times.

CHAPTER 4
AND THEY ALL FALL DOWN

'Sorrow comes to all... Perfect relief is not possible, except with time'

ABRAHAM LINCOLN

Rowers love lie-ins more than most people because training usually happens pre-dawn, when only the birds are supposed to be awake and the world is still content to be in bed. On the morning of 13 June 2006, sunlight streamed through my window, dappling my bed with soft gold and waking me up. I was due to race at the prestigious Henley Regatta in a few days with the Oxford squad, so I rolled over and fell back asleep, leaving birds and sunlight to do their thing.

Just after seven, someone hammered on my door, shouting for Alex. He got up and went out in his stripy pyjamas and I returned to my snoozing. A little while later he came back in and sat on the bed beside me. I sat up half-heartedly, pretending to be curious. He was pale and clammy and looked as though someone had just died.

Someone had. It was my Dad.

I didn't believe him. Dad was OK. Mum had said he was getting better. No, not my Dad. No, no, no, no, NO! Not my Dad. No. I choked with shock, tears cutting down my face and pain raging inside me as I collapsed into a shivering wreck. I screamed and screamed a sound so hollow and alien that it scared me. The whole concept scared me. My Dad was dead. No more. Gone forever. I didn't understand any of it. I cried and cried into the bed sheets, clutching fists of duvet and thumping the bed. My world had just been broken. I was broken. Utterly and completely destroyed; this felt catastrophic.

Somehow Alex managed to calm me down enough to hand me a phone to speak to Mum, and we both cried down the line, agreeing that I should come straight home. Alex said he would take me back on the train and sort everything out with college. I then walked down the corridor in floods of tears to my best friend Roostie's door, knocked and stood there for a moment with my face in my hands, crying some more. I looked up into her frightened face as she opened the door and dissolved into her arms, sobbing with my sad new truth. We cried together and she hugged me tightly, before packing me off to the shower and promising to make me some breakfast.

In the shower the tears flowed thick with the water and I howled and howled until someone knocked on the door to check if I was OK. I had never been less OK. Still crying, I wandered back to my room to change and found that I had no capacity whatsoever to make decisions or think rationally. Even my room felt different now. Only two weeks before Dad had been sat there in his wheelchair. There was the box of the new camera he had given me. There was the card he had written. There he was in a photo. I was silent now, numbed into shock, relying on other people to tell me what to do. I pulled on some clothes and then pushed the cereal that Roostie had made me around the plate, eating a single mouthful and staring into nowhere. I wasn't hungry. I wasn't anything any more. I was just a girl without a Dad.

Alex took me home that morning and I sobbed my way from taxi to train, staring out of the window or at the floor. There is no way I would have made it by myself: everything felt different and confusing, even the familiar routes. I didn't know how I was going to cope.

I kicked my heels as we walked away from the station in Oakham, afraid I might see someone we knew but also afraid of the hurt at home. Dad wouldn't be there. I paused at the corner of our road, and Alex took my hand gently and walked me up to the door. I was trying to be brave, though I can't imagine why. No one needs to be brave when their Dad has just died. As I opened our front door, Michael wrapped me up in his long bearish arms and I cried and cried. Mum joined the hug and assured me that it would be OK. I didn't understand; nothing was OK. Nothing at all. She seemed to have been shocked into some sort of exhausted overdrive, running only on adrenaline and, on the outside at least, she appeared surprisingly normal talking to my aunt and uncle in the garden a few minutes later. I supposed I expected everyone to be bawling their eyes out and I was surprised that they weren't – clearly the shock of a loss does different things to each of us. For now at least it was very public – people were coming to the door to bring flowers or hugs and I see she had to maintain some sort of order on it all. I found Matthew face down on his bed clutching Dad's watch, bawling and writhing, absolutely empty. I knelt down beside him, trying to hug the hurt away, my whole body stinging with the tears. To look at, he was a strapping rugby lad, part man, part boy and taller than me. But today he had been floored with the most almighty scrum of his life and he was broken. Nothing was OK and nothing was normal. I didn't see how it ever could be. Our Dad had died. Yesterday we were five and I had two parents. It had just changed and it could never be fixed. We were now four and Mum was a widow. Dad was gone.

Five days before, Mum had returned home after her night shift as a nurse to find Dad struggling with pain in his back and chest, having been awake all night. He was ambulanced to hospital in Leicester where he saw more doctors than most people see in a lifetime and was tested and retested and investigated. They struggled to stabilise his oxygen saturation levels and so had him connected up to a continuous oxygen pump, apparently looking like Darth Vader. He was sick but stable. As it wasn't the first time he had been admitted into hospital for investigations and no one imagined it would be the last, Mum had said not to worry, and so I hadn't. Mum kept me updated and I sent notes and messages to him, saying that I would be home soon for the holidays to see him.

Five days after being taken in to hospital, my Dad had died. It was the early hours of the morning and very sudden and unexpected. Mum had been on her night shift at the Oakham hospital when she took a phone call to say he was being ventilated. She tried calling for taxis, afraid to drive herself in that state. There were no taxis. Bloody useless out-in-the-sticks Rutland; if only there had been one car willing to take her. Eventually she rang a friend who drove her through the narrow lanes into the heart of Leicester on what must have been the longest journey of her life. He died just moments before she walked through the hospital doors.

Doctors had been baffled by his condition, ruling out a collapsed vertebra and pulmonary emboli and had been treating him for pneumonia. Later, the post-mortem concluded that my wonderful, brave and brilliant hero of a Dad had finally been defeated by pulmonary emboli, or blood clots in the lungs. Despite the tests, they had obviously gone unnoticed – a common issue, I learned.

The day before he died I had posted a letter to him, promising to be back home soon from Oxford, keen to head out birdwatching with him again and teasing him with our usual banter. I picked up the letter from the doormat the day after I arrived home, the day after he had died.

This was now the worst year of my life. I just floated. Memories and thoughts raced round my head making it thump, while at other times it just stagnated, silently. It still thumped even in the silence, and I thought that it always would do. Right from the start I decided that the best way to heal would be to let the grief do its thing; I wouldn't deny it or fight it or run from it, but just stand and face it and hope that one day things wouldn't be so raw.

The day of Dad's funeral was the sort that makes you smile: the trees thick with leaves and full of pretty flowers, the sun giving a sheen to everything beneath a postcard blue sky. Instructions went out to avoid all black outfits, and happily our friends and family did us proud. They wore all the colours of an artist's paintbox, matching the church flowers; one friend was top-to-toe in bright orange, my brother had a pink tie and another friend wore a crimson skirt. Dad would have loved it all, including the fact that his own hearse was late, which meant that Alex had to play *Pachelbel's Canon* over and over again on the organ until we had all arrived.

Clutching my great-aunt's arm, and walking behind Mum and my grandfather, I filed into the church behind his wicker coffin. It was shouldered by family and friends, including my brothers; Matthew only just tall enough at fifteen, smart in a new suit, and Michael looking handsome in his army uniform. I tried not to giggle as they struggled to walk on the very narrow flagstones, knowing that Dad would have chuckled, too. Yet I still couldn't believe it was all happening. Stifled giggles morphed to tears and I felt them slide down my cheeks onto my jacket, soaking the white linen in small patches and dripping onto the bright orange gerbera I had pinned to my lapel.

At the back of the church there was my stand of sunflowers, to match the single stem which I clutched ready to lay on his coffin, complete with a piece of dark blue ribbon round it, Oxford colours. Once the singing had stopped, it was so calm that I decided this was the most peace he must have felt for a long time and imagined him smiling at everyone.

After some welcomes an old family friend, Padre John, invited me forward to the little spot where I had given many readings for carol services in the years before. I knew what it was like to stand in front of a packed house, but I had never read a eulogy. I walked up to his coffin, placed my hand on the rim and turned to face the rows, some smiling, some just staring, all eyes on me and my Dad. As I read, my voice wavered in places, my hand gently thumbing the lavender which Mum had woven into the rim; I felt connected and stronger holding on. In the front row, tears streamed down Matthew's face; Michael had a sad and lost sort of look; and Mum was looking at me in the way that mums do when they know their children are doing something hard, saying 'you can do this; I believe in you', without saying a word.

I got to the bit where I had told Dad about my plans to row across the Indian Ocean one day, and everyone laughed. They laughed again when I said that he, too, had laughed. I announced that I would still be going rowing in 2009 and that I would now be doing so in his memory, raising money for arthritis charities. I broke down as I tried to thank everyone for their support and as I made for Mum's hug through my tears, the congregation started clapping. I was a bit taken aback – I didn't think people clapped at funerals. But it was special, and I felt the sickening sadness sitting alongside a little bit of freedom now; for we had just turned the first tiny corner of our crazy grief road.

CHAPTER 5
THE CRAZY GRIEF ROAD

'Grief makes one hour ten'
WILLIAM SHAKESPEARE

Two days after Dad's funeral I headed to the Hebrides for my basking shark project and a week's camping with Alex. It might seem strange going off on holiday just after your Dad's funeral but life still had to go on and I still had a degree to complete – so there was no option to back out. For most of the time I was out on a boat with a local wildlife trust, surveying and sampling the planktic soup the sharks were feeding on. It felt good to be doing my own research, particularly in my favourite place in the world. Yet grief is still grief, wherever you are, and mine was still raw and bleeding at so few weeks. I often sat on the bowsprit in a teary heap, my stomach knotted, my head throbbing from the happy highs and crushing lows. I think I cried more that week than I had ever cried before in my life. The trouble with being on a boat only 70 feet long filled with six other strangers is that there is no escape or respite for anyone – everyone knew what I was going through. Everyone heard me cry and saw my pain; it was so public. Normally I champion mantras of positive attitude and optimism, yet I really struggled. I didn't want respite; I wanted to hurt and to cry. Those desperate moments in the foetal position or screaming into the waves served as a badge of respect and love for my Dad. Even one day at a time was too much to comprehend sometimes; I lived out each hour according to the schedule of duties for the day and each night called Mum, hoping that Dad would pick up, willing him to jump into the conversation and tell me that he was back.

Going back to Oxford after the summer was hard; I still associated it with all of that hurt and pain of finding out Dad was gone. The year ahead quickly became the loneliest and saddest of my life, darker and lower than I thought possible. Alex was studying abroad for a year and most of my friends were in a state of finals mania. For me, the degree was secondary to surviving. For months I didn't sleep properly, often crying myself into an exhausted heap. I was scared that memories would fade and I hated not being in control of my own feelings, so prone to such intense sadness. I felt volatile and full of rage.

Afraid of exploding completely, I did everything I could to keep some sort of momentum. Rowing was my main therapy; out on the water or training with teammates, I found peace in using my pent-up energy. Without my regular rowing fixes, I am sure that the year would have ended very differently. Just after Dad had died I realised that if I was to survive the grief and complete my degree, then the Blues trialling schedule on top of that would be conducive to little more than accelerated self-destruction. Something had to give, and it had to be that prize – surviving and a degree, in that order, were my priorities now.

Being apart from Alex was both hard and somehow liberating. He found life abroad tricky and lonely and I struggled to convey what I felt in my grieving. It was difficult to communicate and to understand each other. At least alone I could let grief run its course without worrying that I was affecting our relationship. Things at home weren't going brilliantly either; Matthew was in and out of some very troubled times and went off the rails and I spent many hours travelling home. Michael went out to Afghanistan in the early summer with the army and Mum plodded on, holding us all together as best she could. Everything felt so disparate. But at least I had my plan for the ocean.

My principal and tutor were a bit bemused in my yearly meeting with them when I answered their question about my plans after graduation with, 'I'm going to row across the Indian Ocean.' I see now that it probably doesn't crop up too often as a reply, especially when I added that I was going solo.

I had decided to go it alone during the summer after conversations with other ocean rowers. Given that I had dedicated it to Dad's memory, this felt right. It wouldn't be right with anyone else. So I set about figuring out how I would make it happen.

CHAPTER 6
THE PLAN IS TO MAKE A PLAN

'The only cure for grief is action'
C. S. LEWIS

Up to this point in my life I had only ever run college rowing teams, and organised charity balls and school expeditions. In principle, planning an ocean row was simply a scaled up version of one of these; but in practice the step up to pulling off a three-year project with an £85,000 budget, almost no experience, no team and only my student loan as starting capital was monumental. I followed my instinct and took advice, speaking to as many people as possible, making plans and timelines and chipping away at the mammoth piece by piece. In that respect it was just like any other project. Only this time all the energy had to come from within; if I floundered then it would sink. It was my dream and my plan, but I would need a team and a lot of other support to make it happen. Time was an issue, too.

I was still a student, busy with finishing off my degree, struggling with grief, rowing, and I planned to work for a year in between Oxford and the ocean, too. I needed both the time and the money that an extra year would afford me. I didn't really have a plan for working but hoped that it would be something where I could gain useful experience for my future – something to help the CV.

I found the contrast between my long-term goal of the ocean and those days when the grief overwhelmed me exhausting; at times it was as much as I could do just to make it through without breaking down. At others, I couldn't fight it and would spend hours and hours locked away in my room, bawling my eyes out. It felt desperate and empty, but I tried to tell myself that whatever the ocean would throw at me, I would have already survived the greatest test of my life. Tenacity would get me through this and across the ocean.

In terms of fundraising for my chosen charity, Arthritis Research Campaign, I decided to kick-start it by organising an auction of promises down in the college bar one Friday evening. With the help of friends, family and local businesses I was able to put together fifty lots to go under the hammer – everything from photo shoots and a week in an Alpine apartment to perhaps the world's most expensive chocolate brownies. We raised £3,000 that night, a real triumph and boost for the funds, as well as being a lot of fun. I also gave my first talk about life on the ocean, which involved a lot of blagging as I really had no idea what it would be like out there. I had never spent more than a few hours by myself, never been completely out of sight of land and had never rowed on anything more salty than the Isis, Oxford's river. I was amazed and chuffed to have so many people on side; it felt like I was headed in the right direction. That said, they were still only students – I needed to get some bigger money in the bank.

I devoured all the ocean rowing books I could get my hands on, especially solo accounts where I could take away lessons on solitude. The 'alone' part didn't really bother me as I figured that if other people had managed it then so could I; like anything in life it would be a mind game and if I wanted it enough, then I would do it. After all the reading and talking with different folks, I figured that one of the most important skills on the ocean would be the ability to face the highs and lows with a degree of equanimity. Sports psychotherapist Dr Briony Nicholls helped me shape this thinking and, tucked away in the warmth of her little office, she shepherded me through various scenarios and coping strategies, generously giving her time for nothing.

The most crucial part of setting out in the right mindset would be knowing that I had done everything in my power to be as fully prepared as possible, both physically and emotionally. I needed to be confident in my own abilities, safe in the eyes of those whose opinions I valued, and credible in the view of those supporting or sponsoring or following me. Beyond that, there wasn't much else I could do.

My training started while I was still studying at Oxford and it involved all sorts of mad and wonderful things, as well as painful, boring ones, so as to emulate life at sea. There was a sea survival course where, ironically, I had to rescue other people onto a life raft in a swimming pool in

Southampton; in reality there would be no one to rescue me or be rescued on my boat. After a few navigation courses, I spent hours and hours poring over charts and trying to figure out the minutiae of astronavigation – not easy to get to grips with when you're studying at the kitchen table with no stars in sight. One of my favourite bits was a bespoke medical training crash course with Dr Sean Hudson of Expedition Medicine in his idyllic Lake District home. With his wife Caroline, also a doctor, we talked suppositories, rashes and creams over a curry and then the next day he taught me how to inject myself with anaesthetic and stitch myself up, when to use the magic lolly (basically morphine on a stick) and how to cling-film my arm to my chest in the event of a burn. I found it all very interesting, hoping of course that I would never have to use it while also wondering how well I would cope if forced to. For the final part of the training, Sean had arranged for us to do some training on the water, and we spent an afternoon jumping off the local mountain rescue speedboat into the freezing murk of Ullswater, to be picked up and thrown in again. It was all done at high speed and, we liked to think, in the style of James Bond. While it was fun it was mostly irrelevant; in reality, there was no way I would be picked up off the ocean in a tiny boat – out there it would be just me, myself and I. Alone really did mean alone.

That said, there would be shipping, and so I needed to brush up on my radio protocol and gain my VHF licence. For some reason I found the Mayday exercise particularly funny and dissolved into giggles when I tried calling for help. There was something so ridiculous about hearing 'Mayday,

Mayday, Mayday – this is rowing boat *blah blah blah*' over the airwaves. I figured anyone hearing that would think they were going mad and not believe a word of it. Even at this stage, there was a fine line between believing I could do it and then wondering how the hell I would. Having never been so far out to sea that I couldn't see land, I decided that I really ought to check that I liked the oceanic life and so looked for a place on a yacht for a passage across the Indian Ocean, to get a feel for conditions and to experience being out of sight of land. With no luck on the Indian Ocean front, I booked myself a crew place on a 55-foot yacht, on a passage from the north-west tip of Iceland across the chilly waters of the North Atlantic, down the coast of Scotland, through the Irish Sea and round the corner to Plymouth. It was an excellent taster of the routine, fatigue and excitement of life at sea, complete with seasickness, storms and soggy socks and I arrived back in the UK sixteen days later saltier, wiser and with ever more respect for the seas.

Physically, the training had to be fairly brutal to prepare my body for the rigours of a four-month ocean trek, or however long it might be – it's not like catching a train, there is no fixed arrival time. In 2007, while I was still at college and when most in my year were revising (and I probably should have been), I ran the London marathon. The training was a release for me, the long and muddy runs around Oxford a great escape from the struggles of finals; sometimes I would find myself running back to college in tears, exhausted but purged. Race day was intense and scorching hot. Having never run more than 16 miles and with a very painful recent injury getting worse, I found it really tough. To get through the pain I kept reminding myself that Dad had survived far worse pain than any marathon could throw at me and that I would not be beaten unless I was tied to a stretcher and forcibly removed. The Great Toenail Exodus followed a few days after marathon day as I pulled out five nails from my multicoloured and gooey toes, under the misguided notion that they would be better out than in. Bad mistake; apparently toenails can jump out of their own accord and do not need a helping hand. Later on, the mantra 'Toenails hurt more' would be written onto the cabin wall of my rowing boat. The pain training had worked.

My finals came and went at the saddest time of all, coinciding with both my birthday and the last time I had seen Dad one year before. With bloody mindedness and lots of chocolate, tears, rowing and support from family and some wonderful friends, I somehow made it through and received my degree. Another blow came with the passing of our dear great-aunt Broni in July, clocking the second big loss in our little family in two years.

Serendipity had landed me with a job for the following year, teaching and coaching biology and sports at a boarding school just up the road. The post was fixed term for one year. It was perfect: I would have chance to prepare for my row, and accommodation was provided so I could save. The timetable would be demanding but there were regular school holidays and the fact that it would also be a meaningful year, giving me valuable experience of teaching and working with children, made it even better. The school's superlative sports facilities would also allow me to train in style. Bonus.

It turned out that a full-time job in a boarding school surpasses all normal understanding of the term. In my second term at St Edward's I took up the post of matron in one of the girls' boarding houses, with one proviso: that I would not be called matron. My six-day week turned into a six-day-and-night week, with the added trials of a house of seventy teenage girls where, if I was awake, my door was always open to them. And if I wasn't awake then they only had to ring the bell. I guess I was a halfway house, being much closer to them in age than many staff members, yet old enough and experienced enough to show some wisdom. They were formative and valuable times and I came away knowing that one day I would be a teacher.

I also had my relationship with Alex, which at times was proving much more difficult than when we had been together at St Hugh's and even more difficult than when he had been abroad. Alex, a talented and conscientious linguist, studied more hours than I thought possible for his finals and with a single-minded dedication I couldn't understand. It was both frightening and frustrating to him that I was still so affected by grief and that my focus was on my row; equally, I was frustrated that he was so focused on his finals. It was with deep sadness that I eventually acknowledged that we were both headed in completely different directions. I still loved him; I just didn't see my future with him. He did see our future together, which made it devastating for both of us when the relationship came to an end.

Outside of work, I had two major focuses – I needed to raise money and I needed to find a boat. I started to look at the options for the latter and discovered that the aspiring ocean rower can opt for a new build or a second-hand vessel, mostly along the same sort of design. They tend to be between 20 and 24 feet long with two watertight cabins for storage and sleeping, one at either end. Most boats nowadays have composite hulls – usually a foam and glass fibre 'sandwich', making them extremely light, strong and (theoretically at least) unsinkable. Mine was already called *Serendipity*, even though she so far had no builder, no money to pay for her and nothing more than a dreamy notional owner. I didn't even know where to find a boat builder or how to decide what would make a good second-hand one; my only proviso was that I wanted one with character. I decided on the name *Serendipity* quite early on in the plan – while watching dolphins play around the research yacht in Scotland the year before. I love the way that wildlife at sea appears at the most unexpected moment – serendipity in action. The sound of the word strikes a chord with me, too – it sounds a little bit like 'Sarah and Dipperty'. After chats with various people in the ocean-rowing community (yes, such a thing does exist!) and browsing the pages of the Ocean Rowing Society and the Association of Ocean Rowers forums, I decided, with no real consideration of my risibly empty bank account, that I would like a new build. This way I would know exactly how she was built and would be involved the whole way along.

Various names of boat builders were talked about on the forums or mentioned by rowers and I looked into them. The first chap, although highly recommended, didn't ever respond to my messages or calls beyond the first salutary email and so I looked to the next on the list: Jamie Fabrizio and Emily Adkin of Global Boatworks. They had made a string of beautiful, successful boats and were at the time completing a new design for a solo boat, which intrigued me. My first contact with them was met with boundless enthusiasm and an easy rapport; they were clearly the sort of people that make you smile just by being with them. Yes, they could build me a boat; yes, they worked closely with expert designer Phil Morrison and a very good marine electrician; and yes, they promised cheese and baked bean toasties when I visited. And finally, yes, they did this sort of thing all the time. After all, I didn't want any joker building the other half of my team – my life would depend on this boat.

From our initial conversations, I had good vibes about Jamie and Emily, and six months later they were building my boat. Looking back now, I laugh at the serious chats which I had with them on my first meeting, while knowing full well that I had practically no money at the time. I didn't even have the £5,000 deposit, let alone the money for the whole build, which amounted to a figure capable of giving any recent graduate a heart attack. I bluffed through it. I would find the capital, even if I wasn't sure how. I kept telling myself, and others, that it would work out. It had to; I wasn't prepared to let this project fail without giving it my absolute all. Most of what I earned went towards the project and I exercised the full breadth and depth of overdrafts on my various accounts. Sponsorship would be the only way to bolster the sums which I could devote from my own savings, earnings and grants or donations from individuals.

Having heard horror stories about sponsor hunting from other expeditioning folk and adventurers, I was buoyed by early reassurances from some of them that mine was a story likely to attract sponsors. I would be the first woman ever to attempt the Indian Ocean and also the youngest person to do so – all good hooks for the media. The fastest was always open to debates – the previous three successful crossings had all taken slightly different routes and mine would be completely new, leaving Australia from much further south, out of Fremantle. My idea with heading south was to minimise the northward drift which previous crews had experienced, and it would help my plan of landing in Mauritius, a little island a few hundred miles off Madagascar. Six out of the nine previous attempts had failed on this volatile and unpredictable ocean, so I was taking an even bigger gamble with this new route. All of these crossings so far had been from east to west, in order to make the most of the wind and currents. While to land on Madagascar or even Africa would have been somehow more complete and satisfying, I also figured they would be much harder options with the currents, shipping traffic and extra distances involved. So I chose Mauritius as my proposed landing spot – no one had landed there yet on a rowing expedition across the Indian.

The sponsor chasing taught me various things – namely that it would be a brilliant idea either to marry someone rich enough to finance my adventures or to become very skilled at covertly robbing banks. The quest for partnerships was relentless – if I had spare time and wasn't out training then I would be plugging away, researching and trawling for links, sending off proposals and letters, usually late into the night. I talked about my plans to everyone I met and was always on the lookout for good links or possible pots of gold. Of course the end of the effort doesn't always mean money: I had already seen my friend from Oxford, Alex Hibbert, fold two expedition projects after funding issues.

My very first sponsor had the coolest name of them all – Lumpy Lemon, a very funky little design company based in Oxford at the time. I found them in a web search and knew that anyone with a company name like that would be fun to work with. They agreed to come on board, build me a website and help with design work – all very useful as my design skills aren't much better than those of a colour-blind walrus. Another early sponsor came after a round-robin email to friends and family asking for ideas. A school friend passed on his dad's details and almost immediately after my proposal was sent I found my bank balance £5,000 healthier. Another chunk like this was promised around the same time from a chap who got in touch with me – always a novelty in sponsor hunting. He had grown up in Rutland and moved out to Australia but was home for his father's funeral when he read an article about my project. It wasn't all finance that people or companies sponsored either – some offered kit, food, services or their time free of charge or for heavily reduced rates. It was humbling and energising to have so much support and a reminder that success would be down to more than just my ability to keep rowing.

Friends and family also sponsored various aspects, many of them sponsoring 'miles of the row', which I sold for a few pounds each with the promise that I would carry their names across the ocean on my boat, thinking about them as I rowed through 'their' miles. It was a wonderful way of getting as many people as possible involved in the project.

After various articles in the local press I received letters, emails and donations from all over the place, wishing me well or telling me their stories or throwing a few pounds into the pot.

CHAPTER 7
IN WHICH THE ROWER GETS READY TO ROW

'The journey is the reward'

CHINESE PROVERB

One year before I was due to start out from Australia, at the same time as Jamie was laying the first strips of foam along my boat's new frame, I took my first strokes in an ocean rowing boat with an Atlantic veteran, the Hungarian Gábor Rakonczai, out in the baking sunshine of Gran Canaria. It had all come about after I saw an advert by him on the Ocean Rowing Society website, advertising courses on his rowing boat in Gran Canaria. I paid for his flights from Hungary and jumped on a plane, arriving on the island with just a teeny bit of concern as to what I had let myself in for. I had never met him and I would now be living on a 23-foot boat with him for the next week as we made our way round the island. We got off to a slightly embarrassed start when I went in for a handshake and he did the European kisses to the left, kisses to the right thing and we met in the middle with a bit of a headbutt. On our first day on the water we clocked sixteen hours rowing, taking it in turns to rest after the first eight hours. I am surprised we even made it that far – Gábor had been drinking beers all day as I had been glugging my water supply. I guess things are done differently in Hungary. As Gábor slid through the hatch into his little cabin for his first rest, my gaze fixed on the compass glowing red in front of me; I felt like an eager pupil, keen to impress their teacher. Each time the needle wandered I heaved on an oar, pulling the boat back around on course. The wind got up to such a strength that I had to row with just one oar to keep us going the right way and after a few hours my body felt like it was on its way to earning the first salty stripe; that is, that it was bloody sore. The night was beautiful as stars twinkled in the sky and the sea, and bioluminescence swirled off the oar strokes. I was so glad that I was enjoying myself; it would have been awful to discover that I didn't like being at sea in a tiny boat after I had told everyone what I was about to do. I was starting to fall asleep at the oars when Gábor stuck his head out to swap shifts, and so I flopped into my cabin gratefully for some chocolate and a snooze. I have never been inside a coffin before, but if I had to imagine it, then that cabin would come very close. Trying to shake off the shivers, I drifted in and out of sleep, rocking with the waves and trying not to think about being in a coffin, which of course meant that I only thought about being in a coffin. I woke up two hours later to find that

I had to remain lying down in the cabin or face a messy rendezvous with my lunch. Three attempts to get out failed as I was hit back by rushes of sickness, and I fed both the fishes and the deck when I finally appeared at the hatch. After rowing halfway round Gran Canaria we were forced into a little marina by contrary headwinds from where we did a couple of shorter day trips to learn about different bits of kit that had so far been alien to me, such as the sea anchor. Gábor also made me get in the water and scrub the boat's hull clean. I have always hated deep water, but pride made me jump straight in and pretend that I was cool with the whole thing, a complete lie. By the end of the week's training I had a feel both for how many beers a Hungarian seafarer can drink in one go and also what it might be like out at sea; with one year to go I was confident that my planning and training were headed in the right direction.

After finishing at St Edward's in the summer of 2008 I moved back home for the final six months before my planned departure date, in a bid to save money. I took two jobs, working in a coffee shop and tutoring, while I planned, trained and fundraised. It was stressful and exhausting and I longed for the space and quiet of the ocean.

Unfortunately, as with most projects at this time, the global economic downturn meant that my search for sponsors was not as fruitful as it might have been a few years before. At various points I had been ready to apply for a full-blown bank loan; either that or wave goodbye to the project or postpone it. Each time an invoice arrived that my bank balance couldn't deal with, perhaps for the trailer or the final stage of the boatbuilding costs, my hero of a mum said that she would play banker until the money was found, and she continued to plug the gap when the bank balance dipped into the red, even when I was on the ocean. I was frustrated at not having pulled in all the finance I needed, probably more than I was proud at having secured over £40,000 worth of sponsorship. I didn't like borrowing from Mum but equally I was so grateful. It amazes me that she was so willing to help me, even though it would mean some of the scariest moments and most worried months of her life. Mums are the most special sort of people. She couldn't understand why I would want to put myself through this huge journey but she was right behind me from the moment she realised I was serious about it and didn't once try to stop me. Besides running, my training involved lots of hours in the gym lifting chunky weights and hour upon hour on the rowing machine, eventually in our greenhouse at home, which I did come rain or snow through the winter, listening to the radio late into the night and rowing by torchlight. In April 2008 I had also raced in the 125-mile kayaking marathon from Devizes to Westminster. I had no experience in the skinny racing kayaks used for these events and had just two simple aims: to complete the course and not get washed down any of the raging weirs along the way. Given that the fourth and final day of the race was only my tenth time in this type of boat which, by default, likes to rest on its side, i.e. ninety degrees to the upright, I was chuffed not only to avoid death-by-weir, but also to complete the course with only three capsizes and a second place finish. (No one needs to know that there were only two people in my category.) All of this physical preparation was about pushing boundaries constantly and testing myself to find my limits. This is one of my favourite and most frustrating things about endurance: the boundaries are not static, but you keep testing and can keep redefining them. Even when you think you're running below empty, there is always more to give – even if it's just to drag yourself to the end.

Seamanship would be the most important part of my mental readiness – the key would be surviving the elements and staying happy and healthy and safe, in mind and body and boat. Part of this was covered with my weather training and for this I needed a weather man. Not knowing how or where to find one, I asked ocean rower and one of my mentors Roz Savage if she knew any. She introduced me to an effervescent Portuguese sailor called Ricardo Diniz, an absolute god of a human being to look at – tall with deep dark eyes – and great fun to be with. Ric and I spent many months talking weather on the phone and by email, often at odd hours of the day to fit in with our hectic schedules. He would be key to my safe passage across the ocean, feeding me advice and predictions about the incoming weather. He promised to be great value.

Meanwhile, the boat build ticked on steadily and once I had finished my job at school I had a bit more time to go down and visit the little workshop hub where my new best friend was being created. Emily had been sending me weekly updates on her progress and I loved showing off the photos to friends and family as bits of foam and wood grew piece by piece and week by week into a beautiful little boat. I spent a couple of days with them here and there, watching and learning from Jamie and even getting dusty helping out with various jobs. I am proud to say that I screwed in all of the internal fixing points in the forward cabin and made all the flaps for the water outlets, or scuppers, down the side of the deck. I'm less proud of the fact that I got a bit carried away with one of the scupper flaps and made it a few millimetres wider than the rest, which meant Jamie had to redo it – perfectionist that he is. I was confident that she and I were in safe hands. In this day and age of mass production, it was inspiring to see that master craftsmen still build beautiful, solid and strong pieces by hand – the man is really an artist as much as a boat builder.

Halfway through the build I gave *Serendipity* a nickname, borne out of talking about her as though she was a friend – *Dippers* seemed to fit her perfectly. She would be *Serendipity* at heart and on the formal documents, but to me she was *Dippers*. I finally collected her from the workshop in September 2008, bursting with pride as I drove home with my shiny new boat in tow, and bloody nervous too; having only ever trailered a horse box before, it was a novel concept to be towing £45,000 worth of boat up the M4. The first of my friends to see her was Roostie in Oxford who, to my delight and her credit, cooed approvingly in all the right places as I showed her round and let her get inside the cabin, opening hatches and showing her where I would store things, making me feel like a very proud mother. Mum even waited up until after eleven o'clock to see me home and welcome the new addition, photographing her from all angles, even though it was pitch black outside. *Dippers* was plain white at this stage, no sponsor stickers – just shiny and new, brand new, looking exactly like one of the lifeboats you get on the side of a cruise ship. There were three main parts to her – a cabin and deck sandwich, essentially. There was a 2-metre cabin at the back of the boat where I would sleep and which housed the control panel for all my electrics and various storage compartments below my bed. It was tall enough for me to sit up inside and long enough to lie down, but there wasn't room for standing. Through a hatch in the bulkhead was the deck, similarly about 2 metres long and 1.5 metres wide, with a footwell just outside the cabin where my foot plate would go. I would row facing the door of the sleeping cabin, moving up and down on a sliding seat over the deck. Below the deck there was storage space, including my emergency drinking water compartment. The third section was another, slightly smaller cabin at the bows of the boat – all for storage of equipment and food rations. Running between the two cabins were safety rails – one on each side of the deck, there to stop me falling out of the boat and to hold on to in rough weather – something I was especially keen to point out to my mum!

It wasn't just me who thought she looked gorgeous and over the next few days while she sat outside our house she had plenty of admirers, before I took her up to Rutland Water where she would stay, tucked away underneath a tarpaulin in the boat park until I shipped her out to Australia ready for the row. It seemed fitting that she should have her first splash test and most of her outings at Rutland Water, where I had first learned to kayak all those years ago. It was a grey autumn day when I first launched her and my PR manager Adrian had driven up from Oxfordshire to be there. One of the staff from the water sports centre hooked the trailer up to the tractor they use for launching and pulled her round to the slipway. I stood on *Dippers*, grinning the happiest of grins, while he reversed us down towards the water, throwing the bowlines back onto the jetty for someone to tie up when we were floating. She bobbed gently, proudly even, as she sat alongside and waited for me to sort the oars. I had started chatting to her months before, even before she had left Jamie and Emily's, and it was now for real – we were actually going rowing. She felt light and smooth as I pulled away for the first strokes and made easy work of the water; I knew that if she could smile, she too would have been sporting a big grin. It might seem ironic that I did most of my mileage on this inland reservoir, but it was the best option on offer and proved useful for getting to know her, as well as taking family or journalists out for a little row.

Due to time and money issues, my previous plans for a series of coastal trials were whittled down to a single weekend in Devon in December 2008, just four months before I would set out on my row for real. It was absolutely freezing in the south-west that weekend, so cold in fact that I woke to a layer of ice inside *Dippers*' cabin on my first morning. I had stopped for the night in a public car park in Lymington and in between dozing and shivering I woke to hear various intrigued passers-by stopping for a look and a chat. Had I not been so cold it would have been fun to jump out of the hatch and surprise them all, but I was chilled to the bone and decided it wasn't worth the effort. To top it, exhaustion had caught up with me and delivered a honking cold, meaning that my first day of rowing ended after a one-hour battle into head winds in which I barely made it out of the harbour, before I retreated to sleep it off. The next day went swimmingly until I almost ended up on a sandbank. On my way in to my planned destination of Teignmouth at sunset, I met with an outgoing tide and a sandbar blocking the harbour, so had no option but to row up the coast to the very place where *Dippers* had been built, Exmouth. It was cold and tiring fighting strong winds and sloppy seas in the dark, but the stars twinkled overhead and I enjoyed it, in spite of the fatigue, the wet and the cold – perhaps even because of them, in that strange way that makes endurance sports fun. The run in to the harbour nearly ended in a stranding, especially as Christmas lights along the shore were camouflaging the green and red lights of the navigation markers. At least there should be no sandbanks on the ocean, and I would only have to land once.

The following month I spent the entire ten days of the London Boat Show in January 2009 showing *Dippers* off and turning hoarse as I talked to as many people as possible – admirers, enthusiasts and a handful of naysayers. One day I gave a presentation on the main stage and invited some friends, family and sponsors up to officially launch her with some bottles of fizz which had been cooling on ice in the footwell. Late into the night, every night that week, I sat at my cousin's kitchen table in North London typing out emails following up contacts from the day's efforts. Some of it worked, and much of it didn't, but by the end of the week I had a few more important sponsors on board, hundreds of pounds in the charity pot and plenty of people keen to follow my journey. I turned around after giving my sales pitch to one gentleman, who I knew was just bluffing, to find a man and his son smiling at me. 'I work for a vending machine company. What can I do to help?' I smiled at the thought of my very own chocolate machine on the boat and then said that a bit of chocolate would be quite useful and maybe some drinks. He told me to leave it with him and wandered off. So many promises never came to anything and I had learned not to get my hopes up too much, because it was tiring to keep falling from confident anticipation to the lows of a rejection or, worse still, just no response. You can guess how I felt when I answered my phone the following week to hear Brian Tustain (vending machine hero) saying that he had secured me a huge stash of Cadbury chocolate and £2,000. Magic. And it didn't stop there – he fixed me up with an energy drinks supplier too and enough hot chocolate powder to sink a ship.

My other favourite sponsorship story started with a toilet conundrum. I had been trying to work out how many loo rolls to take to sea or indeed if I should just go with the friendliest wet wipes I could find so that they could serve two purposes. Determined not to pollute the ocean, I decided I wanted only the purest, friendliest (to the ocean and my bottom) wet wipes that I could find – cotton, biodegradable and organic. So I asked one of my existing 'green' sponsors if they had any links to any. The phone number of the first of her suggestions was engaged and so I went to the website of the second, found the phone number, rang up and popped the question. Of course they would like to sponsor me – Natracare was a leading brand in this arena of organic toiletries. The young lady on the other end of the line and I then tried working out how many packets of fifty I might need for the crossing. That evening I opened up an email from Natracare's director, Susie Hewson, and within two sentences she had made me cry. In the opener she explained that she too had lost her father too young and so admired my dedication to the cause – things like this always make me cry. In the second sentence, she wondered if £5,000 might go some way to helping to ease my deficit. It was the end of January 2009 and I still had things to pay for – this was a welcome boost to the project bank balance and a perfect bit of serendipity.

Mid February, I posed for final photographs with *Dippers* outside the house. She was now loaded up with most of the equipment and provisions I would need for the voyage – all to be shipped out to Australia by container. There were 500 dehydrated meals, 150 bags of porridge, 10 kilograms of dried fruit, 500 chocolate bars, boxes of cereal bars, treats for Easter, treats for my birthday, treats for when I was sad, treats for when I was happy, a bottle of port, two bottles of eco-friendly soap, four tubes of toothpaste, six different hats, a few hundred paracetamol and three full medical boxes, twenty packets of wet wipes, five books, emergency strobe lights, emergency rations, emergency repair kit, VHF radios, satellite phones, a video camera, solar panels, a water maker, oars and spares, 100 metres of rope, a sleeping bag and a pillow, more spare batteries than I had seen in my life, a British ensign, a Portuguese ensign and a couple of cuddly toys. It was a five-hour drive down to the loading bay in Essex and I am sure I spent most of it looking up into my mirrors to check that she was OK. It took ten men to get her into the container and nestled on her cradle and just one bolt to close the door. It was a poignant moment as I realised that my unique and precious cargo was now just another metal box amid the thousands. I already had a special bond with her and it felt like waving goodbye to a friend, even if I would be seeing her again in four weeks' time. I wished her well as I drove home, an empty trailer in tow, still checking my mirrors most of the way and wondering where *Dippers* had got to.

My final two weeks at home were spent with farewells and parties and last-minute preparations. The hardest farewell was to my Taid, my Welsh Grandfather, old and frail and fading. His huge smiling eyes fixed on me for my whole visit and he hugged me as though it was our last. I wondered if it might be, too, and swallowed back the tears as I drove out of his driveway. At the end of February I found myself at Heathrow having breakfast with a little group of family and my closest friends. Sally Kettle met us there, my friend Anita had driven us down and, after some scheming with Mum, Roostie and Miranda, another of my good friends from Oxford, had surprised me with their appearance – I had already said goodbye to them a few weeks before. As I munched my way through the biggest English breakfast I have ever eaten I tried hard not to think about saying goodbye to them all; I would be flying out to Australia on my own, though my weather man Ricardo would be joining me a few days later to help.

Having worked flat out for the past eighteen months with little rest time, I was shattered but I felt as ready as I could have been. My leaving party stood in a semicircle and I worked my way round, hugging them tight in turn and wondering if I would ever see them again. While we had never discussed that scenario, we all knew it was perfectly possible I might not make it out the other side. Mum wiped away tears as I wrapped her in a hug and she gave me a kiss from Dad. As I rounded the barrier to head through security, my heart raced. I grinned and waved, skipped back for another wave, and then turned my back on the people most dear to me. This was all in the name of adventure. 'It had better be worth it, Sarah Outen,' a voice warned inside my head. Gulp. I wondered if Mum was crying and imagined my little group parting to go home. What the hell was I doing? Gulp again. 'Sarah Outen – you had better come back in one piece,' I growled at myself. My bags were gobbled up by the conveyor belt and I walked through to the other side. Gulp.

CHAPTER 8
KANGAROOS NEXT 14 KILOMETRES

'Gullibility is the key to all adventures.
The greenhorn is the ultimate victor in everything'

G. K. CHESTERTON

A stopover in Hong Kong meant noodles and monasteries. I took a taxi up to a hilltop monastery, where an enormous bronze Buddha smiled out over the rising sun and low-lying mist. I suspect he chuckled smugly, as I did, at the throngs of overweight tourists puffing and panting their way up the long flight of steps to admire the same views he enjoyed all day, every day. I scanned the blue bits of the horizon and tried to imagine my little boat way out to sea, bobbing along under the sun. I couldn't – it all seemed so abstract.

As I sat and slurped noodle soup at a little street cafe, I enjoyed the contrast to the stresses and rushing around of previous months. No one could call me and I had no obligation to anyone; I felt free and calm. So many projects fail due to lack of money or teams breaking up, motivation waning or some other obstacle before getting anywhere near this stage so it felt like a triumph to have at least made it out of the country and to the other side of the world.

After another flight I finally landed Down Under, smelly round the edges after twenty-four hours travelling but bouncing inside with nervous excitement. Struggling under the weight of my impossibly heavy bags I was impressed by the cheery sing-song 'Welcome to Australia' from the customs man at Perth Airport. Less cheery was the hefty bill he later presented me with for the privilege of quarantining the various bits of food that I hadn't been able to ship with *Dippers* and so had brought out in my baggage to go into the boat. I had a thirty-second debate in my head about whether or not to declare the packet of radish seeds which I knew had fallen out of the main seed stash I had just told him about as I handed over the pile of food, but knew that one sniff from an eager customs pup would have me booted out of the country before I had even been allowed in. This would be a serious blow to the plans. I was lucky to be allowed to bring my food into the country at all. Back in the UK, for months I had worked hard to persuade the Australian Quarantine and Inspection Service (AQIS) that it was my sole intention to leave Australia as quickly as possible, I had absolutely no intention of returning and that I certainly wouldn't be selling or giving away any of my ocean food. The normally easy-going and pragmatic Aussies are fiercely (and rightly) protective over their island wildlife, enforcing some of the strictest import and export rules in the world. As I filled out the forms, I was not unsurprised to see that there was no 'Start an Ocean Row' option in the 'Purpose of Visit' box – so I ticked 'Holiday' instead and underneath 'Occupation' wrote boat captain, not brave enough to write adventurer.

Two hours after landing, with all the paperwork now done, I grinned my way to the arrivals exit and scanned the faces for Hilary and Patrick – friends of Alex's family who had kindly offered to host me while in Perth. Ric and I had pinpointed the end of March as a likely departure point so I had a fortnight, which hopefully translated to enough time to acclimatise, receive the boat, pack and sort it all, focus, get a haircut and prepare to push out to sea. As we drove back to my new home, up into the hills behind Perth, I kept pinching myself to remind myself that this was for real. Goodness knows what Hilary and Patrick must have thought – but they were polite enough not to tell me how silly I was being and instead made me feel very welcome indeed.

Over the next few days, I was so intent on getting ready for the ocean that I ticked off 'See Australia' on my 'To Do List' with a single afternoon visit to a koala sanctuary. Here I saw haughty kookaburras survey the world from lofty perches, fed eucalyptus to a narcoleptic koala, and amused myself watching wallabies and kangaroos lounging in the dust. Glad to have seen something of the country, I now focused all my energy on preparing to cast off the bowlines and push out to sea. Hilary and Patrick looked after me like I was their own child. They ferried me about, fed me and pretended not to be bothered by my late-night computer sessions as I waited up to speak to various folks involved in the project in different corners of the world, like Tom Sjoren from Explorersweb who was sorting out all the techy bits of my emailing system from the boat, my PR team Adrian and Amy back in the UK or Robert in America who had volunteered through my website to help record some phone blogs from the ocean.

My first sight of the Indian Ocean came on my second day in Australia with a visit to the leafy suburbs of Perth to meet Caroline and Roger Winwood – the local Oxford Alumni contacts who had agreed to help with some local contacts and generally mother me a bit. From their hilltop house I could see a sparkling blue rectangle in the distance. I whooped with delight – that gem was the ocean. The Indian Ocean. My ocean. Roger drove me down to one of the local beaches, miles and miles of it, and I stood and surveyed the shimmering blue – scanning from far left to far right and back again – scrunching the silky white sand in my toes. It was vast and beautiful and I wondered what on earth it would be like out there, surrounded by it, consumed by it, with no one else in sight, no boats, no beach, and no anything. Just me, my boat and the sea; I was both excited and terrified by the thought, and so I ran down into the warm surf and tried to erase any thought of empty blue seascapes from my mind. Shortly before I left for Australia, I had carefully diverted Mum's attention away from a newspaper piece about an unfortunate swimmer who had been munched on by a great white shark while swimming on the coast of Western Australia, not too far from here.

No fins in sight today, but I kept a careful lookout while I swam up and down, trying not to look edible. Friend or foe: I wondered what the sea would be to me? For so long I had felt it would be friend, and I just hoped that I was right.

Once she had been delivered and taken out of the container, *Dippers* sat on her cradle on the quayside at the Fremantle Annexe of the Royal Perth Yacht Club (RPYC) so that I could do various jobs before she went into the water. The hull needed another layer of anti-foul, the cabin needed padding with foam and there was lots of sorting to do. Except during the hottest midday hours of sunshine, she was generally admired, photographed and questioned from all sides. Everyone was encouraging, kind and very helpful – while also reminding me that I was a daft Pom and should probably book myself in for a head check. It became a little frustrating as my work stopped for the umpteenth time that afternoon and I started my little spiel. 'I sleep in here, I row there and this is where I store my chocolate. She should self-right if we go over and yes, I have spare oars. Water maker in here and solar panels on the top there. Wanna see where I sleep?' Faces lit up as though I had just offered a thousand pounds, and they would nose through the hatch into my cabin, jaw open, eyes wide and generally shaking their head, with mutterings of 'You're one helluva Sheila,' punctuating the rolling stream of questions. They smiled at my Australian yellow road sign with a kangaroo and 'Next 14 km' stuck on my cabin door, asking if I had put it there 'because roos can only swim that far?' People were quite exhausting and so my most peaceful times were spent pottering about quietly in *Dippers*, sorting supplies into different piles as I tried to decide which sort of pile or combination was best. There I had head space to chew over all the bits and pieces that I still needed to, or to wonder at what it was going to be like out there.

That said, I would never turn people away or refuse to answer their questions – I was very touched that people were so interested. They were all so kind as well: I was taken out to dinner on numerous occasions; people brought lunch and snacks to me while I beavered away; another gave me sailing gloves and hand cream; people offered lifts, did my laundry, gave me a bed or a bunk on board for the night and various charms and talismans. In short, I was so warmly welcomed and supported that I felt goodwill alone might buoy me out to sea.

Some of these wonderful people deserve specific mentions. There was Clem, the harbour master. If I had a problem he always had the answer. He also drummed up some local PR for me, chased late deliveries of my kit, drove me about on various missions and to media interviews, let me use his office and generally did everything in his power to make things as easy as possible. I nicknamed him 'Clem, The Man Who Can'. Then there was Geoff the Expert and his partner Janet, both of them experienced sailors. They had originally emailed me to see if I might like to meet Jamie Dunross, a quadriplegic Paralympic gold medallist with plans to sail round the world. I had suggested a quick coffee as I was so busy, but ended up spending hours with them all and they helped me enormously. Finally, there were the two RPYC members who appeared at *Dippers'* side while I was working one evening. 'So, we just wanted to come down and have a look at the crazy gal who would do this sort of thing! I'm Sally and this is Margot,' chirruped the bronzed smile. They were great fun and very good at mothering me.

People also told me about their own adventures, past or dreamed, often saying shyly 'But it's nothing like this' and scuffing over them. I say they are just different adventures – essentially we all go off for similar reasons, whatever the journeys and dreams, and we've all got hopes and fears. So when people said 'You must be so brave', I just shrugged my shoulders, rubbed my painty, dusty hands on my dirty shorts, shook my head with a smile and said, 'We're all brave – we just choose different arenas.' I told them about Dad and his battles and courage, which in turn drew more stories from them. One newspaper photographer wiped away tears as he told me how his father had died a year earlier and he was only just beginning to feel in control of life again; another man choked up as he gave me a little toy duck and told me how it had been from his friend's two-year-old son who had drowned in a pond. In a way I felt like a guardian of these stories, and that I would be journeying for so many people other than myself.

There was a mind-boggling amount of faffing and preparation to be done in those two weeks pre-ocean. As with all projects (particularly those involving boats and in which you have no experience) everything takes longer than you expect, it costs so much that you are required to mortgage all your toes, nothing goes entirely to plan and it can all seem very stressful to the increasingly tired, broke and first-time rower trying to keep all the plates spinning. After a week of making the hot and dusty commute in from the hills, I moved down to Fremantle to be closer to *Dippers* and the jobs list. I slept out on deck aboard *Dampier*, an old fisheries boat that one of the yacht club members had offered me use of, enjoying all the sounds of the marina – boats squeezing against fenders with the gentle slosh of water, wind rattling flagpoles, ropes creaking under strain, the waves in the distance and footsteps padding on the jetty as people made their way back home to their boats.

I was exhausted and feeling a bit overwhelmed by the time Ricardo my weather router arrived, my head sludgy with too many lists and not enough sleep. I relaxed into his bearish arms for a hug and breathed deep. His sole purpose was to finish preparations and help me get out to sea safely; he could take control now. Even though I had only met him in person once before just a few weeks earlier, we had spent hours on the phone talking weather and tactics. It was 11 March and it looked like I had a full week ahead of me before the weather window would let me leave. I needed winds from the east to blow me out to sea for a few days, to reduce the risk of being blown back to shore. Clearing land safely would be one of the hardest parts of the crossing and it would be made all the trickier by the Leeuwin Current, which the local sailors loved to quiz me about. It was quite difficult at times trying to defend our plans and expectations to local people, all of whom had different experiences and ideas about the voyage as well as a wealth of useful knowledge.

It seemed the Leeuwin was a local celebrity – everyone knew about it, namely that it was a fairly strong, not entirely predictable, current which runs down the West Australian coast, pulling things toward Antarctica. It would pull me south as I crossed it, but just how far south was guess work, as wind direction and strength would also be an important factor. The Fremantle Doctor would also challenge my getaway bid. It is a feisty offshore breeze which generally picks up each day, refreshing Fremantle with its dose of cool, salty air. For me, the little rower, it would not be a welcome breeze if it was stronger than a few knots, as I would be in danger of being washed ashore, dashed on rocks and branded a stupid Pom.

As the PR net widened and I appeared on various Aussie radio stations and in the regional newspapers, lots of positive emails and comments flooded my website. Plenty of folks also called me a 'nutter' or 'bonkers' and just a handful of them were sour. I am quite sensitive and briefly got quite worked up about them, before realising that I could use them as fuel. In a way they offered another chance for me to clarify my reasons for the journey in the same way that Ricardo did when he interrogated me. He wasn't trying to put me off; he was just sounding out all my reasoning. He was like a trainer getting his boxer ready to fight, sparring to warm him up and test his reflexes, in order to know that he is fired up in his heart and his hands, but has a lucid plan for the bout. 'Why aren't you scared?' he asked me on the evening that he arrived. I took another sip of my drink and bit my lip to consider for a moment, before looking straight into his dark eyes and explaining,

'There's no time and no need to be scared yet. I'll be scared when I'm out there.' I felt prepared and ready for the ocean now; there had been nearly three years of building up to it and I had done everything I could and was supported by some great people. Besides, I had bloody mindedness and tenacity in my armoury. Ricardo and I both agreed that there is nothing macho or gung-ho about crossing the ocean – there is no place for egos out there and no conquering of anything but your own fears. It is all about sound planning, sensible judgement, self-discipline, respect for the ocean and endurance. The rest is luck and out of anyone's control.

He continued with, 'Where's the cut off?'

I looked back at him with incredulity, fire in my gloves. Did he think I was going to give up? 'There is none. I will have to be a floating body before anyone pulls me off that boat, or very close to it.'

He wasn't satisfied and sparred again. 'What if you realise you're out there for the wrong reasons and don't want to go on?'

I squared up and shook my head. 'I don't do giving up. I'm cool with my reasons. I know exactly why I'm going out there. I'm excited. There is no turning back, buddy, no turning back. I promise.'

He smiled and asked for the bill, satisfied that my gloves were secure and that I had a plan. As he worked his charm with the waitress, I thought about how lucky I was to have such an experienced, level-headed guy on my team. He was already more than my weather man; he was my right-hand man and we were about to embark on the most incredible adventure together. I would rely on him for advice on incoming weather and best tactics for making the most of the good stuff and avoiding the bad stuff. His was the most vital role in my team, the others comprising my PR team, Briony, Sean and Caroline the doctors and my Mum, who had become chief of most things at home. Success would only happen if Ric and I were talking with each other regularly and if I trusted him more than I had ever trusted anybody before. From his home and office in Portugal on the other side of the world in the opposite hemisphere to where I would wield my oars, Ricardo would have the huge task of guiding me safely across the ocean, through contrary currents and stormy systems, and lining me up to land on Mauritius. This wouldn't just be a case of finding the needle in the haystack, this would be more like finding the very outermost corner of the eye on the left-hand side of the very tiny needle in the ocean-sized haystack. It certainly wasn't going to be easy.

As we wandered back to the yacht club I looked forward to a decent sleep over the weekend, glad that I had one week's grace before the weather would be just right for setting out. I felt good – everything was under control now that Ricardo was here – even though I was so drained. He kept telling me to eat more, sleep more, chill out, eat more, sleep more but I couldn't. Ironically, I wouldn't be able to switch off until the ocean, and even then I couldn't really. Mauritius, months and thousands of miles away – that was the next time that I would truly be able to relax. Until then, my focus was the ocean.

CHAPTER 9
OCEAN NEXT 6,000 KILOMETRES

*'The journey of a thousand leagues
begins with a single step'*

PROVERB

'How are you feeling today, my little ocean-rowing girl?' Ric was looking at me intently. I pushed my sunglasses up onto my head so I could see him properly.

'Pretty good,' I smiled back as I sculled with the oars to keep *Dippers* pointing into the waves. 'Shall I row back in or do you want to tow me?' We were just outside the harbour mouth, I was rowing *Dippers* and Ric was with a photographer in another boat. He looked serious and said that he had to tell me something before I made that decision. My mind leapt on to the alert – had I just said something really stupid? Would I be rowing against an outgoing tide or –...?

'How do you fancy going rowing in twenty-four hours? The weather is looking great for tomorrow morning.'

I was silenced. My eyebrows shot up my forehead into a surprised arch and I grinned the wide gummy grin that I always do when I am nervous or excited. My stomach had just knotted itself and I clenched my teeth into gridlock, looking inward at the cacophony of emotion which had just burst out of nowhere. I was going rowing. I looked up at him and nodded, trying my best to look composed and serious. 'Well, if you say it's good, then it's good for me, too.'

We hooked up the tow and their boat pulled out to the length of the line, leaving me to calm my little storm and think of the Final List of Things to Do before tomorrow morning. The list was huge and the clock was now ticking fast – really fast.

I leaned back against my cabin hatch and closed my eyes to the sun, trying to comprehend what was about to happen and willing the gentle waves to soothe me. This was a big day. A definitive day: my life was about to change forever as I rowed into a whole new era. Before the row, after the row: that is how my timeline would read from this day onward. Life was about to get serious and very salty. Departure was agreed for 6 a.m. the next morning and I floated on adrenaline. My appetite had disappeared and Ric kept pushing food my way, while also fending off enquiries and phone calls for me, telling me what I needed to do next and organising the willing helpers.

We worked right through the night to complete everything, with help from club members, friends of friends and people I had never even met before. They were all part of the team now, keen to help and excited to be a part of the adventure. Some were unwittingly signed up to Team Sarah, having arrived for a sociable evening at the weekly club barbecue; thinking they could have a little chat to us as we worked at the boat, they found themselves carrying jerry cans away to fill with water, or were sent off in search of a paintbrush, a pair of nail scissors, a bailer perhaps. We emptied the boat, cleaned the boat, capsized the boat, packed the boat, sorted the gear, resorted the gear, repacked the boat, took delivery of all the food, sorted the food, resorted the food, constructed netting stowage in the forward cabin and turned *Dippers* into a reflective beacon with strips of shiny tape. At one point the pontoon was completely covered with piles of my stuff, leaving any bystanders bewildered by the notion of fitting it all away into *Dippers*, floating alongside. My attitude was that 'if it has to fit, it will'. And it did, somehow, even though I would have to share my bed with two huge 100-litre bags filled with my food packets until I had eaten it all. Respite arrived with a trip to the supermarket and the chandlery – there I was anonymous and free to wander aimlessly down the aisles, deciding on what extra provisioning I needed and whether my last few Aussie dollars would stretch to it. Certainly my bank balance would be very pleased to see me so many thousands of miles out to sea.

As the sunset rolled into darkness, Clem fixed up an outside light on the pontoon, and I left Ricardo and some others sorting the piles into different piles and packing the boat through the wee hours. I sat in the office, wired on fizzy drinks and nerves, making final phone calls to the UK, emailing sponsors and friends with goodbyes or instructions for various tasks. At 2.30 a.m. I climbed into *Dippers* for a couple of hours of rest. But how do you rest when you've got a butterfly brigade marching up and down shouting, 'You're going! You're going rowing!'? I didn't sleep more than a few snatches; my mind was full of thoughts and fears, wanderings and wonderings, and my tired brain buzzed until Ric opened the cabin door to rouse me at 4.30.

'This is it, Sarah, this is it,' I whispered to myself. My toes curled up, my tummy turned, and I took a deep breath before climbing out into the cool dark morning. 'We can do this, Sarah, we can do this.' It was still and quiet, but for the chatter of those who had already gathered or who had stayed up through the night. In the quiet sanctuary of the showers of the club I wallowed under the warm flow, savouring every last drop, reminding myself what it felt like to have fresh water run over my body. I kept pushing the button for more water, each time trying to coax myself out. I talked myself through what I needed to do, and what I would focus on for the next few days. 'Eat. Row. Sleep. Row. Eat. Row. Sleep. Row. Row.' The nerves were chattering quietly, but I felt fairly calm and in control; Ric had ticked everything off our list and there was nothing more to do except get in the boat and row.

More people had arrived while I was in the shower and I felt as though my every move was being watched. I tried to avoid eye contact and conversation and just muttered to myself as I went about my final checks, the realisation of the huge task ahead now dawning on me. Ric handed me a pile of sandwiches and pestered me until I had washed them all down with as much water as I could manage while everyone else was busy with their appointed jobs. Clem had prepared boxes of fruit and a huge bag of sandwiches; Margot filled up the water bottles; Sally was on chart-folding duty. After my breakfast I padded down to the pontoon, enjoying my last steps on land. I climbed on board and then flopped through the cabin door very ungracefully, and much to the amusement of the onlookers. I pointed out to them that it takes a certain art to nip in elegantly through the little hatch – and I had yet to master it.

Ric ran through where the packing team had stowed everything – besides my chocolate stash (which I had loaded up), most of my kit had been packed during my final office session, so the whereabouts of everything from undies to suncream, and from pasta to plasters would be a surprise, for better or for worse. He promised that I would find messages and surprises as I went. Then we hugged and I stepped outside to say my goodbyes. I had known some of these people just a few hours and, beside Ric, none of them for more than two weeks. Yet they had become part of my team and would be a part of my journey and memories of it forever. It was only because of the collective effort of folks like these, here and abroad, that I had made it anywhere near that jetty. This was all a team effort. I wanted to soak up every moment – these were the last times I would have human contact for months. Equally, I wanted to get going. I was feeling a bit sick from nerves and I knew they would settle once I got to the oars. One last phone call to Mum and I would be ready to go. After she told me to be safe and have fun, I told her that I would ring her from my satellite phone once I was out there, slipped in a quick ' I love you' and had to press the red button before either of us got emotional. Neither of us wanted to be the last to say goodbye.

Realising that I hadn't brushed my teeth, I set about one last clean on the jetty, much to the delight of the two agency photographers, who snapped my foaming spit fest from every angle. Then I looked round at the smiling semicircle of people around me before running a final little circle on the pontoon and climbing aboard. I strapped on my safety harness and clipped the line to the boat; *Dippers* and I were now connected and I promised myself (and had promised Mum) that we would remain that way for the rest of the voyage while I was not in the cabin. That was my lifeline, literally.

Everyone was silent as I closed the hatches, fired up the GPS and sat down on my seat, securing my feet in the foot straps. I looked up, tapped the pontoon one last time and they prepared to cast me off.

'THREE CHEERS FOR SARAH!'

Oh my goodness me – what am I about to do?!

'HIP HIP!'

Oh shit!

'HOORAY!'

Heart racing, mouth dry.

'HIP HIP!'

Keep it together Outen, keep it together.

'HOORAY!'

Oh shit, oh shit!

My inner monologue competed with the three cheers and willed me to look composed. Instead, all I could manage was a huge beaming nervous grin before swallowing back a tear and taking my first pull at the oars. Those first few strokes felt perfect as we slicked through the silky black waters of the silent harbour, like an old carthorse slow and steady, finding its rhythm. *Dippers* and I were away and would next be touching down in Mauritius. Gulp. The distance ahead was huge and the ocean vast and that scared me, so I just focused on the song which I had chosen to play through the speakers for those first few moments, 'Don't Stop Me Now' by Queen. We had played it at Dad's funeral as the curtains closed around his coffin and so for me it spoke volumes. Instead of worrying about how far I had to journey, this song reminded me of how far I had already come. All the same, I cried as I sang and I sang as I cried.

Outside the harbour the darkness went on forever. Lights punctuated channels for this, safety zones for that, shipping lane this way and danger over there; red dots blinked, white lights flashed and greens and oranges danced to some unheard beat. I concentrated on the compass in front of me, trying to row on the course Ricardo had suggested. The idea was to push to the north of Rottnest Island which lay 12 miles out, and gradually edge out to sea. A support yacht was going to escort me for the first few hours, just to see me safely away from the main port entrance and so that the agency photographer could get some good shots. I felt so self-conscious with everyone on the support yacht watching me, tracking me, and occasionally crackling some instruction through on the radio. There were some serious sailors on board and I wanted to impress them; I wanted to be credible. I also wanted to go to the loo, but there is no polite way to do it when you have a little troupe of kayaks beside you and a boat full of supporters watching your every move; it was a bucket and chuck it set up so not the sort of thing you do in the company of people you've only just met. I tried to think of other things; not water and not toilets and not the ocean. Not water and not toilets and not the ocean. The stars were a good distraction. They made my world huge, emphasising the dimensions of my new home. And to think that the sea beneath me was only a blip of the space above me – that was weird. My mind boggled at how humongous the world is and how humongous my task was to me, but how small and insignificant it was in the grand scheme of the universe and all that space. Gulp. That was almost as bad as thinking about needing the loo. *Something else, Sarah, find something else. Sunrise?* To the east, dawn seeped into the corners of the night sky, lightening the black through greys and pastel shades to welcome in the day. Not just any day but The Day. I didn't know how yet, but I was sure that this trip would change me.

After an hour Geoff the Expert and his little troupe of kayakers bid me a hugged farewell over the side of my boat and turned back to shore, my last hug for goodness knows how many months; it was a strange feeling and my stomach knotted for a moment as I waved them off. They would be going back to get some breakfast now and a shower, perhaps a snooze, and then they would get on with their day. I would carry on rowing for the next four months before I had another shower. The escort boat played around me, sometimes dropping back to get some wide-angle shots and at others coming alongside for close-ups or to say hello. From time to time Ric whistled like a songbird to get my attention for the cameras or to show me what they hoped looked like a Mexican wave. They made me laugh and I enjoyed the company and our odd bites of conversation, again trying to soak it all up before they turned back for the harbour. They said they would come straight back out to find me in a faster boat to check on me one last time, but it was still a goodbye and I only had one left after this; then I would be completely and utterly alone. Part of me wanted to eke out the company as long as possible; another wanted to get out to sea and another was now desperate for a pee. So in the same moment that I waved them off I dived into the forward cabin to find the bucket and sweet relief.

As the sun climbed higher through clear blue skies, I picked my way through the container ships moored outside the port. They were metal giants, vast as sprawling warehouses. None answered my calls on the VHF radio and I suspected they were all having a lie-in or tucking in to a hearty breakfast. Mmmm. Breakfast. I had been rowing for four hours now and had eaten my sandwiches and fruit a few hours before, so popped inside to find something to munch. I had to throw some sandwiches overboard, regretting that I hadn't mentioned to Clem that I didn't like mayonnaise as I watched them float away; what a sorry waste of sandwich potential. My last for months, lost to the deep. At this point I should probably describe just what 'popping inside' entailed. The hatch door to my cabin was less than a metre across and a metre tall, so involved simultaneously crouching and stepping through into the cabin space — not the easiest of manoeuvres but one which I would need to perfect if I was to be efficient and safe at sea, particularly in the rough weather.

An increasingly boisterous sea followed me round the north of Rottnest and waves bounced up over the side of the boat to soak me every so often. I welcomed the cool contrast to the 40°C heat, which was already wearing me down and at times making me nod asleep at the oars as my tired body rocked up and down the sliding seat, up and down, down and up. Legs, back, arms. Legs, back, arms. Over and over, hour after hour. I longed for night-time, both for the cool air and the opportunity to snooze; I had only clocked about forty minutes' sleep the night before and that was definitely not enough. 'Are we nearly there yet?' I joked out loud and chuckled to myself. Then I let out a few big shouts of nothing in particular, just testing the acoustics of my new home. There was no reply and no echo. Nothing; just the sea doing its thing, gurgling and rippling and fizzing. I returned to the oars and rowed on.

I had been scanning the horizon for a while now, wondering if any of the boats I could see were the Fremantle Sea Rescue Boat RS100, which I knew would be heading out to find me for a final hello and goodbye. There was the fast ferry nipping back and forth between Rottnest and the mainland as well as various other motor boats and small yachts. I waved at some and tried hailing others over the radio. With no response from the waving or hailing, I imagined that I must be invisible. It turns out I was. It took RS100 over twenty minutes to find me when they made it back out to where they thought I would be, *Dippers'* little white cabins lost in the cresty white surf which now rolled with the growing swell. It was quite emotional saying hello when they arrived, never mind saying cheerio. All of those people had come back out to look for me, to be a part of my adventure, and I was grateful to them for it. If hello had been hard, then goodbye was even harder – both to hear and to say. They must have been quite emotional, too – there were mothers on there, seafarers who knew the ocean and folks for whom this was completely alien. It was a bizarre day for us all, I suppose. We reached out in gestured hugs and then waved each other home. The only difference was that they had just 10 miles back to shore and I had over 3,000 before I was home and dry. I waved them into a distant dot, tears washing suncream and sweat into my eyes and making them sting. I hoped they wouldn't have their binoculars out as I didn't want anyone to see; this was a private moment, just for me and *Dippers*. Relief, pride, happiness, sadness, nerves, exhaustion – it all came crying out until there were no more tears inside and nothing left to do but row. The thought scared me a little bit, especially as I would probably have another couple of weeks wobbling while I settled in to the journey. Whatever feelings emerged, I would need to embrace them and relax into all that it threw at me if I were to make it to the other side. I later found out that Ric had summed it up beautifully on my website that evening, writing: 'The task ahead is huge. The first night at sea is always one of mixed feelings. Sarah now has to be born again, into the oceans and gradually switch off from earthly thoughts and emotions if she is to be happy alone at sea.'

As with all major changes, it took me a while to get my head around it.

CHAPTER 10
FEEDING THE FISHES

'A sure cure for seasickness is to sit under a tree'

SPIKE MILLIGAN

Forty-five miles out from Fremantle made a great start for my first day. I ate one of the dehydrated meals for dinner as the sky turned pink, sitting out on deck waiting for the stars to arrive, trying not to think about the waves of nausea quietly stirring inside me. I pulled on some more clothes as the temperature dropped and rowed on through the night, fighting to stay awake and keen to put as many miles between me and Australia as possible. I finally collapsed onto my beanbag bed at 2.00, not even bothering to undress and leaving the thick zincy sunblock all over my face. I was spent and a bit dehydrated, with a little bit of seasickness round the edges; sleep was all I needed and all that I was capable of now. I had been awake and rowing for nearly twenty-four hours. There was no autopilot on *Dippers* so besides setting the rudder and pointing her in the right direction before I turned in, there would be no way of controlling her course while I slept. This close to land, I couldn't afford to drift backwards – out at sea I knew it would happen and I knew it wouldn't be the end of the world. But until I made it clear from the coast, I had to do everything I could to keep her moving in the right direction.

Inside my cabin, wedged in between the two big food bags that didn't fit inside the front cabin, I slept sweetly for a few hours and woke to see a cloudless sky through my hatches. There was one above my head which I had to be careful not to hit as I sat up, and the other was at my feet, looking out on to the deck – both less than a metre across and opened by two swing handles. Outside it was cool and fresh with dew – a welcome contrast to the stuffy and airless cabin. I was feeling sick so I didn't manage much breakfast, especially as the porridge mix looked rather like pale vomit once I had added some water and stirred. I smiled, thinking of Mum and me covered in porridge dust at home in January, mixing up deep bowls of oats and dried fruit, a spoonful of salt, a cup of sugar and half a tub of dried milk. That was the easy bit; vacuum packing it into individual sachets had been some Herculean effort. Once I had tidied away the breakfast clutter and my bedding I pushed on in much the same way as before, making steady progress under the relentless sun. I was already doing battle with sleep monsters and fighting off hallucinations, convinced that Ricardo and Margot were in the cabin, packing things away as they had done the night before I left. I had to keep opening the hatch to tell them to go away, warning them not to be there when I went to bed later. It was all very strange and I hoped they would leave me to cross the ocean in peace; the last thing I wanted was to be haunted the whole way to Mauritius.

By the afternoon of my second day, seasickness had added another layer of fatigue as I alternately nibbled on food, sipped energy drinks and fed the fishes with it all. The wind was also causing me some issues and had shifted to a not-very-helpful direction. Given that it was still fairly calm, I decided the best thing was simply to monitor my course over the next few hours, suspecting that it wouldn't cause too many problems. I was not a happy rower but a tiny part of me was strangely relieved that I could lose myself in a sweet and sleepy oblivion while I waited for it to blow through. How wrong I was. The wind had picked up so much by the third day that I wasn't making any useful progress on the oars. The waves were too much for me to row into and I was just getting blown backwards towards land, watching my newly won miles un-tick themselves on the GPS. To have this happen so close to land was frustrating, and I'm sure I did a bit of crying. There was no use trying to fight it as I wouldn't win, so I decided the best thing to do would be to sleep and deploy the sea-anchor. I had already nicknamed it 'Bob' – a 3.5-metre parachute, 'flown' beneath the waterline to hold the bows of the boat in to the waves, thereby reducing drift and stabilising the craft. Unfortunately, Bob acted like a sail in the current and meant that although we didn't lose much ground to the east, we were pulled steadily south in the famous Leeuwin Current. When I say we, I mean me and *Dippers*: talking about *Dippers* as a member of the team meant that I wasn't alone. It was another of those little tricks that would see me safely to Mauritius.

By now I had already exchanged numerous text messages with Ricardo via my satellite phone. Now came the news that the weather had shifted from what we had previously expected and that the sea would become ugly, uncomfortable and messy as a low pressure system rumbled up from the south.

I later found out that he had written this on my blog:

'My only hope is that this weather system doesn't change its mind yet again and hang around for a day longer or provide stronger winds than forecast. This part of the ocean is known for its dramatic weather and Australian Navy rescues. So we hope.'

I pulled Bob back in after twenty-four hours to see if I could make any more progress. Rowing and sleeping alternately in blocks of a few hours through day and night for the next four days, we were pulled further and further south with only the tiniest bits of progress west. I was going anywhere but towards Mauritius and spent a lot of time crying at the oars in frustration; this was not how my first week at sea was supposed to be. Even so, I managed to put on a surprisingly cheerful bit of chat for Radcliffe and Maconie on BBC Radio 2 one evening. Amusingly, in my brain-mush state I had confused my time zones and when I woke up to wait for the call, I quickly received a worried call from my PR manager Adrian Bell on the satellite phone. Apparently the BBC had being trying to get hold of me for an hour and were concerned that I had been lost to the sea, to sharks or seasickness. I had in fact just been sleeping with the phone turned off to save batteries.

Sitting out on the deck underneath a full moon and a canopy of stars, surrounded by waves and occasionally being rinsed by an over-excited one, I chatted live with 'the boys' in Manchester; it was surreal. Metaphorically, there were a lot of people on that boat already, supporting me from all corners of the globe, and I was pleased to share my experience with the rest of the world over the airwaves. As I pressed the red button to end the call, I marvelled at this little phone which could connect me with anyone, anywhere on the planet via a teeny satellite way up in the ether; we humans have invented some ingenious technology over time.

I had forgotten that Ric was due back in Portugal, so the news was crushing when I heard from Clem via text message that he was en route to Sydney for his flight home. Even in these six days I had already come to depend on him so much for weather information, motivation and morale. He had done this ocean-crossing lark a number of times before as a sailor and had gone solo too, so he knew what it was like to push out to sea and renounce normality for an unknown period of time. That meant he understood something of what I would be going through.

His departure coincided with a worsening of the already unhelpful weather, which made me feel inadequate and powerless, as though all my dreams about this voyage were disappearing towards the raging Southern Ocean. I was just below thirty degrees south at the moment, remembering the whalers' saying that, 'below forty degrees there is no law; below fifty there is no God'. I was scared, I was embarrassed by my lack of progress and I was cross with myself for worrying friends and family. While struggling into the waves in the afternoon of my sixth day at sea, I stopped to look for a ship. My sea-me (a radar reflector) was beeping, which meant that a ship's radar must be hitting it. There was someone else out there, but where were they? The beeping got louder until I eventually spotted a yacht, rising and falling over troughs of waves; I had found it. This was exciting – I hadn't seen anyone since leaving Fremantle a week earlier and had only spoken to one ship so far and they hadn't been too keen on chatting. I held on to the top of my cabin, straining for another glimpse. What sort of yacht was it? Length? Colour? Who was on board? Where were they going? Friend or foe? Most importantly I wondered if it would see us; I hoped so.

I had been struggling to interpret weather and information, so I didn't trust my judgement completely and wondered if I was hallucinating again. But it looked like a yellow yacht was heading straight for us. Apart from hoping that we would rendezvous, I was worried that we might collide. I picked up the VHF.

'Yellow yacht, yellow yacht, yellow yacht – this is rowing boat *Serendipity*. Do you receive me? OVER.'

I was prepared for them not to answer, but to my surprise and delight, a response swam back to me through the squelch.

'*Serendipity*, this is *Spirit of Rockingham*. I am receiving you loud and clear. OVER.'

The name sounded familiar and I frowned in concentration for a second before I realised to whom I was speaking.

'*Spirit of Rockingham*! Is that you, Jamie?' I squealed down the radio, both surprised and excited that my new friend, Jamie Dunross, the quadriplegic sailor from Perth, had sailed out to see me.

I rowed on a bit further to turn us back into the waves, now rolling on a 5-metre swell capped with white. Any meeting with another boat at sea is exciting, but Jamie's arrival was pure magic. To see another person I could speak to was wonderful out here, particularly at this point when I was so low and going nowhere fast. I watched in admiration as he moved in and out of the cabin: here was a quadriplegic man, sailing solo offshore on a 40-foot yacht. What on earth did I have to complain about? Over the radio he said that he had brought something which I had forgotten and I racked my brains to think what it could be. He pulled out Wilson, a painted volleyball named after the *Castaway* film character, from below deck and threw it into the water for me to row on to and pick up. Wilson had been given to me by the boys of Hale School before I left Fremantle, so he was a special addition to my on board crew and I was glad to have him back.

Jamie said that he would circle me for an hour just to make sure I was OK, before he headed back to shore. It would take him nearly two days to sail back in and he admitted that he wasn't looking forward to battling the Leeuwin, which had slowed his progress out to me. I hated that he was watching me struggling. Frustrated and shattered, I cried and cried angrily, pulling hard into the waves and head wind, hoping that he couldn't see my tears. I must have looked like a complete idiot, out of my league and making almost no progress. I admire him for not telling me as much – if anyone knew about fight in this life he did, and he also knew that I would give it every ounce of strength I could muster. He sailed back close in to me for one final chat then disappeared as quickly as he had arrived. I sat down on my seat to cry, my energy all gone and my morale plummeting, not really very keen on this rowing lark any more.

That evening I put Bob out, resigned to the fact that I would be pulled further south and even further off course, but not knowing what else to do. Soon the seascape was a foaming white mess of giants, dancing wildly beneath grey skies, sending *Dippers* and me crashing into walls of water as waves rolled through underneath or into us. Curled up in my cabin, over the next few days I drifted in and out of sleep through some of the scariest hours of my life. Night-time was the worst; at least in the daylight I could sit up and see the waves out of the hatch so that I could brace myself as they charged at the boat, ready for the impact. In the dark my ears provided my only reference, of rushing water, of waves thudding into us and the creaking lines of the sea anchor.

Ric promised that I would soon be out of it, that the current was kicking me south and out into the open ocean; he said that he wasn't too worried, although I think he was just trying to make me feel good. I got quite angry at his suggestion that I was 'so close to being OK and out of trouble' if only I could row a 'teeny bit west'. How teeny? 'Forty miles.' That was not very teeny in my books, not when I couldn't even make one mile west in these conditions. How did he not see that I was as good as 300 miles from clear water? The Australian authorities had a different take on the situation and were concerned. Paraphrased, our phone call went a bit like this; 'Sarah, we're worried you're going a bit too far south, mate.' It was true; I was en route to dinner with the penguins, in some of the world's toughest and roughest waters. The Southern Ocean officially started just a few hundred miles to the south and the no law, no God thing kicked in soon after.

I struggled to remain optimistic amidst talk of rescue and huge bills to tow me in for a restart and I got quite upset, rationale and reason being hard to accept in my fatigued and fragile state. So I thought I would put the question to the floor and see what my friends and ocean-rowing buddies thought. At three o'clock in the morning I rang twice-Atlantic rower and friend Sally Kettle for some wisdom and she agreed in her sleepy state that a tow seemed like the best option. Another veteran rowing buddy, Roz Savage, reassured me that this was the right thing: 'Spectacular ending to first attempt, glorious success second time round: it's what all the best adventurers do.' Her first attempt to leave America on her Pacific row in 2007 ended with a rescue and restart so she knew what she was talking about. Poor Mum – I had these conversations with her too and it wasn't easy. I cried, she cried and I wished it all wasn't happening.

There were ships about and I was worried that we were going to be squashed; I felt overwhelmed and I was getting myself worked up about the options for a restart. Would I tow the boat north? Would I go from Fremantle again? I grew more and more agitated and scared at feeling so small, so lonely and so out of depth, that I was soon blubbering and reaching for the phone to call Sally again. I hate ringing people when I am upset but I was so soothed by the voice of someone who I knew had been out in big seas in small boats and I knew she would make me laugh, too. And she did.

As it happened, the following day saw a significant drop in the sea state and wind strength; it was as though the nasty stuff had blown through to test us. I was quietly proud that we had survived, even if I was a little annoyed at being so far off course. I felt like *Dippers* and I had earned a stripe and knew that although I had a lot to learn still, we had come through some very rough stuff and she had proved her place on the team. With the easing of the seas, I pointed to Fremantle and started rowing back in to shore, calling off the tow. The next two days were like a welcome weekend to my dreadful week; the sun shone, the wind disappeared and the sea smoothed to a gentle rolling swell. This allowed me to do some washing of myself, the boat and my clothes – I was a bit smelly by now and there were splashes of dried sick all over the deck where I hadn't quite made it overboard. For the first time in days I brushed my teeth and washed my hair, which I hadn't done since my last morning on land. My appetite returned as my seasickness waned and I ate everything I could get my hands on, cooking for the first time in a week. The on board kitchen was fairly limited in terms of facilities and consisted of pulling out my little gas stove and a plastic spoon-fork hybrid from one of my hatches and boiling water in the footwell to add to whatever sachet of dehydrated food took my fancy. I loved this new found tranquillity in my feelings and stomach, and I was glad to be rowing again – albeit back to base to loop the loop. Now that I had found my sea legs and was 'in the groove' with a new routine, I decided that I wouldn't go back to shore, but would instead row up the coast to where the Leeuwin Current was narrower, and perhaps offered my best shot at getting through. I was relieved to hear that everyone, including the knowledgeable locals, had been surprised by how much the wind and current had affected my course and this made me feel less silly.

One night on that return row I listened to Mozart's *Clarinet Concerto* through my speakers on deck as I paddled under a blanket of silver stars; that piece will forever remind me of the deep peace and contentment I felt at that moment, rowing through inky seas, with bioluminescence twirling off each stroke. The sea stayed smooth and I surfed up the coast, helped by following seas. Late one afternoon, I spotted a pod of about one hundred spinner dolphins chasing each other across the sea, cavorting and somersaulting, while the horizon to my left showed signs of land. I rowed outside of Rottnest Island on the evening of day ten, under a dramatic sky of pinks and reds, enjoying the fact that I had something other than sea to look at, but on the other hand a little bit nervous at being so close to land and ships again. I was on high alert and slept in short bursts, waking regularly to check for ships, while trying not to disturb the tern who was hitching a ride for the night, perched on my forward cabin, his black head tucked under his wing, showing only one eye to the world.

At three o'clock I woke again and puzzled over why the cabin looked so different. There were two sets of very dim lights on each side of the cabin which I had never seen before. They were the LEDs of the cabin lights. I noticed that all of the other lights on the boat were either off or extremely dim. The VHF radio display no longer glowed orange and the voltmeter read way below what it would normally do. Clearly, something was very wrong with the electrics. A phone call back to my electrician in the UK and some investigation left me with no option but to radio in for a tow. It would be stupid to carry on with a problem like that, especially given that I was just 10 miles out of Fremantle, from where I had launched eleven days before. I guess some things are just meant to be.

Either way, I decided that it was a blessing in disguise and had proven to be a damn good shake down for the ocean ahead; in short, a 400-mile practice run. Some asked if I would be going home and I laughed – I wasn't going to step down that easily.

CHAPTER 11
THE ORANGE INQUISITION

'Drag your thoughts away from your troubles... by the ears, by the heels, or any other way you can manage it'

MARK TWAIN

Life on dry land exploded into a maelstrom almost as soon as I stepped off onto the jetty. There was my first (and actually illegal) mistake – I hadn't warned the Australian authorities that I would be back on their shores until after I arrived. The second mistake was in telling them that I had left my boat and been out for a meal (also illegally) before I had been quizzed and vetted and officially 'welcomed' back in to Australia. I was threatened with every punishment under the sun apart from being pushed out to sea in a small boat: namely monstrous fines, destruction of all my food supplies and impounding of my boat. The issue was that I had effectively just imported all of my food (and myself) into their country illegally. The food issue was particularly naughty because of all the strict rules about imports and exports to protect their island wildlife from invasive species. As a biologist I salute the stringency, but as a rower I hated every bit of it. After much growling and scowling, the customs heavies decided that I was just a very bad wannabe ocean-rowing Pom and signed me back into the country with some fines, metres and metres of yellow tape marking my boat out of bounds, and pages of rules and restrictions about just what I could and couldn't do with my boat and food.

The Orange Inquisition is an amusing little memory nowadays, but in my tired and on-the-verge-of-tears state it was anything but. Two of the Australian and Quarantine Inspection Service (AQIS) inspectors had been sent down to the yacht club to go over my boat with a fine-tooth comb and look for beasties and nasties, remove anything that presented a threat, cordon off anything that I was allowed to keep and take notes to help AQIS decide whether or not I could keep all, or any, of my food. Given that this freeze-dried food is expensive and had all been packed neatly away into the hard-to-reach corners of my boat, I was floored by the suggestion they might leave me with nada. It takes a certain knack to look comfortable in a little ocean-rowing cabin and it is impossible to look good while foraging about in all of those well-hidden hatches where my supplies had been packed neatly away. Watching those two AQIS monkeys struggle inside the tiny cabins was the only funny thing about that process; until they spotted where I had spilled a packet of teeny red radish seeds on the deck and spent twenty minutes on their knees trying to pick them up with wetted tissue paper. After that they returned to the cabin, where the smilier of the two, a friendly chap called Damien, pulled out an orange from one of the stowage nets and held it up into the sunlight, looking at it cautiously. Glancing up at me through knitted brows, he asked me what I was going to do with it. I looked at him as though he had just asked me something in Polish, and tentatively suggested I was thinking of eating it. I wasn't aware you could do anything else with an orange.

'Am I allowed?'

'Only if you eat it now, down here on this boat, give me the peel to put in this ridiculously large yellow quarantine bag and I then sign this form here to say you've done it, spray you with pesticide and push you out to sea.' I considered for a nanosecond, pushed it away and told him to do what he wanted with my orange. I didn't want it any more. 'TAKE THE DAMN ORANGE!' screamed a raging imp in my head. Thankfully, I don't think Damien heard the imp.

A lemon came next. It, too, was scrutinised by the frown and latex gloves. He wiped a bead of sweat from his forehead, struggling under the pressure, and then called out to the gloves in the other cabin. 'What do you reckon to this?' Inquisitor no. 2 forced himself out through the hatch, matched the frown of his compadre and looked up seriously. 'She can keep it: the sticker says it's from Australia'. Deep joy: lemon one, orange nil. Sadly, leaving Australia in a hurry wasn't on the 'Can do' list from AQIS – I wasn't to move my boat at all or to touch any of the yellow tape or forbidden objects. Nothing should be added or removed until further notice had been given, meaning that I was grounded for the foreseeable future. This also meant that I could be assured of rest and sleep and food for a few more days on shore while I waited for decisions from the AQIS powers above. Or so I thought.

Rest and sleep actually didn't figure very much at all as I tried to get my head around the logistics, formalities and general decompressing from my Warm-up Lap. Everything felt out of control and seemed too big and complicated, as things do when you're tired and emotional. There were important decisions to be made about the plan for my next attempt, such as where I would be leaving from and when and how I would get there if it was from further north. There was a lot of talk of trailering the boat north, of rowing it north, even one mad idea of having Jamie tow me north in his yacht. It seemed everyone loved the bloody north. Arguments for going further up the coast were based on differences in currents and winds; it was also where previous attempts on the Indian had left from, but Ric was still keen that I stay put. Coupling all that with simple things such as my not having any clean land clothes anymore (only very smelly ocean clothes) and being absolutely dog-tired, I had a teary break down on the phone to Mum, reassuring her that I was fine but not fine but would soon be fine… 'Honestly, Mum. If only [sob] they [sob] would let [sob] me [sob] back out to [sob, sob] sea.' In spite of all the lovely folks around me who were offering to help, I felt swamped and quite alone. My team were scattered about the world and I was driving everything myself again and after two hectic days on land I cracked. As the tears rolled down my cheek onto the damp patch of pillow below, I consoled myself with the knowledge that the ocean would be much simpler. Now all I had to do was get back out.

Fortunately, nothing major needed to be changed in the set-up of *Dippers* and the kit and there was nothing too catastrophically wrong with the electrics either. It transpired that the batteries were in fact just fine, apart from some mis-wired connections – not my fault – which meant that the batteries hadn't been charging as efficiently as possible. The power issue had been a combination of, rather embarrassingly, my playing my music too loudly and rowing north for the last few days, which meant that the solar panels hadn't been charging nearly enough for my carefree, power hungry (and I now realise, quite naive) lifestyle. I didn't mind the little bit of egg on my face, though; it was better that I had learned these lessons just offshore rather than far out to sea.

After a week on land I was worn out. Stressed, tired and emotional, I wore my sunglasses permanently, to hide the tears which were now in my eyes most of the time. The lovely Margot (one of my surrogate Aussie Mums) rang me up and invited me to her family home for the weekend, away from the sea, promising I could sleep as much as I wanted, that she wouldn't talk about rowing and that she would feed me up with home cooking. Finally, did I have any requests? Bed, shower, sleep, bush walk and a supermarket trip: my needs were simple. The weekend was wonderful; to be away from boats and interested onlookers with their barrage of well-intentioned questions was so relaxing, and to be with a family a real comfort.

Feeling renewed and awake, and with the blessing of the AQIS that I could keep all my food and head out to sea without having to pay the long list of punishments and fines, I now had headspace to make important decisions about my point of departure. There had been quite a lot of debate and discussion over the options. I made a list of pros and cons for each place, bearing in mind that Ric was right-hand man in my team, I had little money and I had already annoyed customs. My gut instinct said Fremantle. I had friends here now; I knew what it was like to row out from Challenger Harbour and after all, I had said I would, so I would damn well prove that it could be done. Everyone still felt that if the wind hadn't shifted as it did, then I would have made it out to sea safely the first time around. Departure day was named as 1 April and Ric was confident that the new weather window would be enough 'to blow and row the hell out of Australia once and for all'.

On my final night on land I was raring to go, the nerves helping to keep me focused. Geoff the Expert had helped me pack the boat; some new friends had kindly taken me on a supermarket run and generously footed the bill; and I had been lucky enough to be visited by British rowers Guy Watts and Andy Delaney. They were due to be setting out from Australia in a couple of weeks' time in a rowing race with eleven other boats, also aiming for Mauritius. I had not wanted to be a part of the race as I didn't want to pay the £15,000 entry fee and felt I had more flexibility and control over everything if I did it independently, leaving from Fremantle instead of Geraldton in the north, for example. We had met in Southampton the year before and kept in touch intermittently, each conscious of everything the other was doing to prepare for the ocean. We exchanged telephone numbers with promises to keep in contact on the water and I reassured them that it was great out there, while I showed them round the boat and passed on what I had learned. We hugged and wished each other well for the journey. 'SEE YOU IN MAURITIUS!' I shouted after them as they left me to my final packing, hoping that our arrivals would overlap and that we both made it across in one piece. We would both fight many battles out there, some the same and some different – I envied them having each other but at the same time I loved my independence and all that would bring to my journey. For dinner, I went out with my Aussie friends for pizzas and beers and even landed myself a new sailing jacket, after complimenting Jamie on how warm his looked. It is the first time I have ever done that and been gifted with the item in question, so I well recommend it. Note to self: compliment more people more often on their clothing.

As I wandered along the jetty to *Dark Energy*, the yacht that someone had kindly offered me to sleep on, I looked across to *Dippers*, bobbing gently at her mooring and shining brightly in the moonshine. She looked like the runt (albeit the beautiful one) of the litter surrounded by all the gin palaces and posh yachts and suddenly I knew that I should sleep in her tonight; it didn't seem right to leave her. I stepped over the safety rail and crept quietly through the hatch so as not to wake I don't know who, and took a moment to run through a list of things for the morning.

Diary entry: 31 March
'It's eleven o'clock at night and I leave at 8.00 a.m. Rather less frantic than first time round and

I'm looking forward to a proper sleep. There's a pile of food to be cut up and I've stacked all my bottles for filling; Margot, I'm giving that job to you. Customs are coming at 7.00 to stamp me out of Aus and then I am officially 'Gone Rowing' and not coming back in a hurry. I'd just better get across in one piece. I'm feeling confident. Ric says the weather is the best it's been for four months too, so I've got the best chance possible now. Let's nail it.

Goodnight Australia.'

I slept deeply and dreamed of nothing, waking to a soft dawn and the first well wishers, all wrapped up against the stiff cool of morning. It felt right this time round; *Dippers* and I were off.

The club was already buzzing with activity, and I felt uncomfortable being the centre of attention. There were even a few sets of people I had never met before; they had driven from a few hours away to see me leave after hearing me talk on the radio or seeing my news in the papers. Jamie had kept his kids back from school, and people had taken time off from work – I was so touched that all these folks had come along, but it was a bit overwhelming. Two shiny grey dolphins played round *Dippers*, encouraging me to get going and reminding me of Ricardo, whose company in Portugal is called Delfinus, Greek for dolphin; it was as though he was there in spirit.

I skipped my way through a little set of thank-yous, beamed at Geoff to push me away and took my first strokes as he called for three cheers. In a rowing boat you look back on where you have come from, so I drank up all the details of the crowd cheering for me, standing up to wave as I rounded the first corner of the harbour. There I had to fight back tears as I spotted Clem and Rob, two key players in my Aussie team, waving from one of the yachts. Others had run round to the harbour wall and waved from there. Two boats followed me out those first few miles, one a kayaker dressed in bright orange, his face pasted in thick sunblock. I enjoyed the company and we chatted our way out into the choppy water, by now glistening brightly in the sun. The other was a motor boat and had my new Mauritian friends Lina and Gerard on board, who I had met a few days earlier via the chap in Mauritius helping with preparations for the finish, along with Guy and Andy, the two rowers.

As it was 1 April, we had played a little hoax by photographing me taking an outboard motor and 600 litres of fuel on board, stating that this was so that I could rescue myself if needed. Many of my blog followers were caught out and my team on shore told me of comments pouring in to my website congratulating my good sense while lots of others tried to work out the maths of the engineering. Even experienced sea-folk such as my friend Geoff Holt were hooked ('Arghhh, I can't believe I was duped!'). I just hoped that I wouldn't later be branded the fool. Some had been surprised at my going out to sea a second time, but they clearly didn't know me and had never seen me fight. I was no fool and I was not fooling around; I was serious and optimistic about the ocean and my ability to make it to Mauritius in one piece. Or else why on earth would I be doing it? That evening one of my sponsors wrote a lovely message on my blog, asking me to, 'Take care and remember that it is only a challenge. Failure is no disgrace – the taking part, the effort is what matters.'

For now, I had an ocean to row. If I failed again, then it wouldn't be for want of trying.

CHAPTER 12

AND ALL I ASK IS A SUNNY DAY WITH WHITE CLOUDS FLYING

'Wherever you go, go with all your heart'

CONFUCIUS

I was more than pleased to be on my way once more, and grateful to have sunshine warming my muscles and a gentle sea nudging me helpfully in the right direction. When the motor boat turned back to base after a few hours I stood and waved and waved and waved, following their boat with my eyes as it shrank first into a smudge and then to nothing. Andy and Guy would join me on the ocean in a few weeks' time in their own little rowing boat, *Flying Ferkins*, though we fully expected never to see each other out there. Each of us would be blown by winds, pushed and pulled by currents across the waves.

'Now that I don't have this boat escort, I can hang my knickers out to dry,' I told my Dictaphone once they had left and I pushed on past the moored shipping. These metal leviathans represented both my potential nemesis and source of rescue, should we get too close or I need assistance on the water. I squinted up at them, wondering who was on board and where they would go after docking in Perth and whether our paths might cross out at sea. Not that I would be any the wiser – none of them answered my attempts at a hello on the VHF radio. I smiled to think that these beasts would cross the ocean in a matter of days, clocking top speeds of around 30 or 40 knots. My voyage would take up a significant chunk of my year; however, I was sure that mine was bound to be more fun and full of adventure. It had to be – I had 500 bars of chocolate on board. How many boats can lay claim to such a fine chocolate-to-crew ratio? Rations aside, I knew my ocean crossing would be incredible.

My Warm-up Lap had shown me that I needed to manage my rowing and resting patterns more effectively this time and so I took short rests during the day, snoozing or stretching out in the cabin for maybe ten, twenty, forty minutes. While out rowing I drank up all the details of land while I could still see them, wondering when I would be back again, hoping that it wouldn't be too soon. Fremantle's Maritime Museum curved into the air like the Sydney Opera House; the cranes and containers of the port looked like a pile of children's building blocks; masts of sailing boats waved in harbours and, as I moved further up the coast, the towers of the city stood proud. Beaches stretched out a bright white along the shore; swanky apartment blocks and high-rises climbed into the sky behind and life trucked on as normal for those on land. Only I had started a new adventure today.

Instead of turning out to sea after Rottnest Island this time I made use of the inshore current which tracks up the coast. The breeze picked up a bit through the afternoon, cooling the sun which scorched the deck and made me skip over it from my rowing seat to my hatch, burning my toes. Even though I felt more queasy than I did hungry, I nibbled my way through the day and into the night, trying to avoid the dehydrated meals while I still had more interesting 'land food' to graze on. There were the boxes of fruit and jam sandwiches that Margot had chopped up for me and some fresh muffins too, which I ate faster than anyone on shore would ever dream of doing. On the landless side of my boat on the right, the sun dipped and turned the sky a dusky pink; meanwhile to my left the night-time show of lights on land had begun. It made for a lovely first evening back on the water and I was glad that whoever had picked the day's weather had been so kind and thoughtful – it was just what I needed to settle into this strange new world again.

I rowed on until the night was treacle black and filled with diamond stars, heading to bed around midnight. Although I was tired and just wanted to wrap up in my blanket and sleep, I made the effort to go through my routine of wet-wiping off the suncream, applying moisturiser, talc and hand cream, cleaning my teeth and so on, as much for the sake of my clean fresh sheets as my own cleanliness. I had a run of text messages on my satellite phone from friends and family, as well as from Geoff the Expert and Ricardo – all positive and encouraging, and happy with my progress of twenty-something nautical miles so far. The last thing was to fill in the next line of my logbook and mark the day's end on the GPS, check that all my gear was stashed away safely and then I was free to drift on to dreamland, my weary muscles applauding the rest time. I slept lightly for a couple of hours before checking my position and that of any other boats in the area then slept again some more; after a whole week of long, full sleeps it would take a few days to get used to being on alert again. It was great to see that, thanks to favourable winds, I had gained sea miles in the few hours while I slept and pleasingly all in the right direction. I was still nervous of a rerun of the Warm-up Lap, but trusted Ric's forecasting of fair winds for at least seventy-two hours.

A stiff breeze blew over the next few days and the waves grew steeper, blowing from a useful easterly direction so that we were treated to some exciting surfing. While they weren't as big as the waves we'd seen on the Warm-up Lap, they were certainly testing me, warming me up for the bigger stuff to come. Phil had designed and Jamie had built *Dippers* to be a real surfer chick, and although it was nerve-wracking to whizz down wave sides at high speed, I felt sure that I couldn't have had a better boat for company. With each hour that passed I grew more confident in my own abilities to captain her, too, and began to enjoy surfing with her. Surfing a rowing boat is like any other surfing. You line up square to the wave, paddle hard as you feel the back end lift and steer down it by digging one or other oar into the water as a pivot, squealing, whooping and swearing as required. I loved learning how she moved and tracked in different conditions and how I could make the most of them to pull in more miles. It was electrifying to race down waves, tummy lurching as on a roller coaster, the wind in my hair and inevitably a few waves sloshing me. Often the scupper flaps on the side of the hull would be forced open by rushing water, which flooded the deck and filled the footwell, leaving my feet even soggier than normal. The scariest moments were when I couldn't hold our course and we carved into a wave, broaching under the weight of the water dump crashing in over the side. Those were silent screaming moments as I braced every muscle in my body, sometimes letting go of the oars to grip the grab rails as I faced the wave growing up into my sky, a tower of blue or turquoise edged with white. Once I had clocked that we had come through it and hadn't been capsized, it was a race to get back on the oars and line up for the next wave, often hollering triumphantly as I pulled hard to swing the stern round. Being thrown off the seat as an oar got caught in the water or the boat heeled over was neither extraordinary nor something I wanted to repeat more often than necessary; we often balanced on that fine line between feeling very excited and in fear of a complete wipe out. Although we had run a successful capsize drill in dock I didn't want to test *Dippers'* ability to self-right out at sea and would be happy (and very lucky) if I made it to Mauritius without rolling at all. All in all, the adrenaline was delicious and I was addicted.

Less addictive was the sight of my hands and feet. After only a few days they were already disintegrating from being wet all day; layers of skin sloughed off my palms and the soles of my feet, leaving them a white and soggy mess and my cabin speckled with shed skin. I was only completely dry at night when I could take all my clothes off and let everything air. My bum hurt, stinging from being constantly wet and salty; sitting on my cushion outside was like sitting on hot, itchy drawing pins, which didn't bode well for the months ahead. Initially it was too hot to wear waterproof trousers, so I just wore Lycra shorts; some ocean rowers swear by rowing naked, but to me that seemed like trekking 1,000 miles in hiking boots but no socks. The mix of sweat, water and salt meant that saltwater sores and boils were becoming a permanent feature of my Lower Decks – red and, as their name suggests, very sore. To keep it all as calm as possible and prevent deep infection I made a regime of applying talcum powder, zinc oxide cream, iodine and lavender oil a daily ritual, sometimes thrice daily. By Day 9 I was brewing some monster boils and I was convinced that I had trench foot. 'I don't know what it looks like, but I'm sure that it would look like this if I did have it. They're falling apart,' I told my diary. I looked forward to being dry and desalted at the end of the day in the same way that I looked forward to the re-warming of my toes and fingers if it was really cold. For even when the sun was shining, a wet windy day meant a chilly day at sea, calling for waterproofs and fleecy hats.

Lying in my cabin I could get a feel of the day by looking out of my hatch, listening to what the water was doing and feeling for the boat's motion. Hearing and feeling a wave slam over the top of the cabin or into its side suggested a very wet day ahead. I always drew out my preparations inside on these days, savouring every last moment of dryness. The first thing I did every morning was turn on my satellite phone to check for messages. Then it was tablets, toilet, teeth clean, logbook, before prepping to go outside properly for breakfast and rowing. Pulling on wet shorts usually made me gasp with the coolness and the sting of the open sores, but at least once they were on they started to warm up with my body heat. I slipped into my waterproof top, a shiver running through me at the feeling of cold rubber on my skin, then smiled as I pulled on my fleecy neck warmer and hat. Next came the damp and cold safety line around my waist, suncream and sunglasses, and I was ready to go outside. I judged the day's opening by timing how long it took for the first wave to sluice me with its morning greeting, which quite often happened as I slinked out of the cabin, dousing me with cold salt and sending water running down the back of my neck to invade my warmth. This was made worse in the second week when my waterproof trousers split down the seam of the crotch, rendering them fairly useless and not in the least bit waterproof. If only I had brought my heavy-duty salopettes. Instead I had listened to various rowers who had said I would only need normal waterproof trousers, the sort you use for walking. Clearly my kindly sponsored Berghaus trousers were only meant for walking, not rowing across oceans, and my rowing friends who had advised them hadn't had such messy weather on their Atlantic runs. Next time I'll take the heavy-duty stuff as well.

In many books I had read, ocean rowers seemed to take this continual drenching personally, holding a fiery vendetta against the sea. I tried to avoid this and each morning I would smile (or try to) as I stepped outside to breathe in the sea air, all fresh and salty. No matter how tired or sore I felt, a lungful of it filled me with renewed energy for a moment at least. I shouted a greeting out over the waves, 'GOOOOD MORNING WOOOORLD!', perhaps closely followed by a squeal as a wave came in. Every day was a good day by simple virtue of the fact that I was alive and living the dream. I was both a day closer to Mauritius and another day down the grief road – all happy progress. And for me it was better than being stuck in an office and driven by someone else's routine; the ocean was just the ocean, doing its ocean thing and I had to live by its terms. So while I might not enjoy being soaked continuously by feisty waves, I loved the way it was so changeable and fickle, how its forces were calmed or fired up in a flash. That was one of the reasons I had set myself this challenge in the first place. I was in love with it, waves, storms and all. There was so much energy out there, raw and elemental, and I gained my own from this. I had seen big waves on my Warm-up Lap and had experienced some very heavy seas on my Atlantic yacht passage in training, but I knew that this crossing would test me far more than I could ever imagine. The ocean always had many more gears and always had surprises. My blog readers knew it too, especially the old sea dogs among them. An Australian ex-naval-officer wrote a note along those lines one day, halfway between joking and jeering, 'Remember the sea is a hard taskmaster and the Royal Australian Navy likes a good rescue!'

On the subject of blogging, my website was being kept up to date by my Mum and my PR folks, Amy and Adrian, and once my web people at Lumpy Lemon had figured out the techy aspect, I was able to upload blogs directly from the boat, using the satellite phone and a tiny handheld computer. It generally took a few minutes while the phone searched for the satellite connection and then fed all the data via space back home to the server. Mum then played postie and copied and pasted all of the comments from the blog into emails for me to read – all in all a great facility to have, even if it was painful for my bank balance.

CHAPTER 13

BECOMING A SEA ANI

'Strange is our situation here upon Earth'

ALBERT EINSTEIN

One week in and I had the blues. I was swinging between soaring happiness and quiet glumness, admitting to my diary on Day 7 that 'I don't think I would ever want to spend 100 days at sea by myself again.' This was not a great thing to be writing when I had many more lots of seven days ahead of me.

'TO BE OPENED AFTER ONE WEEK AT SEA' read the envelope. Inside the little card it said, 'Thanks for being such a grand girl. Just to let you know I'm thinking of you and Dad would be proud. Love Mum.' Tears and smiles refreshed me and I muddled on for another day.

I refused to confess my state of mind openly to anyone else, though, and hoped it would be just a passing stint.

After all, I had just swapped life in the real world for life in a completely surreal one. It was my dreaming which had got me there and it was my rowing which would get me safely to the other side. Never in my life had I been so wholly liable for my own safety or single-mindedly committed to one task. I found this beautiful and scary, liberating and restrictive; it was exactly what I had wanted. I still wanted it. I was just finding it hard to adjust. And the ocean ahead was mind-bogglingly enormous, a huge swathe of emptiness between the two islands on my chart, with only a tiny little red line where I had plotted my progress so far. This mood popped up on and off for another week, set against a general feeling of all-round culture shock. All this and the solitude, sun and hours and hours of rowing were turning me into something like a hormonal teenager, crying one minute and hysterically happy the next, generally a bit confused by all the feelings and not really knowing how to reconcile them. My only real option was to row on, of course, which I found easier said than done at times because it was so tiring. It seemed that I had two settings – tired or really tired – and I found waking up in the morning really hard and getting out of bed even harder. I got angry and frustrated at myself, worried that something wasn't quite right and already doubting my ability to last one month, let alone four. The mood swings were exhausting, too, and I found that I got distracted easily, getting up from rowing after half an hour to find something else to do and so on and so on throughout the day, interspersing bursts of rowing with other activities.

I eventually confided in Ric, who assured me that he understood early voyage blues, that it was all perfectly normal, absolutely to be expected and perfectly curable. All I had to do was 'become a Sea Ani'. A what? A Sea Ani. It is his very own concept and word and, according to him, a Sea Ani is where you become so happy on the ocean that you feel a bit guilty at not thinking about land any more – you are at one with the sea, the gull's way and the whale's way, and all the associated drama, laws and energy of the ocean. You have to become a beast of the ocean, if you like. Bring it on! I currently felt like a schizophrenic fish out of water, my emotions volatile, and all the time sweating and toiling and rapidly growing bored of my bad singing. I was frustrated that it was taking me so long to settle in to a life which was so simple; each day I had only to row west and stay happy. How hard could it be? Apparently impossible, until I had shaken off the shackles from land and could focus fully on the ocean.

It wasn't just the blues that I was contending with – I was also vomiting my way through early-voyage seasickness, which meant I had to force myself to keep snacking to replace my energy stores. I enjoyed the 'land food' that I had brought along for this adjustment period, perishables such as fruit, muffins and bread that would soon run out and last only in my memories until Mauritius. 'How did I ever think that ten packets of biscuits would be enough for a whole ocean? I'm three down already,' I had written on Day 6. My food bags and snacks allowed me around 5,000 calories for each day, but I still expected (and rather hoped) I would lose a lot of the weight I had piled on before leaving. I generally grazed throughout the day and night, starting with porridge for breakfast, often eating it as cold gruel if the sea was too rough to boil water safely in my little gas stove. This would be followed by regular snacks of seed bars, chocolate, dried fruit and nuts, with some dehydrated meals thrown in and various random treats. In my bid to stop scurvy I had stashed away some fresh fruits and vegetables, although these didn't last long. Before I had left Australia, Geoff had written on my cabin bulkhead, 'Fresh fruit is very much overrated – hardly worth thinking about really.' I cursed him with a smile each time I saw it – later in the voyage, fresh food and fruit teased my dreams. I often woke in the night, tasting and smelling food from home with all its textures and flavours; there was no enjoyable texture to any of my food. Dehydrated meals varied between very sloppy and squidgily stodgy, and flavour was in even shorter supply. As I coaxed myself into finishing off a packet of Mush X, Y or Z, I cursed the salesman who had convinced me to buy from their company, luring me in with promises of discounts.

On my Warm-up Lap I had discovered that strawberry protein shakes tasted as bad on the ocean as they did on land; I gave away as many of them as possible when I repacked the boat ready for round two – completely illegally, I later discovered. My friends at the AQIS would have been suitably unimpressed. They had cordoned off most of my food with yellow tape and heavy-duty cable ties, not to be removed until I was over 12 nautical miles out to sea and therefore outside of Aussie waters, which meant leaving many of the shakes on board. This meant extra weight and, as I was 112 per cent convinced that I wouldn't drink any of them, I decided to empty a few overboard. Unfortunately, it wasn't only the sea which changed colour. I discovered that a downwind deployment resulted in my receiving a spraying with strawberry talc and in the end resigned to rowing the extra weight; it had to be better than death by pink, but to this day the smell still makes me gag.

It took about twelve days to push off the continental shelf, rowing through steep and boisterous waves. Day 11 was particularly wet and windy, slogging through grey and cresty seas. The warmth of my dinner packet held against my tummy cheered me as I huddled with my back to the waves, trying to work out if it was better to see the waves flying towards me or not while I talked myself into eating another mouthful of mush. As I cleared up after dinner, rinsing out my stove pan overboard, somehow I let go of it and lost it to the deep. I lurched over the side to try and grab it but it was gone – we were running with the waves and all I could do was curse and growl at myself as I watched it waft down to an eternity on the seabed. As this constituted a loss of 50 per cent of my cooking capability I didn't know whether to laugh or cry, and I was just considering the pros and cons of each when I looked up to see the sky go black. Something was soaring low over me, and my first thought was of planes. A 3.5-metre wingspan and mottled brown body suggested otherwise – these wings had feathers. My teatime visitor was the biggest of all the winged voyagers in this world, the mighty wandering albatross. I whooped in delight as I watched him cruise over the waves, making light work of the watery walls which had hampered my progress since morning. Life was good – I would trade a pan for an albatross any day.

The morning of Day 16 provided a rather too exciting start to proceedings. My sea-me radar alarm invaded my sleep – it beeped if it was hit by another boat's radar – and I lay awake on my beanbag for a moment with my eyes closed, timing the gaps between the beeps as I tried to discern what the sea was doing outside. At the same time I was half-heartedly flexing each of my major muscles, coaxing my stiff body into action. Peeling back my eyelids, yawning and not feeling very energetic, I stepped clumsily outside to see who was out there. I was met by the dull dawn breaking on an even duller sea, and with a slap in the face from an over-excitable wave was kicked into action. There was no boat in sight even when I scanned with binoculars on three separate sweeps so I put out a few calls on the VHF, giving my position and asking whoever may be there for a wide berth. 'Sécurité, sécurité, sécurité. This is rowing boat *Serendipity*, *Serendipity*, *Serendipity*.' I gave my position and heading and finished off with 'Wide berth kindly requested as I am small and limited in my ability to manoeuvre. OUT.'

I turned up the volume and listened carefully, but there was nothing, nobody. After a few transmissions, there was still no boat and, as the alarm wasn't too insistent and it was way before 8.00, when I had planned to wake up, I decided I would just catch a few more snoozes and hope for the best. Bad idea; I was woken up ten minutes later by the sea-me going berserk and this time when I popped out on deck and swept the horizon for ships I saw a very large one making easy work of the 2-metre waves as it headed straight for us. Completely naked, I stood on the deck with radio in one hand and holding on to my cabin roof with the other, alternately repeating my VHF call and waiting for a response. Still no reply. I could feel my heart starting to beat heavily and as the ship surged closer, I could pick out details – the lifting winches, the windows, the flags, the name painted on the side, even though I couldn't read it. Things weren't looking good. Ocean rowers had been squashed by big boats before so there was no guarantee that the captain had even noticed us yet or even would do – it was very possible that it could run straight into us and not bat an eyelid. The ship was about a mile away and still bearing down; my heart was now hammering even louder and my mouth going dry as I tried to line up the angles and calculate whether or not and at what point we would be squashed. As I looked at the bow wave rolling surf over the water, I remembered reading Pacific Ocean rower Jim Shekdar's account of passing a ship too close for comfort and being rolled out of the way by the bow wave – I just hoped that the same would happen for us if it came down to it. I couldn't row out of the way – that would take too long and I wouldn't be able to radio while rowing. So I carried on my barrage of requests for this juggernaut not to squash me. After what seemed like an age, a reply crackled back through the airwaves:

'Small boat, small boat, small boat – this is *Prince of the Netherlands*. Do you require assistance? Or are you just one of those mad adventurers? Over.'

Oh, happy days! Yes, I was a mad adventurer and no, thank you, I didn't need any help. The kind captain altered his course and said he would pass on word to the Australian authorities that I was still alive. We wished each other a safe journey before I watched and waved at the *Prince of the Netherlands* until it disappeared from sight, still completely starkers but very chuffed to have spoken to someone. Most never replied and it would be months before another ship responded to any of my VHF calls.

While trying to fend off the blues and seasickness in those early weeks, I also did regular battle with various impish voices in my head, which taunted me if I finished rowing early for the day or stopped for another snooze in the afternoon, goading me to row for longer every time. One might be shouting '*Carpe diem!*' and hammering on my cabin wall, pointing to the message I had written there. One told me to 'Get up and row!' and another shouted at me to 'Make the most of now!'. Some days that was easier than others as I tried to justify the value of spending an extra hour or two in bed. This was a marathon, not a sprint, after all. Prior to my row, sports psychotherapist Dr Briony Nicholls had helped me with strategies for situations like this. We had concluded that the dynamic nature of the ocean and its weather systems would require a flexible rowing schedule; that is to say that if the weather was good I would row and make the most of it, and if it was gnarly I would tuck up and rest. It was all about optimising opportunity as well as listening to my body and its grumblings. Success was going to be about equanimity and taking life one day at a time, sometimes just one stroke at a time. Some days would be about thriving and others would be about surviving. As such, instead of setting a schedule of X hours a day, I had given myself a single goal – simply to row and rest as much as I could, so that I could be as efficient and effective as possible.

Each day (or as often as required) Ricardo texted or emailed through the weather forecasts and also advised me on how best to route through or around the action. I loved it when he talked of good wind coming my way or praised me for progress, and I always dreaded downloading my emails if it had been preceded by a text message asking me to check my email inbox for this usually meant bad news. At times I struggled to meet his brief, whether it was to 'head to this lat and long' or 'push north 40 miles to find new wind'. I was comforted when he assured me that the best thing in these early stages was to just go with the flow and, if it was possible to row, to do the most efficient thing. In short, any mileage west was good and we could fine-tune the north or south part later on as we needed. Even so, there was concern among some of my blog followers watching my track on the little map on my website that I was already way above the green line and heading too far north. This green line was a fictional, theoretical and very smooth line on the map joining up Australia to Mauritius – a line I later called the racing line. My own track was definitely not a racing line and there was disbelief in some quarters that I would make it. Maybe Mum needn't have forwarded those messages on to me but she did and I continued to read them and chew them over. In my head, I was aware that these were early days. Yet I was a bit frustrated that their chatter bothered me; I needed to focus on my game and Ric's instructions and nothing else. It would be one of the most important lessons to learn and take home from the waves back into land life: listen only to the voices that matter. I hadn't got out to sea by listening to people who had said I wouldn't do it or that I would be shark bait. This was no different.

An important step came around this time. A blazing sun shone into the purest, brightest, bluest hue I had ever seen and all was mirror calm, crying out for me to jump in. I had debated the mid-ocean swim with various sailors before leaving land; on the one hand being in the water goes against all natural instincts because the boat represents safety but on the other, it is so enticing and alluring. I knew that to immerse myself would be to venture into a whole new world. Indeed a brave new world, too, for I had never before swum in water so deep or so far from land and swimming in deep water terrified me. When I say deep, I just mean deep enough not to see the bottom – even a metre or two can freak me out. I so wanted to do it and my muscles ached for the coolness, yet my logical head was trawling up memories of being swept out to sea on a rubber ring as a child when I had been too scared of jellyfish to swim back to the beach and had to be pulled back to shore by a watching bystander. As I wondered how many people could lay claim to swimming in a pool 4 miles deep and quietened the imps in my head, I stripped off. 'I'm going swiiiiiiming!' I squealed half nervously and half excitedly to my video camera as I tied on my extra long safety line and donned my mask and snorkel. I stood on the edge of the boat, leaning back on my safety rails and had one last look for fins and sea monsters. A bird wheeled in the distance, foraging for dinner, but there was nothing and no one else; it was silent and empty, just me and the lonely sea and the sky. Instead of jumping in with a whoop I just froze, eventually stepping back on deck for a quick pep talk. I took a deep breath and stood up for another go but again, I didn't get any nearer to the water. Kneeling down, I stuck my head under the surface, just to reassure myself that it was OK. Of course it was, so I got back up on my perch, ready to jump. Once more, I froze and so there I remained, egging myself on until the boat had keeled over so much that I slipped and fell in with a very inelegant splash. I was in just long enough to register that it was both very blue and way too deep to comprehend, when a little black and white striped fish looked up at me and growled. I squealed and leaped out, my first foray ending almost before it had started. I was so chuffed to have made it into the water and confident that I would jump in to fix something if I needed to. But I am not ashamed to admit that I was more than a teensy bit scared. Scared of what exactly, I am still not too sure, for of course the fish didn't really growl. (And he was only 8 centimetres from fishy nose to his fishy tail.) In fact, on second inspection he was really rather sweet and I'm sure he said, 'How do you do?' I was enchanted, and all the more so when his mate appeared. In their stripy little jackets they were calling out to be named Tweedledum and Tweedledee, so I did, and appointed their stripy collective The Tweedles. They would be my friends and follow me to Mauritius; pilot fish by name and pilots by nature, they are escorts of most ocean wanderers, boats, beasts and other flotsam. My deep blue swim was a triumph, therefore: I had semi-conquered my childhood fear of swimming in the ocean and felt that, now I was on first-name terms with the locals, I was well on my way to becoming a true salty beast.

CHAPTER 14

RED CARPET WEATHER

'Water is life's mater and matrix, mother and medium.
There is no life without water'

ALBERT SZENT-GYÖRGYI

Ricardo called it Red Carpet Weather when the wind blew from the east. I think he meant Magic Carpet Weather, referring to the way it magicked me along in the right direction to gain sea miles, but it ended up being called Red Carpet Weather. It was our favourite sort of weather. The initial forecast that we had based all the decisions on for my April Fool's Day departure had suggested helpful winds for a week or so and happily, they continued to blow for more than a fortnight. Following winds made for perfect surfing weather, with waves rolling towards Mauritius, helping us in the right direction, even as I slept. Oh, how I loved this rowing lark; you don't get free miles like that by your own two feet, eh? Some mornings in these early Red Carpet days, I took advantage of the weather and used the opportunity to do something other than rowing. Sometimes I might use it to clean either myself or the boat, but on a few mornings I slept for an extra hour or three, the time being determined by the temperature of the cabin and by how sticky and sweaty my sleeping gear was. Generally if I was tired, I would only wake up again when the air in the cabin was so stifling that I doubt any oxygen remained at all. Until this moment, extra sleep was mostly very welcome and very sweet. After waking up on these mornings I would try to get out into the air as quickly as possible, whilst working out how productive my coasting had been. The bubble compass in the bulkhead showed through to the cabin, so with a quick bit of maths I could work out our heading. A little look at my red ensign through the back hatch gave me an idea of what the boat was doing relative to the wind and either elicited a warm smiley feeling at the thought of free miles or a rapid leap outside to swing the boat into a better position. Then there was Einstein, my GPS, wired into the deck outside, who would reveal all the twists and turns and wiggles of the night's drifting. The anticipation of finding out my position teased me and sometimes I saved it until after breakfast if I knew it was going to be a good one. One morning I woke up after a particularly satisfying sleep to find that we had run nearly 30 miles in the twelve hours since I had stopped rowing. Even better was the fact that it was all in a perfect line due west.

Of course, it wasn't always like that; the ocean is full of intriguing and feisty currents and eddies which do not always act as useful conveyor belts for the ocean rower, as my Leeuwin Current experience had shown. I could tell if I was in a current by the temperature of the water and my progress relative to the wind, waves and my own rowing efforts. Ric would also warn me if I needed to head in a certain direction to avoid a contrary current that might push me backwards. I had heard of ocean rowers and kayakers looping round for two weeks or more in an eddy before being slingshotted out, but some currents were jolly helpful and carried me along a useful track, or at least rectified any mischief caused by another part of the same system. Between Days 8 and 11, each night as I slept the boat was pushed round a series of eddies, curving the top half of a circle. Had I not rowed west again the following day, I would have looped complete loops on my tracker. Thank goodness the weather was calm enough to allow me to row or else I would probably have been drawing polo mints far earlier in the voyage than I would have liked.

As we left the coastal shelf and ventured out in to the deep ocean, the waves grew steeper and the wind blew harder. Everything, it seemed, was getting bigger and scarier. I found it both thrilling and terrifying at times, and always tiring from the physical exertion and the focus I needed to stay safe. It was good to have the ten days of the Warm-up Lap in my head as a reminder of my ability to cope, though it was still a challenge. My inner monologue was turning out to be quite a chatterbox and I talked myself through most tasks, however small they might be; I couldn't afford to lose focus or make a mistake, so I had to make sure that voice stayed measured and calm at all times. As with any survival situation, when feisty waves are threatening to wash you overboard, your thinking is crystal clear – there is no space for extra noise.

Outside the boat, I felt like I was in control at least; inside the cabin all I could control was how many bars of chocolate I ate. Less than 2 centimetres of boat wall stood between me and the waves, meaning that every sound of water came straight through, a bit too loud and clear for my liking at times. Sometimes it wakes you up. There's no reference but for the sounds. You might feel a whoosh and acceleration down the wave, but sometimes you can't work out how big the waves are. Perhaps it's better that way. Even on a pond-like day when water gurgled gently and swirled round the rudder, the boat was never silent. I found this rather comforting, especially as I grew to know all the different noises and what they meant. As sea state increased through wavelets and slightly bigger waves into the sort that charge about like monsters, the noise would build. In hindsight, earplugs would have been a good idea for those noisy hours in the cabin, and industrial spec ear defenders would have been genius.

Boisterous seas always curtailed my rowing at night-time; I felt it was better to be safe and end before sundown than to push on in dubious and volatile conditions, particularly at this early stage. A big bright moon and following seas made for irresistible night-time rowing, but with waves rolling into the boat broadside my heart was racing and I was soon soggy and bruised in the ribs from being bashed by my oars or hurled into the safety rails. Being dumped on by waves in the sunshine was not great but I might at least have a chance of warming up a wee bit; at night-time if I got too wet it might get critical. With no one to take care of me I couldn't risk getting hypothermia, so a few too many sloshings generally sent me inside. One such night in my third week at sea I finished rowing just after sunset. After tea I went through my usual routine of sluicing my Lower Decks with iodine, powdering with talc and plastering with zinc cream. An hour later it was stuffy in the cabin so I opened the back hatch, just a fraction, and put it on the latch. A sliver of a breeze crept in and cooled the air, soothing me. I was just considering how crap it would be if a big wave came and got us wet – and guess what happened? A chuffing big wave came along and back-ended us, giving us one hell of a ride down the wave. My sleeping bag got rather wet, which was no fun and I decided that I couldn't risk opening the back hatch again unless it was a calm day, for fear of a capsize. If we rolled with a door open it would be curtains for the project and for me, as *Dippers* wouldn't come back round.

Rain was a different matter; I have always loved the sound of water hitting roofs, be it on tents, boats or buildings. Gentle rain, lashing rain, sideways rain, warm rain, cold rain – I'm not fussy. I just love the feeling of being cosy, snug and dry from the wet. On the ocean, rain means fresh water and sometimes the opportunity for a bit of a shower, or at least a token wash. If I saw a big squall on its way I quickly stripped off, filled a bucket with seawater and soaked myself, rubbing in my tangy shower gel (biodegradable and organic so as not to annoy the fish). If the clouds did as they threatened this was great and I rinsed in fresh water; if they decided to play the tease instead, then I was left freezing

My lovely Dad. Smiling on holiday in 2005

The flying press-up – Operation Fit and Strong!

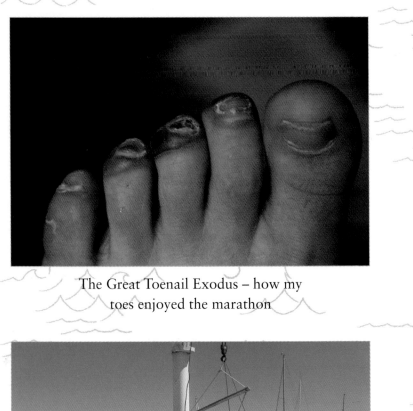

The Great Toenail Exodus – how my
toes enjoyed the marathon

Dippers arrives in Australia

My first day at sea – Friday 13 March 2009

A glorious sunset at sea – my favourite time of day

The control panel for the electrics with emergency
instructions and little anecdotes written on the wall

Masters of the sea – a juvenile Indian yellow-nosed albatross

Snoozing at sea

A triumph – one month at sea!

Day 56 – the birthday feast

The Tweedles

Land Ahoooooy! Day 124 – 24 miles to go

Not very good at walking to start with!

Hugged and hugged again – an emotional reunion

Ricardo and I – we made it!

in the buff and covered in bubbles, which had to be rinsed off in a bucket of seawater once more, of course throwing more salt over the very salt I had hoped to wash off. Funny times at sea.

A squally evening on Day 17 looked to be the start of something more serious. The skies were stormy and the waves growing, which meant new wind was on the way. 'Here's an even bigger one!' I squealed into the Dictaphone as we raced down a wave; 'Wohoooo!' I laughed. Winds arrived with each set of clouds and then died down again as they passed over, before another massive wave set and cloud line rolled in from the distance. The big white tops were phenomenal, rolling on a 10-metre swell. I rowed non-stop for five hours, then went for a snooze.

I woke after my rest to find white water everywhere and some bloody big waves. 'I'm glad Mum can't see; she wouldn't be very happy,' I told the Dictaphone. Feeling a bit queasy I took a seasickness tablet and lay back down in the cabin for a few minutes, before digging about for some snacks. A Crunchie went down very well, though sadly it came back up even more swiftly a moment later, thankfully straight into a well-timed plastic bag. A vomity cabin would have been unbearable. Chuckling at the sad waste of my Crunchie, I switched on my satellite phone and hoped for some messages. Roostie was at work (and clearly trying to procrastinate). I sent a message back, telling her that it was getting messy outside and that I was tucked up for the night already, wedged in and bracing myself against rogue waves. She asked if I was ever scared by the noise, or did I find it comforting? Mostly it wasn't too scary, I replied, but hearing a crescendo race towards the boat while I waited for the inevitable slam was fairly frightening. Luckily, some of those ran themselves out and crashed elsewhere. After a long exchange of messages I said cheerio and carried on resting. The lights were on and my phone was too so that I could pick up any incoming messages and I nibbled bits of spiced cake, calm and relaxed, calm and relaxed. Or at least I was as calm and relaxed as I could be, given the watery mayhem outside. I checked my watch – only just past sundown – and acknowledged that it was going to be a long night. I snoozed gently, reminding myself that I was oh-so-very calm and relaxed.

A nanosecond later I was slammed into the cabin wall. *Dippers* was suspended mid roll, apparently deciding whether to go right over or come back up. Water rushed in through the vent on the hatch and I screamed, willing her to come back round. She had done it in Fremantle; she knew how to do it. Come. On. *Dippers*. Save the rolls for another day, my friend.

The roll back to upright was as violent as the first and I was shaken. *Oh shit, I'm scared now.* I'd been on the roof of the cabin, stuff was everywhere, the food bags had squashed me. I had only just been telling Roostie how I wasn't scared; here I was now whimpering and too frightened to go out on deck and get my helmet out of the front cabin. Up to now I hadn't needed it, but with roughed-up seas I couldn't risk another big knock like that without a helmet on: I had to go outside. Even if I failed, at least I would know I had tried. Only a fool doesn't have at least a little go so there was really no choice. Not wanting to get my clothes soaked, I stripped off and clipped my safety harness round my waist; the buckle snapped shut, cold against me, and I shuddered at the thought of going on deck. Bracing myself against the lurching, I drew a deep breath and I visualised each little step in the process. The other end of the boat was only a pace and a half away in good weather, but I knew that once I opened the hatch it would be a race to get outside, clip my safety line to the deck bolt and close the door again. Stinging salty spray whipped across me as I peeped out and I shivered as a wave landed straight on top of me, gritting my teeth and tensing my muscles against the cold. The deck was lurching, rising and falling as waves rolled under and into us. The moon shone brightly behind grey shadowy clouds and the air was filled with spray and spume. Gripping the safety rails I crouched low to face the incoming waves, pulsing my legs against the boat's rhythm. Opening the forward hatch, it was clear that the Grand Slam had shifted my kit into odd positions; a welly boot was lodged out of place, the grab bag had come loose; things which had been on the left were now on the right. I grabbed the helmet and put it on, jamming the heaviest bits of kit back into their proper place – *Dippers*' righting ability was in part reliant on heavy gear being stashed low down. It was too dangerous to do everything now; I needed to wait until it had all calmed down. My inner chatter talked on, putting the fear into a box and telling it to stay there until some other time. I picked up the few odd bits which hadn't been washed out of the stowage pockets on deck and made a dash for the cabin, taking another soaking.

Inside once more, I felt spaced out; I was drowsy and woozy, worried that I might fall asleep and not wake up. I was also scared that it might happen again; one boshing definitely did not preclude another. I had no way of tying myself down inside the cabin so had been hurled at full speed head first into the side of the boat. Note to self: 1 centimetre of foam camping mat round the cabin is not enough to protect the amateur head banger. My head thumped as I struggled to keep my eyes open so I decided to send some messages via the satellite phone, trying to make light of it. I knew no one could help me; I just wanted someone to talk to for a moment as I felt very alone, very tiny and very scared. Ric made me laugh later when he sent me a message saying, 'Stop trying to break your boat with your head!' He assured me that he was confident she wouldn't ever roll past ninety degrees, and I tried to remind myself that we hadn't capsized fully and that it could have been a lot worse.

The next morning, deciding it was time to find a little present to cheer myself up, I settled on a large jiffy bag which had instructions to 'Only open if you're feeling really low'. A complete stranger had given it to me when we were filming a short piece down by the river in Oxford one day. I felt pretty low and in need of a smile, so I opened it up. Joy of all joy! Four bags of pork scratchings! I scoffed the lot within the hour and wished for more; the salt and the fat and the crunch was sublimely delicious. Another note to self: take copious supplies of pork scratchings on next adventure. Unfortunately, after the Grand Slam the salted pumpkin seeds in the food hatches were now soggy and destined for fish food; on the upside, Roostie promised to look into pigeon-posting a malt loaf across the waves. So it wasn't all bad, even after a boshing. In fact, it had served as a relatively gentle reminder that the ocean was a wild and unpredictable place.

CHAPTER 15

HAPPY SOCKS

Happy socks (n) (pl.) [happee sokks]

By Day 22 I had come through some fairly rough stuff after departing the continental shelf, leaving me cold, tired, wet and with disintegrating feet and backside. Surely all this was a ticket to an early finish each day? Well, not according to the imps in my head. They goaded me, saying that Ellen MacArthur wouldn't do this because she was cold or because she was gaining free miles with the wind. Captain Scott would have carried on. Dad wouldn't have stopped. *So you're not going to do that. You're going to sit there and row until as near to six o'clock as you can get.* With winds gusting 20 to 30 knots and water flying everywhere, the last week had been challenging; surfing down some of those watery walls, I just pulled in the oars and held on. I was living on a mix of adrenaline and fear, but despite the messy bits, I was very content and loving it, fear and all. In the final run in to the end of the day, as the sun set and my eyelids longed for bed, I willed the sea not to throw water over my head. I'm quite a calm person so I usually smiled, albeit wryly, when this happened just before bedtime. But I sometimes screamed a bit too; a good yell does wonders for the soul, especially when you're shivering and wet. The cabin was my sanctuary; inside I could dry out, warm up and snuggle down into my cosy bedding. Even if my sleeping bag was soaked, my woollen blanket stayed warm even when wet, though it did make the cabin smell fairly vile – think teenage boy's sports bag and then double it, add a whiff of salt and a splash of unidentified boat odour and you've got the musty damp of Eau du Cabin.

Give me the smooth bitter bite of a fine gin with a cheeky twang of zesty limes, all iced up in a long glass with some tonic, and I am happy with life. Give me a sea view at the same time, and you will have just made my day. Sadly, Jamie had forgotten to install the ice maker and bar on *Dippers* and so sipping gin with the sunset only ever happened in my head. I did have a Gin Machine on board though, a piece of kit so important that I talked to it each day, and so expensive that I had nearly opted for the manual one to save the bank balance; had I done so, my life at sea would have been quite different and even more bloody hard work. This is because the Gin Machine was my one-stop flick-a-switch route to fresh water each day, and the manual version would have meant hours spent pumping instead of rowing. Fortunately, the swanky electric desalination pump took only TLC and kind words, and when it went wrong, a bit of Vaseline. It is a fantastic bit of kit, powered by the sun via the batteries, which drive the pump to squeeze seawater through various membranes and filters, pushing out the salt by reverse osmosis. The result was fresh water, fairly tasteless but for a twist of salt. Usually a few hours of the Gin Machine whirring away in its little hatch filled a jerry can of water to last me a day or two, and I only had to make sure the batteries were nicely juiced up with sunshine. This was the tricky bit; contrary to popular belief, the Indian Ocean is not always a sunny place. There were many sunless weeks on my voyage when water was in such short supply that I only used it for drinking and rehydrating meals. Laundry was way down the list of priorities at times like this and I mastered the art of turning things inside out and back to front, re-wearing them and refreshing them occasionally with a squirt of perfume. Yes, perfume, and I don't care that you're laughing at the fact I'm probably the first adventurer to take a bottle of perfume on expedition. It made me smile and also prevented me smelling myself out of business.

During one week of grey, my water ran dry; the batteries were all juiced out and there was no sunshine nor any forecast for any. A rower with no water will struggle for a while and eventually dehydrate and die; it is serious stuff to be faced with no fresh water and no tap to fill up the tanks. This is why I had 90 litres of emergency ballast water stowed below deck. It acted as extra weight to help *Dippers* to self-right, but was also there in case I needed drinking water. In another bid to save money I had filled my jerry cans with tap water from the quayside in Australia rather than buy posh sealed bottled stuff. Unfortunately, any thoughts of sterilising processes had escaped me completely, and so eight weeks later it didn't smell quite so fresh. Nor did it look it either; a mouldy carpet had grown over all of the cans and the first one I opened had orange blobs floating around in it – lots and lots of them. They may even have been swimming, too; I closed the lid quickly, not stopping to investigate. I had the 'Survivor drinks own urine to stay alive' headline running round in my head as I reached for the second can. What if the whole lot was ruined? Hmmm. I inhaled gingerly, remembering the time our chemistry teacher had proffered us a vial of sulphur dioxide and we all keeled over after taking an enthusiastic whiff. This one looked OK and smelled just like all things do on a boat after that long at sea, so I went for a little glug, swilling it round my mouth. Ugh! I spat it out; it was stale and pungent. But at least things weren't growing in it yet, or if they were then I couldn't see them. And even if they were they weren't orange, so that was a bonus. Worried about draining my precious supply, I cut my drinking allowance and rationed the water for three full days, willing the sun to shine. After three days I was a bit dehydrated but still wanted to play it safe – I could do this for a few days yet. That week, more than ever, I realised that water is the key to life; here I was on an adventure struggling to make enough water, yet there are a billion people in the world with no access to clean water. It was a humbling eye-opener and I realised that the ocean is one of the best places to learn about resource management, for what you forget to take with you, you do without. And you do everything you can to make sure you don't run out of the crucial stuff. Or you're buggered.

Everyone should have a pair of Happy Socks. They are cosy and capable of soothing mind, body and toes after a salty day on the ocean, or indeed after a long day in the Real World. On or off the water, I champion Happy Socks: happy socks make happy days.

I know what you are thinking; I bet you are wiggling your toes and questioning your sock ethic, asking your toes if they are happy. My Mum invented Happy Socks, made with that curiously clever wool that changes colour from top to toe, the sort you thought were cool as a little person, uncool through your teens, but are now keen to wear again. A brand new pair was made for my voyage and I knew I could count on them to cheer me from my toes up after a hard day at the oars. Once I had shut up for the night I would strip off, wash, checking for sores and mould, and then put on some dry clothes.

It's probably a good idea to talk about ocean laundry at this point, too, as lots of people ask about this. First thing to note is that you only attempt it if the sun is shining and the sea is calm enough to dry everything; for if you wash too much stuff and the sun abandons you, then you get left with damp mouldy clothes and a stale cabin. I hung my newly washed knickers and socks from netting inside, and

I might wake up to find a pair of shorts stuck to my face, they having found their way onto my beanbag as I slept. Of course, usually I would put on a fresh pair of shorts (I only had two) or a clean top (I only had three), enjoy the relative freshness for a moment, before being drenched by an errant wave.

My attitude to ocean hygiene was that I should keep myself clean enough to avoid infections and stay healthy, but not use too much fresh water; dehydration was a bigger threat than intoxication and so the priority for water was to drink and then to wash. The main task, therefore, was rinsing the tidelines out of my rowing shorts to protect my Lower Decks from chaffing and general rot. Not wanting to harp on too much about it, but feeling the need to share my discomfort, I shall sketch out a little idea for you. Imagine sitting on a cold damp mat, in cold damp shorts, in cold damp trousers on a little boat, being pitched about by rather salty, cold, wet waves. Not only do you appear to be sitting on some sort of trapped nerve, sending numbing pains down through your legs, but the flesh on your bottom is red raw. Salt sores have set up camp on your bottom and thighs and prickles run all over your skin each time you move; you need to talk yourself through some tasks because it is so damned painful. On wet days you will squirm so much that you can't sit or stand for more than a moment in one position and every time you need to use the bucket, you have to rip fabric from skin as you peel away the shorts, scratching salty crystals across open wounds. Swearing fills the air as you pull them back up. This was me and my bottom, unhappiest on the wetter days. At the end of the day and sometimes in between rowing shifts, I tried to have a look at the mess, twisting round like a dog chasing her tail. Red mountains and oozing volcanoes everywhere – it was like a Martian landscape, pitted and pinnacled with carbuncles and bumps en route to boilhood. I remember one in particular which rubbed so much that it drove me mad; it felt like Everest at the top of my buttocks. Declaring war I went for the big squeeze, relieved as the lumpy yellow pus exploded onto the deck. Better out than in, I thought, as I doused my entire mid section with iodine, wincing as each wound flooded and gasping with the sting. The gaping hole filled and refilled with gunk for days afterwards, adding another scar to the collection. But these would be war wounds to be proud of; I was working hard for them.

While we're on the subject of Lower Decks, I should perhaps describe the toilet. Of course it was all en suite – I just had to open the cabin door for the most picturesque al fresco loo experience in the world: a changing landscape with each rise and fall of the waves, perhaps a fiery sunset or a starry night, bioluminescence sprinkling alongside in sparkly trails. Of course I was often unlucky and soaked by waves or rain clouds, but it was worth it for the views and I never did fall off completely while in action. It was a very simple system – use a bucket and then chuck it overboard. The trick was in timing the throw and doing so downwind: rebound on the day I ate a whole bag of dried mango in one go would have been disastrous.

Laundry was a very rustic affair, either done in a bucket of saltwater hauled on board or right in the sea, using friendly biodegradable soap. A few ocean rinses before a final fresh water dunking and all was done. Being so dependent on the ocean and weather for all my needs, like water and power and washing, felt very primal; I think we lose that connection with nature on dry land with all our gizmos and gadgets – life can become very clinical and controlled. The scent of even relatively clean clothes on the boat was always welcome, though in fact everything that I cleaned on the boat just went from smelling rough to smelling slightly different. Sometimes I happened upon something fresh from land, like the fourteen pairs of vacuum-packed knickers that I found one day. I hadn't smelled anything so fresh since Australia and it reminded me of Mum, and how all Mums seem to feel the need to iron anything that leaves the clean washing pile. It's funny how smells conjure up memories from home; at one stage I have to admit I even enjoyed smelling a pair of socks which had been used and reused again and again, honking like deliciously ripe old brie. And that's probably why I liked it – there was no cheese on my boat and I dreamed of rich cheeseboards and stringy mozzarella on pizzas.

I learned some important rules about washing. Firstly, ask yourself if you really need to wash when there is no one to be freaked out by your athletic aromas. Secondly, it is time to wash your pillow case when you actually have to peel it from your cheeks in the morning. Third, it is important to wash your hair at least every two weeks and to remove as much salt and suncream from your face each day as possible. It might sting as the salt will have crystallised, but you'll cope. The fourth rule is to tie all washing securely at all times; winds and waves can and will whip up from nowhere and steal prized clothes in an instant. My highest casualty rate was three socks and a pair of shorts in one day – a sad loss. Finally, my own rule was not to wear my Happy Socks on deck for fear of saltwater ruination and also not to wash them until Mauritius. My towel fared slightly better, and was washed a full two times on the voyage. Mothers, I am confident your teenage boys would love this life of ocean grime.

CHAPTER 16

RUBY PORT AND RED CARPETS

'All the world is beautiful and it matters little where
we go... the spot where we chance to be
always seems to be the best'

JOHN MUIR

'I'm not sure if the porridge has gone rancid or
if I ate too many wine gums as an entrée, but I
have just fed the fish with my breakfast...'

Blog, Day 30

Apart from this, 30 April was a very good day at sea. The
sun was shining in a crisp blue sky as cauliflower clouds
whipped across peaky seas in an easterly wind. All this made
for a very smiley rower and another stonking mileage for
the day. After a few days of delicious Red Carpet Weather,
I was due to cross over the one hundred degrees east line

later that day, marking my first major easting of longitude. For those readers not au fait with latitude and longitude, they are the grids crossing lines on the globe that mark the degrees east and west of the Greenwich meridian (longitude) and north and south of the equator (latitude). I needed to reel in the longitude to get to Mauritius (i.e. distance from east to west) and I didn't want to lose too much latitude (i.e. fall too far south or run too far north). This meant that each degree was a milestone and to knock off ten degrees was a big step as it meant crossing over into a whole new set of figures, or decades as I liked to call them. Moving from the Australian side of one hundred degrees east into the double figures of the 'nineties' was a huge step. I had started out at one hundred and fifteen degrees east in Australia; Mauritius lay at fifty-eight degrees east so each decade of degrees from now on would represent one fifth of the remaining journey nailed. *Just a little bit further to row now, Sarah…*

It was super special to be crossing this line on my thirtieth day out there. The One Month at Sea mark had been a big milestone in my head since Day 11, which had marked the longest time I had ever been by myself. However I looked at it, one month was a significant time to spend by myself and at sea; I was a real beast of the oceans now and content on the waves. Surely this meant I had earned my first salty stripe? I thought so and was as high as a kite all day.

It was all about progress, which meant increasing confidence, increasing happiness and reducing the distance between me and my goal. While I was now in love with the Indian, I still wanted to make it across to the other side, so days in the bag (or chalked up on the wall in my cabin) were days both to be proud of and to be thankful for. There was no easy ticket to the beach in Mauritius and I would have to fight all the way in, so each day really was a gift.

Another day on the ocean also meant another day of healing; I already felt that I was more at peace with Dad's death, just by making it to the ocean. Every day since he had died I had considered a healing day, a badge of honour for surviving and moving forwards, however slowly that might be. In short, Day 30 was a triumph, a real whistle-blowing, horn-honking, and sing-and-dance-on-the-deck-beneath-the-stars sort of moment. I also had a letter to open from Mum that day, always a treat. Today's was a card with a gorilla on the front, lazing in the sun. Inside it read, 'So proud of you. Make sure you get enough rest.' Not one to disobey my own mother, even at long range, I dutifully went to my cabin and snoozed through the midday sun. To say it was delicious is a gross understatement – it was divine; both mind and body certainly felt like they had rowed for thirty days now and so I welcomed the downtime. To round off the afternoon I indulged my new-found love of deep ocean laundry and did a wash, hanging the clothes out on deck to dry, singing to the waves as I did so.

Following on the festivities of Day 30, I welcomed May to the party in style. As the sun prepped its bed for the night in skies of silky pink, I opened the bottle of ruby port which Ricardo had given me when I first met him. It had been at the London Boat Show in January and he had come over from Portugal especially to meet me and be there for the launch with friends, sponsors and bubbly. The deep corky pop was a delicious sound and I breathed in the smooth redness. I also swallowed back some tears as I brought it up in the air for the toast – this was a big day. To start with there was a splash for the sea and a splash for me, glugged straight from the bottle. Next I raised the bottle to the sky and toasted everyone who was special to me and had helped me this far. Then it was *Dippers'* turn – and I poured some on her bulkhead as I thanked her for being my teammate and friend. By the end of it I was very warm and a little bit fuzzy round the edges. Poor old *Dippers* came off rather worse, and looked like she had been in a messy fight when the port dried to a dark red stain. I looked out to the horizon and wondered where I would be in another thirty days. Which decade of degrees would I be in? I hoped I would be out of the nineties and storming well into the eighties. For now it looked as though someone had pulled candyfloss across the sky, wispy like a fairy's outfit. Tiny grey mushroom clouds sat on the skyline, set against a backdrop of bright blue, making my very own piece of ocean very special indeed.

I hopped inside the cabin and picked up the phone, keen to share my excitement at having spent a whole month on the ocean. Annoyingly, it was lunchtime in the UK and so all I got was answerphones. Down with time zones, so over-rated; out here on the ocean I was running on ocean time and doing just fine. I cursed the Real Worlders and rummaged about for some celebratory chocolate.

CHAPTER 17

TALKING TO MYSELF AND TO THE WORLD

'I love not Man the less, but Nature more.
From these our interviews, in which I steal
From all I may be, or have been before'

LORD BYRON, FROM *CHILDE HAROLD'S PILGRIMAGE*

On 1 May I opened another letter to celebrate my first month at sea. Well, that was my excuse; in truth, I was just useless at rationing them and was keen to know what was inside.

> Hello, Mum calling. I expect you're out there surrounded by sea. Calm, I hope, with waves that aren't too big and that it's been a good day for you. That your bum isn't too sore and that you don't have too many blisters.

She also wrote out a little passage she had found somewhere, full of philosophical titbits and stirring musings about life, struggles, perseverance and, rather amusingly, the importance of staying headed in the right direction. Did she not know how tricky it was to steer a little rowing boat across the ocean? Ah, my lovely mum. Without her help, I wouldn't have even made it to Australia; emotionally, logistically and financially, she had been a rock. Like my dad, she had always encouraged us to follow our passions, however mad they might be. Michael was serving in the army and enjoyed hurling himself out of aeroplanes and Matthew enjoyed flying round dirt tracks on motorbikes at great speed, so we hadn't chosen the gentlest of hobbies. Yet still she supported us and helped pick up the pieces when we got in a pickle or came a cropper. She would probably have argued that this is what mums are for, but really, ours was super special. Getting across the ocean was made all the easier by having her daily emails and messages on the phone. Not wishing to leave any space in the text messages, she always filled them up with kisses if she had nothing else to say and often just typed all the words into a continuous block of letters, without any spaces at all. Clearly this was in a bid to be efficient, but it sometimes made for a good little deciphering task at my end. Mum was very much my HQ by now, too, replying to and filtering emails, paying bills and plugging the bank balance when it looked unhealthy, as well as being the best PR in the world. She said that she couldn't walk through town at home without being stopped every few steps by people asking how both she and I were getting on.

I looked at the photo of Dad on my bulkhead, smiling and relaxed in Wales on holiday the year before he died. It was the first time the five of us had all been away together in years, and it was lovely. I wondered what he would think of it all and I knew he would have been proud. Had he been alive he would have been HQ Manager, Email Whizz and Technical Chief. He would have loved it all. And he knew about sailing and oceans so he would have helped me out with those bits, too. Grinning back at his smiley face, another tear rolled down my cheek – I missed him. Out there I thought about him often and I talked to him, too, imagining what he would make of certain situations and which bits he would find funny – because Dad was a laughing man.

After all this time talking to myself, my boat and the visiting wildlife, I was mostly content in my own company. Having said that, the scariest moments usually made me reach for the phone to let someone know I was having a bad time, and there were a couple of occasions when I rang home and would have enjoyed a pint in the pub with my friends. Still, I knew there was nowhere else I would rather be and it was good to have the option of speaking with the outside world, even if I didn't want to use it. Each day I sent at least one email to Mum to assure her that I was alive and I normally exchanged messages with Ric about the weather. Friends topped up my inboxes with random chatter, scientific articles from time to time and musings on the outside world. My friend Siena even emailed me the clues for *The Times* crossword one day and then sent me the answers a week later. All these things made a real difference to morale, even if connecting up the satellite phone was a complete faff, after the Grand Slam in the early weeks had broken the connecting clip for my phone and data card. This meant that after a painstaking typing session on the tiny screen of my tiny computer with an even tinier stylus, I had to grip the two pieces of kit together and orient them to find a satellite. While the technology was incredible it was just like any piece of clever kit and perfectly capable of breaking and misfiring, which was especially annoying when call time was so damned expensive.

Besides a weekly phone call home, I had interviews with radio stations and news shows. These days were always much anticipated and I looked forward to the chance to speak to people without worrying about who paid the phone bill as the stations always rang me. It also meant exposure for my charity, too. Before I came away I had switched from raising money for Arthritis Research Campaign to a support-based charity, Arthritis Care, so that my fundraising efforts would go to different areas of arthritis – one research and one care based. I left Perth with £1,000 banked for the latter and it was rising all the time with donations from all over the world. One chap heard me on BBC Radio 2 and donated £500 and there were a couple of anonymous £1,000 donations later on. Whether it was five hundred or a fiver, I was touched by the generosity and amazed that people were tuning in from both hemispheres to get the latest on my saltwater boils or the chocolate store. It was clear that vicarious living was important and exciting to people. It's what we do by reading books or watching films and it's what I still do by following other expeditions; we thrive on it and feed off it, planning our own adventures of whatever size suits, fuelled or inspired by others'. For days in the lead-up to these media interviews Mum phoned round everyone she could think of, putting them on standby, including my dear Taid (my grandfather) in Wales. He sat up late to listen through the television when I was on *Radcliffe and Maconie* and, with his hearing and eyesight fading, it was as though he was hanging on to life while I was away at sea. When I had said goodbye to him in February, I hadn't expected to see him again. This made every phone call to him an extra special bonus and I loved it that he could tune in to hear me. He had been an English teacher and whilst the dementia and strokes had ruined much of his short-term memory, he still had the most wonderful store of poetry banked. It was through poetry that we connected now and I learned poems to recite down the phone to him, always excited when he joined in or took the lead for a verse.

Having media interviews meant that I could go from speaking to nobody at all for five days to perhaps four or more people in one session, which felt like a real festival. I often popped inside ahead of time to wait for the call, sometimes using it as an excuse for a sneaky break, cunningly finding ways of drawing it out a bit longer. There was no point in my getting comfortable first – the satellites were in charge, so it meant that if the little display on the phone showed only a bar or two of signal, I had to find a position where the phone talked more happily to the satellite. I always smiled when producers rang to check the line and asked to speak to Sarah; who else did they think they would be speaking to? Sometimes I asked them to wait a moment while 'I went to find her' and was amazed that it worked every single time. An engineer then checked my sound levels before I went on air to talk to the presenter. It was always a strange thought, that I was being broadcast into the living rooms and cars and offices of people going about their normal lives, while I bobbed around in my little boat in varying states of undress at whatever hour of the day or night the station required. A broken transmission was annoying, even though I chuckled to think of the calm voice saying, 'We appear to have lost her there...' just as you see them do on TV. In another studio would be a rather worried producer ringing me back, keen to know that I hadn't just been eaten by a shark or swamped by a rogue wave. No, it was just the satellite connection. If, for whatever reason, an expected call didn't make it through to the boat, the sea was usually treated to an earful of fruity language and grumblings. Didn't these folks appreciate that I had an ocean to row and no time to waste? What did they think I was doing out here? The rant generally made me feel better until the worried email or message popped through and made me feel a bit guilty that some people might have been disappointed or worried.

My favourite was the *Radcliffe and Maconie* show on BBC Radio 2; 'the boys', as I affectionately called them, touched base monthly to become my best media supporters. My interviews with Stuart and Mark, such genuinely lovely and funny blokes, were a mix of banter and chat, with the added treat of being able to request my very own choice of track. We even had a few 'in' jokes. One day I was telling them how uplifting it was to see an albatross after a pretty pants day. For me, 'pretty pants' meant pretty crap but for the lads in the studio, it was a celebratory day of fine ocean lingerie. That's why I doodled a pair of 'pretty pants' on my wall. With no fresh clothes on board, there were definitely no pretty pants for another few thousand miles.

With long distance communication, miscommunication can happen quite easily. I had never appreciated it before but, alone and restricted in my ability to discuss things, I found it wasn't hard to go off at a tangent and take a message in the wrong way or get worked up by something perhaps fairly trivial or easily explained. To try and get round this, Ric and I decided we should be in touch as often as possible, and at least once daily. One day, Ric asked me to update him every six hours via a text message sent to his email account as he was going away from his computer for a few days. I did so but had no response from him for three full days. A very strongly worded email from me to Portugal worried him enough to contact Mum, and assure her that he had sent a pile of messages that obviously had been lost in the ether. We decided that if I didn't hear from him when I thought I should have done, I would ring in to touch base. It was crucial that we understood exactly what the other was thinking or saying – my life might depend on it, so there was no room for falling out or errors. I trusted his judgement implicitly and respected his interpretations of satellite charts, so he really did have me in his spell. If he was worried, I was worried; if he said it would be OK I would try and believe it, too. Trust and clarity were everything.

CHAPTER 18

ANOTHER GOOD RUN

*'This time, like all times, is a good time,
if we but know what to do with it'*

RALPH WALDO EMERSON

The run-up to Day 40 was perfect; I was whistling along the top of a high pressure system reeling in the miles and enjoying the drying time offered by the toasty sunshine, both for me and my rotten bottom. Then came the Empty Quarter, the bit in the middle of this same beautifully stable high pressure system where there was no wind. Not a whiffle, nada. Ric called it the Second Sector, having previously told me that the whole crossing would be divided into three, possibly four, sectors of weather, all defined by the weather rather than any particularly geographical point or delineation. For general warming and recuperation this hot still weather section was great news; for my daily routine it rather scuppered things, however, because by midday it was too hot to row. On one day I complained to my diary that 23°C felt 'a bit nippy' now that I was so used to temperatures of 40 plus out on deck. I shifted my schedule so that I rowed earlier in the morning, took a break through the hottest hours and then rowed on into the night under starry skies. It was exhausting enough on a cool day, but to be clocking ten or twelve hours of rowing every day in extreme heat was punishing. During the middle part I generally washed myself or my clothes, had a little swim (if I was feeling brave) or caught up on emails and blogging, perhaps even enjoyed a little snooze. Falling asleep was no problem in the heat – the cabin was like a sauna; it was waking up and getting out afterwards that was tricky. The stuffiness of the cabin left me sticky with sweat and semi-comatose, stretched out like a tired dog on its back, tongue hanging out and legs at all angles.

Windless really does mean windless in the middle of a high. The water was absolutely still and quiet, glassy calm with not a ripple or a splash or a wavelet, except for *Dippers* and I. Although it was never completely silent, it was a bit eerie to have so little sound apart from my own. The little solar vents still whirred softly and if I moved about the boat then I could hear the water gently tickling *Dippers'* hull. I was so attuned to the different sounds that the tiniest variation or surprise had me on the alert. In these hot and windless days, I relished the help of some currents sluicing us westwards. In still seas, you have to work hard for every single centimetre on the chart, so my rowing was slow. Ric had warned me about this and told me to row extra hours

ANOTHER GOOD RUN

to maintain a decent mileage of twenty to thirty nauties. So I did, eager both to impress him and to push myself. Even though this was my journey, it had become his, too. He did his bit on the charts back in Portugal, often staying up late into the night to check on my progress or rising early to see that I was safe; out on the ocean it was all up to me.

He was a friend as well as a weather router now and we were growing to know each other very well, despite the fact that we were thousands of miles apart. With the tracker providing almost instant feedback on my course and mileage, I felt like he was constantly watching me. The day he sent me a message to say that the tracker had gone silent made my stomach churn; I suddenly felt really alone. If I plopped overboard, no one would even know where to look. It turned out that I had just leaned on the switch while I was getting changed, inadvertently knocking it off. I often looked out from my cabin across the little deck and watched for the flashing green of the tracker unit. It was a saucer-like gadget, bolted on top of the forward cabin, busily beaming out information about where I was and how far I had (or had not) rowed that day. I was so far from anyone yet so close and connected. Various people asked me if I would have coped with the expedition in days of yore, without the use of satellite communications. I was determined that yes I would, of course I would – I loved the ocean so deeply. But did my tracker anxiety prove my theory wrong? Either way, it was useful both for my safety and Mum's sanity and it also made me smile to think that my squiggly track was keeping people entertained over their cornflakes each morning. I think it would have been hard if it had been removed, but I would have coped – you have no option at sea.

It was the same with my music. While I often just cruised along in my own thoughts, enjoying the sounds of the sea, I valued having the option of listening to music or audiobooks if I wanted; enforced silence could be frustrating. I had set out with the option of playing music through waterproof speakers on deck or using my iPod with headphones – the latter was far less demanding on power as it didn't need to be plugged into the mains. A little later on in the crossing, I had a silent boat for a full seven days, partly because I had broken my headphones on Day 10, partly because there wasn't always enough sun to charge the solar panels. My solar panels were on the back of the boat facing only one way, and if the sun wasn't directly on them then they didn't charge fully. I hadn't even considered it before setting out, only nodding when the boat builder suggested this position, saying that is where they had been placed on *Dippers*' big sister. Consequently, this meant that my batteries were sometimes too low to power everything; my Gin Machine then my communications ranked as more important than music, which meant I was left a prisoner amid my own rather limited repertoire of songs. Amusingly now but annoyingly at the time, the only songs which I could remember in full were school hymns, making the seas both well blessed and cursed that week. Having broken my first set of headphones within the first two weeks at sea I was frustrated that I couldn't find a second pair: I had a second pair of most things, so why couldn't I find the bloody headphones? The only upshot was that my rummaging turned up some other treats – a bottle of wholegrain mustard, three packets of sweets and a book of poetry, all very welcome additions to my pantry and library. I hoped that I had forgotten to pack the headphones as I would probably struggle to see the funny side if I found them when I reached Mauritius. I concluded that they must have missed the boat and consoled myself that worse things happen at sea.

I had a cutlery conundrum which was almost as frustrating as the headphones headache. Having started out with what I thought was a healthy supply of three plastic fork and spoon hybrids (called sporks), by one month in all had been broken and repaired multiple times. Apparently thirty forks would have been more appropriate. The day my latest spoon repair hadn't broken after a full twenty-four hours in service stood out as a veritable triumph. I found it amazing how a broken fork had the capacity to make me growl and shout when I was tired, hungry and really not in the mood for innovating. Third time round on the same fork and the growls were generally replaced with wry smiles and more fruity language; it was only a fork, after all. Eventually, the winning repair involved supergluing a length of broken plastic to the fork head, and wrapping it in lengths of cord before caking it in more glue. This was actually an improvement on the initial design for the most part, though the twine also acted as a catch for bits of errant dinner, making the whole thing look rather horrid and probably a bacterial holiday camp. Still, I avoided illness so all was good.

Flat seas may have been exhausting but they provided some stunning views. With no sea state to talk of, not even the slightest ripple of a wavelet, my horizon was pushed out further and it seemed like I was staring beyond the edge of the world. No wonder the early explorers worried they might fall off. I found that the beginning and end of each day were the most dramatic for this, particularly the sunsets. Wherever I am on the planet, I always love this time of day and the chance to sit quietly and be absorbed in the moment, for the moment and by the moment. It was often the point that I stowed the oars and started closing down the boat for the night, sitting back against the hatch of my cabin to watch the skies morphing through the colours of an artist's paintbox. Reds deepened before blues darkened and folded in around the ocean, wrapping a sequined coat of soft black around my world. It was a full 360 degree show – the whole dome of the sky lighting up to soak the sea in colours. Day 40 was particularly beautiful and went into my diary as a trip favourite:

'The peachy moon is rising through a purple strip of sky, surrounded by blue clouds, grey in places. Above, gentle pink twirls have been teased across it, like the fibres of fleecy wool being drawn out across a weaver's knee. A peachy streak in the west and then following the horizon round, the sky turns orange, red and blue in the east. The swell is a good ten foot high so each time I rise to the top I am treated to more and teased by the edges of the picture when I roll off into the trough. We love the sea.'

I also loved the arrival of new wind. After a few days of no wind at all, even the slightest whisper of a few knots felt sweet, not only because of the improved mileage but also for the opportunity to snooze a bit longer without too much guilt. When storms were afoot, I loved watching the sea state change from mill pond to monster – it was dramatic and often scary, not knowing what lay ahead or how hard it would beat us. It generally started with a swell rolling through, making rowing very tricky and holding a course even trickier, especially if it was from the wrong direction. The wind would pick up and start scuffing little lumpy bits into waves, which would then sort themselves out into marching lines and so they would grow. In a few hours it could be a raging mess, foamy and spiked with watery mountains. I didn't always need Ric to tell me that this was about to happen – a sharp rise or fall in my little barometer let me know, and sometimes I noticed headaches. It had taken just a few weeks for me to become pretty well versed in the clouds and what they forecast. High wispy trails lying in a different direction to any others in the area meant that big winds were on the way and I knew to expect trouble. Towering nimbus clouds represented the advanced party, marching out in warted cauliflower fashion, forming up on the horizon, preparing to charge. My heart rate and the sea state would rise as the barometer fell. Ric hadn't forecasted anything like this for a while now, so I was pleased to row on unhindered.

CHAPTER 19

REELING IN THE NAUTIES

'The soul of a journey is liberty, perfect liberty
to think, feel, do just as one pleases'
WILLIAM HAZLITT

Day 43 saw me running west at speed; in the previous three days I had covered over 150 miles with a fresh following wind. As the GPS showed less than 2,000 miles to go, I was happiness personified. Ric was stoked, too: 'You are making perfect progress and the weather will remain so for seven days.' Looking outside, however, I wasn't convinced, as the wind was revving the sea into a ruffled mess and nimbus clouds had gathered into a lump on the horizon. It looked fierce as I put the oars to bed, so I put on my Happy Socks and helmet and snuggled down for the night. As I listened to the wind increasing I didn't quite believe Ric's declaration that out here clouds also meant the weather was calming down. He had predicted 'no wind Thursday' in a few days' time, but other than that one calm spot the week's prophesised helpful weather might mean crossing the halfway line at eighty-seven degrees east in a week or so. It was only a few hundred miles away and my most recent daily runs had given me my biggest daily mileage yet, a stonking 58 nauties (my own word for a nautical mile) all in the right direction – a new course record for *Dippers* and me.

I reached the ninetieth degree of longitude a couple of days later on Day 45, chuffed to have made it, now a full sixteen degrees of longitude out from Fremantle and hoping that within a day or two I would be on the other side and into the eighties, closing in on the halfway line. I toasted my ninety degree day with port, laughing at the bottle all wrapped up in my camping mat, looking like covertly packaged Prohibition-era moonshine. Before evening drinks, I had a good wash and shaved my legs, which was always a real treat. On land I see shaving my legs as a chore (albeit a rather necessary one) but out there I loved it because it made me feel ladylike again and as fresh as you can get on a boat. I followed this with a clean Lycra rash vest, another treat, even if it only smelled marginally less repellent than the one I had been wearing. It was baggier than I remembered now, too; I was obviously losing some of the bulk I had piled on before leaving home. My tummy was smaller, my shoulders were very muscly and my calves were shrinking away to nothing with their lack of effort. I even found that sitting down without any cushion was uncomfortable – something that had never happened to me before as I have always had more than enough of my own padding. This was all a good thing of course (it is exactly what I had bulked up for) but I hoped I would have enough to see me through to the other side, especially as I was still struggling to eat the custard puddings because they made me feel sick. In fact, I had completely given up on them and was emptying them overboard at every possible opportunity. This automatically cut out nearly 1,000 calories a day from my rations and so I decided to set myself the challenge of five spoonfuls of chocolate chip dessert instead. It didn't really go very well because while mixing the powder and water 'until smooth and creamy' as per the instructions my repaired fork got stuck in the concrete mix and snapped off. There was more innovation needed, apparently.

Each day as I pulled the oars in for the night, watching the water droplets drip off the blades and back into the ocean, I wondered at all the strokes they had taken and all the ones left ahead of us before we reached land. Thousands. Millions, perhaps? There were a lot, that's for sure. Each one was quite literally a dip in the ocean. I sniffed and sat up straight, gently fingering the back of my neck and shoulders, wincing a little at the landscape of knotted muscles, amazed at how they just kept on rowing, day after day, week after week. I reached forward over my legs and enjoyed the sensation of weary muscles being stretched, knowing that the pain would ease and tomorrow I would be able row on some more, renewed and refreshed, even if only a little. I sat up and mopped my forehead, rocking slowly up and down the deck on the sliding seat, breathing in the ocean and relaxing. Looking down at my hands I pulled at some skin which had blistered on top of the tough line of calluses – they were cracked and dry, and needed a good session of hand creaming and massage if they were to survive another day. I curled one foot up onto my lap for a stretch and promptly fell off the seat as it slid out from under me. Sitting on the cool damp of the deck I tried again. Euugh! My feet were wrinkled and white, and it looked like the lines and whirls of my footprints had been scoured by a knife. I eased off a few dead shreds of skin and threw them overboard, stopping when I made them bleed. A wave sloshed into the back of the boat, shunting us forward and sending sheets of water rushing over the top, straight over my head. I shivered and squealed as it ran down my neck; it was time for some Happy Socks and bed. I quickly tied off the oars and the seat, checked that the deck was clear and leapt in through the cabin door. As I shut the hatch behind me and flopped into the squishy mounds of my beanbag, I gave a little whoop, high-fiving myself for another good day. Then I lay there, still and silent, enjoying the warmth and feeling cosy inside *Dippers*. She was like a best friend now, my protector, and I was hers. We needed each other and I already knew that I would miss her when all this was over so I patted her sides and said thank you. As I did a virtual body check, running up from my soggy toes to my knotted neck, I concluded that while I was tired and battered, it was OK because I was happy tired, the sort of satisfied exhaustion that comes when you know you willed your body into a corner and made it work and fight until it was too tired to go on. I was winning in my own way; making progress, looking forward to my birthday in ten days' time but mostly excited about sleep and getting off my rowing seat.

The satisfaction was all the more complete because there had been no indecision about carrying on or stopping that day, as I often battled with the imps in my head as to whether I should stop early and rest or push on and clock more miles. The competitive part of me always wanted to reach a milestone, be it a certain distance to go until Mauritius, or reaching another degree of longitude so to have reached ninety degrees was satisfying. In the opposite corner, the sensible imp always pushed for as much sleep as my body needed. The human body is a remarkable fuel gauge – it gets hungry when it needs more fuel and gets tired when it needs rest. The response time is so acute and accurate that I found even a few hundred calories or an hour of sleep made a huge difference. The wonderful British comedian Eddie Izzard wowed the world with some extraordinary marathon running at around the same time that I was splashing about on the ocean, running forty-three marathons in fifty-one days. He likened it to driving a car with the needle on the fuel gauge near to empty, topping it up a tiny bit and then running it dry again. By this stage in the journey, I knew exactly what he meant. I was tired and hungry most of the time – I just got used to it and that's how I carried on. On mornings when I woke up feeling like a comatose slug, I knew that food and water would tip the gauge back into the black fairly quickly. If I still felt no better after an hour or two rowing, there was no option but to stop and snooze. It was all about being efficient.

My biggest indecision often came at sunset, as my world grew shadowy and black. The trade-off between racking up miles and staying comfortable and dry was a tough call. The times I rowed for sixteen or eighteen hours were punishing and the following day I always slept until late, utterly knackered, the tank completely empty. Equally, when the seas were sloppy and the rowing difficult, the decision to stop was easy. But if the sea state was rowable and I was feeling OK, I often donned my warm gear and rowed until treated to my first drenching. I never tired of night-time rowing and I loved gazing up at the stars, sometimes learning the constellations, sometimes just staring. Life out there was so peaceful, my life was so uncluttered. I lived out my routines by the rhythms of the sun and moon and really did feel like I was a part of it all – a tiny speck maybe, but part of the drama nonetheless. The contrast between the immensity of this voyage in my eyes, with the insignificance of it in the grand scheme of things, was quite humbling but also quite comforting too. Whatever happened to me and whatever decisions I might make, the world would still turn as if nothing had happened.

Light pollution on land can really ruin our view of the night sky. Out at sea it is as black as black can be, which makes moon rises very impressive. On Day 44 I had watched the most stunning I have ever seen; it was like something from a fairy tale. Thick nimbus lined the front of the stage, lit up by the rising moon behind which then turned them gently yellow, embossing them with deep shadows and sending silvery shafts of moonlight back down to the ocean below. It was easy to imagine an artist sitting on some scaffolding painting an angry Zeus into the picture, leaning out from his cloudy lookout to zap the mortals in the world below.

CHAPTER 20

A NIGHT OUT WITH BOB

'A smooth sea never made a skilled mariner'
ANON

It turned out that Zeus was about to lean out and vent his fury on my little bit of Indian Ocean. Just a day after Ricardo's promise of 'perfect' settled weather, he emailed to say that I would have some interesting stuff happening. Whereas the last weather zone had been defined by little wind and lots of stable high pressure, the next one would be rougher, with more wind and more rain. So long as it was in the right direction I didn't mind. The thing is, he couldn't be sure exactly when this third sector might start – it wasn't like arriving at a Tube stop, apparently. Only after some consistent changes in the weather patterns would we know that I had arrived. Ric's prediction for the week ahead showed changeable weather with fresh weather bubbles blowing through, often with 40 knots of wind and thundery rain banks. That is a lot of wind, even in a big boat. There wasn't a lot I could do but row on and make the best of it until I was unable to row. I imagined that if the winds really did blast from the south and the west, then my westward progress would be annihilated, so my rowing would be about damage limitation rather than making new miles. I didn't want to go too far north, so the southerly winds wouldn't be welcomed at this stage.

As it was, I was being transported south in a current, which I found mildly annoying but useful for juicing up the solar panels, which hadn't seen the sun for a few days as we had been rowing north-west, meaning that the batteries were rather low. I was already rationing my water and had even opened my spare jerry can from the forward cabin. I always seemed to be walking on a knife edge with my water supplies.

Day 45 wasn't the happiest of days on board *Dippers*; the wind howled and the swell was big and bouncy, certainly not the calm that Ric had forecast for the few days ahead. There I was thinking that my daily run of songs was keeping the wind gods in good spirits, but perhaps they weren't so fond of my medley. Early evening, we happened upon some huge cloud banks, stretching right across the sky, which brought both rain and a wind shift. Unfortunately, we were being blown back towards the Australian side of the ninety-first degree. Having tried to row against it, across it, over it, under it, through it and around it all day with no westward progress at all, I called on my sea anchor, Bob, to reduce the collateral. I was shattered.

It wasn't just my mileage going a bit pear-shaped either. While investigating the extent of rusting in my tool box, I had found that every single one of my spare fuses had been enjoying their own electrolysis party and were now disintegrating and useless. This meant that if any in the system should blow up, I would have to do some creative swaps to solve the problem. I just had to hope it wouldn't come to that. Most mariners will agree that the electrics are the soul of a boat, especially in our techie age; if they go down, things can get critical. Things didn't get any better when I reached for my camera and discovered that the desiccant sachet had burst inside the waterproof pouch, exploding granules everywhere, some even wiggling their way into the camera body. 'Oh why did they let me out to sea in a boat by myself?' I shouted at the waves, which were by now pushing me in completely the wrong direction. I hung my head and mustered a little laugh; in the grand scheme of things, this was nothing at all. I had already nipped under the '2,000 miles until Mauritius' sign, which meant that well over 1,000 now stood between me and my Aussie mates and that made me proud. So while it wasn't my favourite pastime to be drifting back from whence we had splashed, I was sure that I was stoked with sufficient bounce to treat the evening out with Bob with a little smile. Most importantly I was OK and *Dippers* was OK, which meant that life was good really. And when life is good, a Mars bar is a perfect way to celebrate. So I found one and ate it, making it three in one day.

Unless you live in a chocolate factory, three Mars bars a day is rarely sustainable. If only it was; I reckoned I could comfortably put away five a day and still have room to spare. It certainly wasn't sustainable where I was because I had only taken a box of forty-eight out to sea with me and I have always been useless at rationing treats. Chocolate was mostly munched immediately upon discovery on my boat, and I actively searched through my day bags to find more. A quick fix of a few bars and I was sorted, not bothered by knowing that finite really does mean finite and that I would have to endure a chocolate-less run in to Mauritius. I was resigned to the fact but found that I couldn't do anything to stop myself: I am a die-hard chocoholic so the urge cannot be ignored. Any woman will sympathise, I am sure. I bet they're reaching for a Mars or two now in solidarity. In fact, before I went away, when journalists asked me what I was worried about, I said that it was a dwindling chocolate supply. They all laughed. Yet here I was just over a third of the way into the voyage, anticipating the loss of a critically endangered species. It only made me smile because it reminded me of a car journey with Dad when I asked him if he would like a Mars bar. Of course he would. 'Oh yes, so would I. But I don't have any – I just wanted to know if you wanted one,' said I, and chuckled loudly.

Still, Mars bar or no, I had to find good things to keep my mojo ticking. A visit from my second favourite fish that evening, just as it started pouring with rain, did just the trick and made me smile. Bluey the dorado was my second favourite; first place being claimed by my faithful Tweedles. A few more of Bluey's mates arrived as night fell and they swam alongside the boat, glowing like silver torpedoes.

Even later on when I went out to brush my teeth and check on Bob, they were still cruising alongside.

Overnight we shot south and gained a barely tangible mile to the west. Wahooo! I smiled at the contrast with the week before when I had made perfect westerly progress with the minutest of deviations to the north and south. Now I was excited about any sort of progress at all, almost counting it in metres, not miles. I loved the sea for exactly this reason – it is fickle and ever changing.

The next day (Day 46) was even wetter and even slower, but although I barely made 4 miles west, I was calm and content. I still relished the simplicity of my days and being so unstressed in comparison to my 100-mile-an-hour lifestyle at home, where I ended each day by making lists of things to do the following day. Out here, I made lists each day of all the reasons to smile, even if it was as basic as 'Thank goodness today is over.' After all, what wasn't killing me would be making me stronger and I was sure that I was growing all the time, expanding my comfort zone and pushing my limits. And that is always good, even if you only notice afterwards. So far the most noticeable changes were in my confidence, patience, and in my pain and fear thresholds – all of which were expanding. I was more chilled out than I had ever been and had gained a sense of perspective. Generally after any ruffled feathers, I could put things into a positive light and move on; if it wasn't a matter of life or death then it wasn't worth worrying about. I think my sense of humour had changed a bit too, warping slightly, perhaps inevitably, after so many days laughing at my own jokes and at things which otherwise probably wouldn't be funny at all.

All this clutter-free headspace gave me plenty of time to think about life after the ocean and what I might do next. I had hoped I might find a golden ticket with an answer on it, but so far I was firmly undecided between teacher training (the sensible life) and the adventure of further expeditions. Swinging wildly between the two, I often started off the day thinking sensibly and then finished it by dreaming of more adventures, using my GPS to zoom in and out on countries and plan routes. After a few weeks on the waves I had set my sights on the world and started to scheme about a human-powered trip around the planet. I was loving life on the blue stuff, and I wanted to experience land crossings too, meeting people and discovering places. Of course, I couldn't be sure how I might feel when I reached Mauritius. Who knows, I might have a Sir Steve Redgrave moment and say, 'If anyone sees me anywhere near a boat again, you have my permission to shoot me.' Given that Sir Steve then went on to win another Olympic gold medal after saying those immortal words, I decided it wouldn't do any harm to change my mind later on.

By teatime on Day 46, the wind had veered to the north, big cumulus clouds were marching in from the horizon and Bob came back out to play as we started losing ground. Ric's rough stuff was on the way and Zeus would soon be making mischief. The corona around the moon added to the sense of foreboding; while they are beautiful to look at, they always give mariners the willies, for they signal nasty stuff ahead. Around this time some of my blog followers, bless them, told me that the all-female crew of the Row Angels, part of the race fleet, were passing about 20 miles to the south of me, and suggested I might like to meet up with them or perhaps talk on the radio. I loved the idea in principle, but in practice it would be impossible. VHF radios only work on 'line of sight' (i.e the aerials need to see each other); for our little rowing boats, only one metre off the water, this would be possible only if we were in ironed-out pancake seas and within a couple of miles of each other. I was chuffed to have held them off for this long; with four of them rowing it had taken them nearly thirty days to overtake me. Not that I'm competitive or anything.

I appreciated all of the blog followings, messages and emails forwarded through by Mum, particularly the lively debate stirred up when I posted news of my recent swims. There were the jokers who said they had spotted my white bottom on Google Earth, the lady who warned me of shark attacks and pleaded with me not to do it again, and plenty who were very much in approval and indeed a little bit envious. One chap implored: 'Ignore the nervous nellies, Sarah. If courage were the issue you wouldn't be where you are. Help us all feel what it is to be truly alive in a world that is not of our own making. You go girl.'

Absolutely, mate. That was the essence of all of this, even on a day when I ended up 5 miles closer to Perth than I had been after my breakfast or on the rainy days or the anchor days. Any day and every day, I wanted to feel alive; I don't think there can ever be anything better than that.

CHAPTER 21

LOOPING THE LOOP

'We must free ourselves of the hope that the sea will ever rest. We must learn to sail in high wind'

ARISTOTLE ONASSIS

I woke to a stuffy cabin on Day 47, growing damp with drips from the leaky light fitting in the cabin roof, and restless after twenty-four hours out with Bob. Miles continued to un-tick themselves on my GPS as the wind blew us backwards. I had a pick-me-up Cadbury breakfast and tried to stay upbeat about losing my hard-earned miles. The biggest struggle for me was the waiting game; I am such a competitive person, even with myself, that I didn't like to sit around and do nothing, especially after all the good progress of recent weeks. It didn't help that it was so boring inside the cabin. So I tried to tell myself that it is better to be utterly bored than to feel nothing at all – if it ever came to that, that would be a time to really worry.

Looking out across the waves through my little hatch while I nibbled at the chocolate wrapper, trying to pull off every last trace of chocolate, it didn't look too heavy outside and I toyed with the idea of rowing. It was raining very heavily so I would be guaranteed an instant soaking and the seas were really too heavy to make any ground at this time. I tucked the idea away in a box, trying to employ some of that recently learned patience and instead lay down to snooze and make use of the enforced rest time.

I did manage some rowing that day, albeit only for a few hours and at the pace of a geriatric snail. It wasn't great for morale and I approached dinner time feeling low. I wanted biscuits but only had one packet left and didn't want to eat them this early on. I also craved hearing sound other than my own voice but my batteries were struggling, so I couldn't afford to play any music, not even one little song. I had also been soaked all day and was now soggy and cold, and still behind on mileage. So I did what most folks do at such times – I rang home to rave a bit. Phone calls home always work wonders; Mum listened and cooed in all the right places, and then filled me in on all the news. With just 3 miles left to row until I regained all my lost ground to the west, I rowed on into the night for a few hours, making almost intangible progress. I finished at the oars after a full day's rowing, but having made only 7 miles in the right direction. I didn't like going to bed while I was still behind on the mileage but I reassured myself that there was no point in exhausting myself unless it was urgent; a marathon not a sprint after all, Sarah. 'Please let us end up west in the morning,' I murmured as I snuggled up onto my beanbag for the night. I still wasn't very good at going the wrong way, not for three days in a row. As you can imagine, it gets a bit old hat after a while.

Looping the loop at sea in a rowing boat is big news: I don't mean capsizing, just moving forward into new territory after a backwards wiggle with contrary weather. It felt like a fresh start, an opportunity for some progress. Day 48 felt like this when I woke up with just a one-mile gap before I looped my loop. One tiny mile. That equated to fifteen minutes' worth of walking on land or of rowing on a surfing day, yet it might be impossible if the wind played tricks on me. There were lovely messages from my blog followers during that period of poor weather, all of them very encouraging after seeing me losing miles. It felt like I had hundreds of Mums all saying 'There, there, dear – you can do it.' One in particular made me smile inside and seemed to sum up everything that my voyage was about:

> Every great undertaking in life, even the smallest ones, are opportunities for finding within yourself something you didn't know you had, and these awakenings always come with a price. The discovery comes when all the cheering stops and when the task ahead is greater than the task you left behind. The universe is wide open in front of you. How and why I found you I do not know and I cannot fathom what you are doing. The silence you are experiencing is a gift – listen carefully to it. It is within you and without you.

Indeed, the task ahead was still greater than that which I had completed and yes, the universe was wide about me. On the silence I wasn't so sure; normally I looked at it this way, but now I was so bored of my own bad singing that I craved some new tunes. I was being tested and I guess I didn't like it. If only the sun would shine, then I would have music. I would also have enough juice in the batteries for my water maker to run, too. By now I only had half a litre of water left in my day tank, meaning a breakfast without porridge.

I decided to convert the electric pump into a manual one. As I stumbled through the manual, unscrewing bolts and teasing pistons and coupling pins apart, my language flipped from controlled and annoyed to no-holds-barred swearing. I couldn't find the right spanner and I later discovered that I didn't have the one size that I needed. I had thirteen others but not the right size. What a muppet. Why hadn't I checked before I left land? Then I discovered that the unit had been mounted in a place so awkward that I couldn't actually pump it manually at all. If the batteries went completely, it would be useless and I would have to row 20 kilograms of redundant kit. I smiled; I would get over it. I had to; there was no one else to do it for me. I opened the hatch to let some air into the stuffy cabin and try and quell the waves of nausea that were gurgling from below. I rested my head on the bottom part of the hatch and breathed in the coolness from outside, listening to the gentle rocking of the boat and tried to put it all in perspective. Two hours messing around with it hadn't been much fun but at least now I knew. And in a way, once you realise you have no control over something, it becomes less of a worry. Nonetheless, with all this dodgy weather and the run of little mishaps my emotions were swinging quite wildly and I needed to gain some sort of control over it all. After I had reassembled the water maker I was ecstatic to find we were about to complete the loop and start breaking fresh ground again. I turned the boat into the sunshine while I stopped for lunch and rounded it off with a call to Andy and Guy, my friends on *Flying Ferkins*. I always enjoyed speaking to them and finding out where they were. Out of all the six boats left in their race (six had dropped out by now), they were the only ones I knew and had any contact with. Twenty minutes or so flew by as we swapped stories and weather forecasts like old sea dogs. My ears pricked up when they mentioned that they were due a storm at the end of the week. Looking at my sea chart we were only a few hundred miles apart, which suggested that their storm would be mine, too. I wondered why Ric hadn't mentioned anything yet.

After hanging up, I put storm thoughts aside and carried on rowing. I felt chirpier now that the batteries were juicing a little bit and that I was charging all the little devices with my flexible solar panel, which I hadn't thought to use until now. I'm not sure why really, but it just hadn't occurred to me. I hung it over my cabin door and tied the corners down to soak up the sunshine. It was helping solve my power problem and the cells were all iridescent, so it was a welcome change from staring at my cabin door. I often stuck printed poems up there to learn but had overdosed somewhat since having no music. There was something cathartic in the latest dumping overboard of pudding and protein shake too, despite the sprinkling of pink protein shake that coated me and the boat. As the offending powder drifted off, I drifted onwards to Mauritius. My day was made brilliant by the discovery of a packet of jelly babies in one of the hatches, all squashed up into a loaf. Eaten in one sitting as the sun sank into the sea and painted the sky pink, they were a welcome treat and spurred me on to row well into the night. By then, the moon was waiting until nearly midnight to put in an appearance, which made me think I ought to alter my watch. Besides fixing up interviews with the outside world, time zones weren't that important, but I did use my watch as a guide. A big bright moon shone down on the sea, now chopped up by an increasing wind. I said goodnight to Orion, hopped inside and went to bed.

In the cabin, I fired up the sat phone, excited about downloading the daily emails and messages. The GPS revealed that I had just 24 miles before I crossed into the eighties and I was determined to get there tomorrow. Opening up my emails, I had to realign my goals a bit. The first in my inbox suggested that maybe I wouldn't make it to the eighties the next day; Ric had titled his message 'The Calm Before the Storm'. Gulp. Perhaps tomorrow would be about survival instead of the eighties.

The essence of his message was that a big low pressure system to the south of me was going 'to munch me in its fangs'. My happyometer took a bit of a nosedive, and then lurched a bit when I read that the folks in Fremantle would be battered by it too, with winds of up to 45 knots forecast. Suffice to say that this was one heck of a storm flexing its muscles across the entire ocean area. Ric predicted just two days of clean weather afterwards before another system rolled in. 'Suggest you gain some miles before the big blow blows you back.' What did he think I had been doing, I thought? And did he think one day's rowing was going to gain me many miles? He signed off by saying that the following week would be more civilised and noted that 'this one won't provide much progress at all', just in case I hadn't worked that out. With his optimistic hat on, however, he pointed out that I would gain other experiences, and assured me that it would 'spice up my life a little', urging me to enjoy it. Hmm, I couldn't promise that but beneath the fear I was a little bit excited. Even though Ric had assured me that I had seen worse storms, it had been a while since I had seen wind that strong and seas as big as this would bring. I scanned back over the email again, my eyes resting on the key facts: 'will be hit pretty hard... it will paste the entire sea area... gusting... Wednesday will be worst...'

This meant I had one day to row as far west as I possibly could and prepare the boat for what lay ahead – potentially three days cabin-bound, dehydrated, smelly, hungry and scared witless while the storm blew through. Exciting, eh? This was to be another of those feeling alive in the wrong sort of way moments. Tomorrow I would have to make sure I had extra food and water in the cabin and everything stowed away properly. If we took a hit or capsized, then I had to be certain we would be safe. I went to bed slightly nervous and wondering how many miles

I would lose over the next few days. I hoped it would be less than a hundred but I knew I wouldn't make the eighties for a while yet.

CHAPTER 22

IT WILL MUNCH YOU IN ITS FANGS

'The only thing to fear is fear itself'

F. D. ROOSEVELT

I slept perfectly until dawn on Day 49, dreaming of nothing more curious than running races and custard tarts; the sea does weird things to your dreams. A grey dawn slowly grew into a dazzling display of reds and oranges; rows of clouds covered the sky, all running in different directions. Although beautiful, it didn't bode well at all; in fact, it promised fury and some monster waves. After a quick breakfast, I rowed all day until the swell had grown so big that I could make no useful progress westward. Towering nimbus clouds moved closer and closer, bringing with them wind, turning the benign swell into rows of peaky waves. They were impressive but I was nervous and my ears seemed to ring from my thundering heart rate, which had pounded all day. I sang to try and keep my morale up, in between making lists of things to do before the storm came. I had lined Bob up on the deck in readiness, so now just had to haul him up over the safety rail and let the lines run overboard, gazing into the deep as he drifted out like a big yellow jellyfish. The waves were too big to row through now and I was spent after a day's rowing, so all I could do was leave Bob to hold the fort. I checked the rig twice to make sure it was secure and in no danger of entanglement, before sitting down to a quick tea on deck. I huddled around the stove while it boiled, hugging my knees up to my chest, keen to get warm but also keen to enjoy the fresh air. I had many hours in the cabin ahead, and I knew it would be anything but fresh in there.

After re-stowing a few bits and pieces, I went inside and checked my emails. Ric predicted that the next three days would provide 'the most interesting squiggle of the whole trip', but he stopped at that, saying that all the satellite pictures were showing very unstable weather systems and different files were contradicting each other and he wasn't sure what to expect. In short, anything might happen. We were both nervous.

I noticed that Ricardo had helpfully copied Mum into his initial storm-munching email. I wasn't sure if I liked this or not, but decided to trust his judgement. After all, he had been involved in more ocean crossings (both as sailor and shore team) than I had dreamed of, so he presumably knew that pre-storm honesty was the best way forward. If only he could have avoided putting 'you' and 'munch' and 'fangs' in the same sentence, she might have been less apprehensive about it all.

As I lay on my beanbag filling out my logbook and listening to the waves growing more boisterous outside, I thought back over the last few weeks and how lucky I had been with the weather. To have lasted so many weeks without a proper battering was remarkable, really. I didn't pray because I'm not in the least bit religious, but I did spend some time thinking about faith. I had a lot of it: faith in my boat, faith in my team, and faith in myself. With hope, dear old Bob and a stash of chocolate, this was all I had now.

I popped the logbook away, pulled on my helmet, switched out the light and rolled over into the foetal position, often my default position for going to sleep, with Alberto, my stuffed-toy albatross, tucked under my arm. I never have been a toy-hugger, but out on the ocean all by myself I found it comforting, especially in the rough stuff. It wasn't exactly the way I had hoped to spend my half century at sea, clocking fifty days on the ocean with a forty-hour stint in the cabin. It was made all the more frustrating by the fact that I had managed to row to within 12 miles of the ninety-degree line again the day before. I felt like a climber making an assault on the mountain and acclimatising progressively by going up and down repeatedly: only a climber knows it will improve their chances of success.

After a full forty hours of not rowing, I wrote on my blog:

> It's 20 knots, gusting 25, at the moment and rising. Not too crazy yet, but still eating away

at our miles run and throwing us about. Whole system is looking very unstable and we're not entirely sure what will happen; Ricardo reckons it won't hit me as hard, or for as long, as he first thought. Fingers crossed. Maybe we'll escape the fangs yet.

For nearly two full days, *Dippers* and I were boshed in stormy seas, losing 18 miles to the east. I was scared most of the time and got a soaking every time I stuck my head out of the door. Every so often, I would take my chances and nip out on deck for fresh air and to use the bucket, to check Bob's lines and to measure the wind strength with my little anemometer. I measured gusts of at least 35 knots but I imagine they were stronger at times, making for very excitable seas and a bumpy, often uncomfortable ride. If you think Bucking Bronco crossed with the waltzers at the fair, crossed with the sort of roller coaster where your tummy gets left behind, crossed with rolling down a hill in a barrel, I think you'll be nearly there. Add in lots of creaks and groans and slams as the boat gets thrown, a dollop of unsullied fear and the fact that you are thousands of miles from help, and you'll probably have the feeling just right. And if you haven't done so already then you need to partially starve and dehydrate too. All in all, being cabin bound in rough weather is not much fun.

Stormy seas in a small boat by yourself in the daylight are one thing, but on a dark night are quite another. Things got really exciting when the sea-me started bleeping in the early hours, indicating that a ship was near. We hadn't seen a ship since Day 16, and yet it appeared on the roughest night yet, when my tiny boat was indistinguishable from wave tops. I spent two fraught hours on the VHF in the hope they might hear my requests not to squash me. I heard no response. I am not ashamed to admit that it was one of the scariest nights of my life, although I evaded the squashing.

Another triumph was listening to a few hours of Richard Dawkins' *The God Delusion* above the raging winds. It was a somewhat daring and hilarious feat, for without headphones I could only play things through my on-deck speakers. In a loud raging sea this meant I had to sit by the hatch, opening it a fraction to hear the words, and then pulling it shut quickly when a wave washed over the boat. Suffice to say the sea was better practised than I and we had a face full of salt on more than a few occasions. A friend pointed out how wonderfully ironic this scene was, Prof. Dawkins' atheist book being broadcast loudly to the heavens. As ever, with any reference to this learned man, I received a barrage of comments on my website, many very critical of my non-religiosity. I was content on the non-godly side of the fence and anticipated that I always would be. Why would I change or even want to? I have knowledge and experience of science to understand the world so I don't need any sort of god to complicate matters. Why would I need religious faith when I had faith in my self? I was coming to believe that this was the most important thing of all.

During the storm I did a live interview with Jenni Murray on BBC Radio 4 *Woman's Hour*, the first time I had touched base with them since I left the UK. I remembered our first

meeting and all the giggles because the item before me had
been about a sex toys website, so as I slipped quietly into
the studio and shook hands with Jenni, there was a lot
of buzzing in the background, which we both found very
funny. This time they were keen to find out about the highs
and lows of my journey and about what had frightened me
so far. I thought of a long list but decided that this storm
lark was probably up there near the top, mostly because of
never knowing quite what might happen, and made worse
by the fact that at night you lose all visual input and rely
only on sound, which makes it all the more intense. It wasn't
very comfortable and I spent a lot of time clock watching,
willing the time to hurry up and get me through to dawn.
'Wahooooo!' I yelled to my Dictaphone diary at six o' clock
on Day 51.

> 'We've survived the night and though it's wild
> and I want it to end, at least it will be fully light
> in a few hours. It's picked up since yesterday
> and we've had quite a few waves crash right
> over the top of the boat. Outside the clouds
> look hideous, but I have to go out and stretch
> my legs – two days on that stupid beanbag is
> not comfortable.'

Apart from the rest, I did enjoy one thing during the mad
weather – and that was all the birds that appeared to flaunt
their aerobatic skills. Sometimes there might be four or five
or six wheeling about on the wind, from tiny storm petrels
just tiptoeing daintily on the surface of the waves through

to the giant petrels and albatrosses that cruised about like cool teenagers at an ice rink on a Friday evening, master gliders.

After forty hours the weather had eased enough for me to haul Bob back on board, though I skinned my knuckle in doing so. It would take a while to heal out in the wet, but it was a small injury to show for the two days of rough weather. As the wind dropped, the waves got sloppy and quite scary, creating the most almighty surfs. A couple of them really freaked me out and on one occasion I thought we were going to pitchpole, which is the worst sort of capsize, where the boat rolls end over end. Thankfully we didn't and just got sluiced by some thunderous waves instead, bobbing back up fully rinsed, top to toe.

Once it was all over, the things I enjoyed most were the simple freedoms that I usually took for granted in good weather – to go outside and stand and stretch and do anything other than lie down, to eat something other than chocolate and biscuit bars. After two days, I was a bit bored by a diet of treats. I rowed on, pleased to have made it through the storm fairly unscathed and buoyed by Ric's assertion that I had done well to keep it together so smartly, and that my 18 miles lost to the east was 'actually bugger all in the grand scheme of things'.

One of the questions that Jenni asked me on the radio was how I was coping with the isolation. All in all, I think I was doing well and thriving on it, being bored by my company only occasionally, and I definitely didn't consider myself lonely. It just made everything more intense, both the good and bad bits. I found that being alone meant I was much more aware of everything going on around me, keen to look at new things or listen to new sounds. Right now, I was glad to be the other side of my first half century out on the waves and loving the sweet rich tunes of life at sea as a soloist.

CHAPTER 23

TINNED PEACHES

'It's when you're safe at home that you wish you were having an adventure. When you're having an adventure you wish you were safe at home'

THORNTON WILDER

'Why is it that I always seem to be headed into the biggest storm clouds?' I pondered to myself as I tucked up for the night on Day 52, with just four more sleeps until my birthday. I had gone practically nowhere in the previous seven days apart from round in circles, so was looking forward to a new system of wind and the opportunity to chip at the 180 miles between me and the halfway line. It was now an obsession, and at any given time of the day I knew how many miles until ninety degrees and how many until halfway. I can't say that I liked my happiness being so reliant on my progress, but it's not surprising when you

207

are alone in challenging circumstances with one simple measurable, and what sometimes seems like an out-of-reach goal. When the focus is so pure, the outcome and progress can become all consuming and all important.

When I stepped outside the following morning I found the biggest kamikaze flying fish to date lying on the deck, shiny, lifeless and staring into nowhere. I still felt very lucky that I had so far avoided having one leap out and slap me in the face, as they often flew straight into the hatch behind me with a thud or skimmed low in front of my eyeline at high speed. There was always the risk that one would land itself somewhere out of sight and fester a while before being noticed; what if I found one dead and dried, stuck to the back of my head or snuggled down inside the hood of my jacket? So I had to be vigilant at all times. I had also read about squid recently in Thor Heyerdahl's exuberant *Kon-Tiki*, which recounted the Norwegian anthropologist's hilarious and daring adventures sailing a raft across the South Pacific with five other men and a green parrot in order to prove his theory of the colonisation of Polynesia. After retrieving some from the roof of their cabin, they hypothesised that squid must be able to squirt themselves up out of the water like a jet-propelled blob of jelly. Scary, eh? Especially as said jelly blobs have suckered arms and a sharp beak. Even if it did sound rather intriguing, I preferred not to have any try out their suckers on my boat.

The sea was still settling down, which meant that every so often a huge roller would, well, roll in from the south. Squalls blasted through regularly, sending me leaping back inside through the hatch to avoid the wet. On the plus side, squalls and sunshine mean rainbows, always a pretty diversion. At the end of the day I finally made it to ninety degrees east again, after so many failed attempts to cross it. 'HAPPY, HAPPY DAYS!' I shouted. It had taken us so long to get here that I brought the port out to celebrate. I also rehydrated my solitary packet of freeze-dried berries and pretended that I was eating it with a delicious pavlova and lots of cream. It was a fine day.

Ric's forecast was not so fine, and he predicted more of the same thundery mess as another system rolled through beneath us. True to form, I rebalanced the happy scales with 58 grams and 259 calories of deliciousness in the form of a Mars bar, made even tastier because I had found it while looking for dried mango which, although rather tasty, was easily secondary to the joy encased by the ever rarer red and black wrapper.

I felt at one with the sea again as the wind eased further and I enjoyed a starry night. All I had to do was open the cabin door and I was treated to a view that took my breath away. I had my confidence back now after the storm and confirmed this with an email from Ric, which suggested he was also sure that I could nail this, even with incoming bad weather. 'Keep it tidy and keep it together,' he wrote, reassuring me, 'All will be just fine. You're a water creature now with all your fishy friends around you. They will be sad to see you go.'

Go?! I still had nearly 1,800 miles to clear before I made it to Mauritius, though I knew already that I would miss them when we went our separate ways. He was right, they were friends now.

As always, the good stuff didn't last long and I spent Day 54 with Bob out, sweating in the cabin as the rough stuff that Ric had predicted blew through. It created some big, steep waves, close together and messy, which were frightening too as the boat took a few violent slams right over on her side. Outside I might get washed overboard with a cold salty slap from the sea, and inside I was in danger of suffocation from the stifling heat. It seemed like a rock and a hard place and I wished for it to end.

It now felt like I had taken a step backwards again, and I was exhausted by the flux of my volatile emotions. I was frustrated at such stilted progress and, as often happened when I was really tired, also missing Dad; I couldn't believe that it was close to three years since I had last seen him just after my twenty-first birthday. As I lay there in tears, I realised that it was the first time I had cried in weeks. Truth is, I still missed him and that hurt. Looking back on it now, it seems a sorry picture, a young woman out on the ocean crying her eyes out. But it was restorative and healing, helping me ditch a bit of the frustration of only making 50 miles west in ten days.

It was a wonderful feeling to get back out on the oars on Day 55 to have another shot, even if it meant pulling Bob back on board. This was never an enjoyable task, especially in the dark of the early morning, the night specked only by a few remaining stars and a sliver of a crescent moon. It involved heaving various ropes, hauling them up and over the safety rails and easing the huge parachute up out of the deep with them. With the rise and fall of a sloppy sea pulling against my every move, and the odd rogue wave drenching the boat, it gave the same results as a heavy gym workout. The day grew to be grey and dull, a palette of shades rather than colours, and by early afternoon I was struggling to smile; so much for a sunshine cruise to Mauritius. I put on my orange-tinted sunglasses and transformed my world into a glowing seascape, making everything happier in an instant. An albatross then joined us from nowhere and soared up and down the wave crests, looping back round and round again to take a closer look at us. He was accompanied by a pintado petrel, which seemed keen to be close to the boat. As I rowed on across the rollers, he flapped his stubby little wings to regain his position and sat on the water once more, eyeing me up. The juxtaposition of the 3-metre giant and this black and white spotted, rugby-ball-shaped clown the size of a coconut was amusing and added to the warm feeling I had summoned up from my lethargy. It wasn't such a grey day after all, particularly as the next was 26 May, my twenty-fourth birthday.

It started with my magically waking up at midnight and checking in with the emails and messages. After a few days of radio silence from the website because Mum had been away, I was overwhelmed by the birthday messages she had forwarded on and the donations to the charity, encouraged by her calls to throw a few pounds at it in honour of my birthday. Before Dad died she didn't ever use a computer, but now it seems that she was addicted, thanks to my row. I had saved a tin of peaches for the occasion and at midnight I was so close to eating them that for ten minutes I sat with them in one hand and my Leatherman knife in the other before I made myself back down and save them until lunch.

I was chuffed that I managed to save my cards and presents until morning, too, and instead went back to sleep for a few more hours. Then I sat up in bed munching snacks while I rifled through the bag of cards and little presents that had been stowed on board, to work out which I would open first. I savoured each message, sticking the cards all over the wall of my cabin. It must have been strange for everyone to write these many months in advance so that I could take them with me, probably not too sure of what they should write to someone so far out to sea all by herself on her birthday. One card even had a badge on it and they all brightened up the cabin hugely, as did the sunshine, which arrived for the first time in days. I sang happy birthday to myself at the top of my lungs as I treated myself to a bucket wash and a splash of perfume, before setting to the oars. With the sun out it was glorious and I enjoyed the rowing, even if it was a pitiful mileage. I didn't care – it was all towards Mauritius and my birthday lunch was just around the corner.

It consisted of vine leaves and butter beans, washed down with a little bottle of champagne – all of which I had bought in a rush in Australia as a last-minute thought about having a celebratory meal on this day. Roostie had thoughtfully cut out a picture of a birthday cake from times gone by and had written that she really hoped I was happy. I sat back and thought about it, concluding that I couldn't have been happier, but for an airdrop of real cake. I had spent the morning debating at what time I could legitimately ring Mum. First I thought nine o'clock, then I thought eight and then I decided seven would be OK – this was quite a special day, after all. So after lunch I touched base at home, waking Mum out of a deep sleep, a little bit annoyed to find out that I had missed her call at my breakfast time. She had waited up into the night to try and ring me to sing 'Happy Birthday', apparently! This being quite a unique way to spend my birthday, it also attracted some press and I did interviews with various stations, many from the BBC. One of my favourites was with the World Service, who had taken some time to research things and asked some slightly different questions. I had to stifle a chuckle when he thanked me for taking time out to speak to them, since I must have a lot on. As it happens I had looked forward to speaking to them all day.

My final interview of the day was to be live on the BBC Radio 2 *Radcliffe and Maconie* show, my favourite of them all. Unfortunately for me, it meant waking up at two in the morning, so I was very grateful when my brother Matthew rang me at one o'clock to say hello. Poor little man, he was having a rubbish time because of a knee injury and exams, and I felt sorry to be so far away.

It was always fun speaking with Radcliffe and Maconie as they were such good fun and very supportive of my mission. They brought a lump to my throat that night because Mark said that it was like I was one of the family now and they were proud of me. Coupled with all the messages and donations to the charity from around the world, it made me feel very warm and very loved as I closed my eyes on the most original birthday of my life.

CHAPTER 24

SERENDIPITY KNOCKS

*'The sea is everything… an immense desert, where man is
never lonely, for he feels life stirring on all sides'*

JULES VERNE

On the ocean, everything positive was used as fuel, and each
and every little bit of progress became worth celebrating,
especially when I knew that it could be dashed with a few
hours of contrary, fickle winds. My diaries are riddled with
talk of weather and mileages, right down to tiny fractions of
miles travelled this way or lost that. At times I was obsessed,
locked in a battle between frustration and trying to look at it
all with equanimity; sometimes the sensible side of me won,
sometimes the frustrated imp did. Messages from Ricardo
back on shore didn't always help my mindset, partly because
they either left rather too much detail for my imagination to
fill in or just scared me witless. 'When he tells me I am brave

and then drops into the conversation that there is a front headed my way, I know we're in for a walloping. Arrgh!' To his credit, there was plenty of encouragement and good advice, too and I liked it when he acknowledged that I was doing well and making sound progress.

> Take care my little ocean rowing girl, you're doing a top job in getting this job done. When it hurts just keep going, dig deep and focus. If you can keep it together now, then you will make it through to the other side. Just take each day as it comes, one step at a time. I'm with you all the way.
>
> Your mate, Ric

Day 61 saw the return of the decent Red Carpet Weather. The hardest thing through the loops and wiggles and time out with Bob had been maintaining morale, so it was great to feel very upbeat as I waved goodbye to May and welcomed in June, surfing with toppling rollers in the sunshine. After fifteen days of some of the slowest rowing known to mankind, we had a full day hoofing towards Mauritius, leaving fewer than 1,700 nauties left to go. Result, made all the more special by a visit from another Sooty albatross. They were mostly Sooties that I was seeing now, and two different subspecies at that – one paler than the other. I never tired of watching any of the birds, but the albatrosses were a class apart, and I always greeted them with whoops of delight, fading into awestruck silence and a sort of reverie at their mastery of the waves.

The albatrosses weren't my only regular visitors and I was glad that the Tweedles had managed to stay close by in spite of the stormy weather. Each morning I greeted my stripy cavalry and did a fin count. Over the last few weeks the troupe had steadily grown to around thirty fish. People laughed when I told them that the fish were my friends, but it was true – I felt like I was in good company with them swimming alongside and under the boat. Their bow riding always made me smile, too, mostly because I had never considered that we might travel fast enough to create a bow wave. While the conversation might have been a bit limited, it was always good to see them rushing over to nibble the remnants of dinner when I washed my cooking pot overboard or to have them school around me when I went for a swim. It was entertaining and comforting somehow. With no one else around, I found that I held on to all signs of life very tightly, mesmerised by anything that flew or swam or floated past.

As well as gaining in number, the fishy folk had also grown in size, with a cohort of Senior Tweedles leading the pack. At first, the title of Tweedle le Grand was bestowed upon a fine fellow of 15 centimetres, before he was usurped by The Right Honourable Monsieur Tweedle le Grand, a champion at over 30 centimetres long. A perfect size for dinner, one might think, but I had already declared that fish were friends and not food. In the early days I tried fishing with the hand line my brothers had given me, but was secretly pleased that I didn't catch any; the thought of eating one of my friends was awful. Besides, I had already lost my only suitable cooking pot overboard and apart from the Tweedles, the other fish I had seen were far too big for me and I would hate to waste one. Given that the world's fish stocks are being plundered so brutally that they are set to collapse in the next thirty years, I felt I ought to do all I could to save them, not eat them.

At any rate, I was too busy rowing to fish at the moment. As we welcomed in June, Ricardo had given me an ultimatum:

YOU HAVE 6 DAYS TO GET TO 25 DEGREES SOUTH IN ORDER TO MAXIMISE YOUR RED CARPET. I AM TRYING TO GET YOU NORTH ENOUGH OF THE HIGH SO THAT YOU STAY IN ITS EAST TO WEST FLOW.

I was surfing well in the wind and enjoying the sunshine and effort well spent in meaningful progress. By Day 65 we had clocked 200 nauties since lifting Bob five days before and had fulfilled Ric's request, also rowing over the halfway line, so I was very buoyant. That night, having clocked 50 miles in the right direction, I did what any good mariner might do and made mango jelly to celebrate. Don't let anyone ever tell you that you can't make jelly without a fridge, because they're wrong; it might not have been very solid or elegant but it made for a wonderful breakfast.

Trying to stretch out my back while I gargled the mango jelly round my mouth, I heard a loud 'Prrfffff' from just off the bows. 'IT CAN ONLY BE...!' I squealed in excitement, and swung round to see the large, smooth, black back of a whale cruising gently by, enjoying the salty air. I saw three surfacings; whether we had just one whale or more, I couldn't say. It was more than twice the length of *Dippers*, I estimated, around 15 metres of beautiful whale. I was speechless. It was these moments I had come to sea for, serendipitous encounters with true beasts of the ocean. My mind boggled at this gentle giant and I longed for it to stay near me. My ultimate aim was to swim with one, but this chap (or chappess) was gone too soon, heading into the setting sun and fiery horizon and I probably wasn't brave enough anyway.

Unfortunately, Ric's latest message wasn't so thrilling and brought warnings of a weather shift:

> BAD NEWS. THE FRONT HAS CHANGED ANGLE AND SO TOMORROW WHEN THE FRONT HITS IT WILL BRING SW WINDS FOR AGES AND AGES. NO RED CARPET FOR AT LEAST 7 DAYS. NEXT WEEK WILL BE SLOW. LARGE LOW THURSDAY. AFTER THAT LOW IT LOOKS LIKE YOU FINALLY HAVE A GOOD STRETCH AHEAD AGAIN. BUT LOTS COULD CHANGE STILL.

Instead of tucking up the oars for the night, I decided to make the best of it and clock some miles to the west while I could. It was sobering, but after wrapping up in layers and filling my belly with snack bars I took up my seat with a calm resignation; I would do my best and hope that the forecast was wrong. There wasn't much else I could do apart from sing, which I did to stay awake as I rowed late into the night. It wasn't like my student days where I could pull all-nighters on a whim. I got tired more easily now, no doubt something to do with the 1,500 miles and the two months I had already rowed.

True to Ric's prediction, the wind arrived from the south-west, and so with the dawning of Day 67, I found myself growling as I shipped the oars and deployed Bob to stand guard, taking myself on an unwelcome cabin holiday. Everything was grey as I tucked up inside to wait for the bashing. Unfortunately, this coincided with finishing the last of my five books and I was left with two technical meteorology and seamanship tomes, neither of which was at all inspiring. If only I had taken more books along. While packing I had argued that this was a rowing trip, not a reading trip, and had decided that six would be plenty. I had even justified the weight by noting that they would all make useful mops in the event of a flooding; not at all considering that they might be sanity-saving forms of entertainment. The sea wasn't rough with the new wind, so after a little snooze I left the cabin for the fresh air and took the opportunity to clean and dry out the boat, rid the hatches of mouldy damp and assess the food stocks. While the stores weren't overflowing with goodies, I was pleased to see that I had managed to save a few treats, including a bag of Minstrels which I decided to keep for my century at sea, now just over thirty days away. That night there was a spectacular display of thunder and lightning, accompanied by a hammering rainstorm and a wind shift to the west, exactly the direction I didn't want it to come from. I shrank from the thought of how long it would take to reclaim the miles and continue rowing west – we had already lost 20 miles in one day and there was a full week's forecast of westerlies.

As I woke the next morning, my sixty-eighth day at sea, feeling a bit like I had been punched by a heavyweight boxer all set to pummel me again, I knew that I would drive myself crazy stuck with Bob out all week. I was already restless and ready to row, so I decided to try and row by day and call on Bob by night. Heaving the rudder right over to pull me into the wind, I set to the challenge. As usual, the biggest challenge of all would be maintaining mental composure. Even if I were to row right round the clock I would still lose mileage, potentially hundreds, but I knew that it would be worse if I did nothing at all. My plan was to try and keep the wind from stealing all my miles by rowing north – hopefully there the weather would be less changeable and contrary, and I would have more chance of scooting along at the top of the high pressure system.

The rowing that week was brutal and demoralising. Trying to row across the waves was punishingly difficult and also rather miserable with lots of cold water sloshings. Albatrosses became ever more important to my morale and I searched for little treats, such as a new silk sleeping bag liner or a bit of music. My northward track meant little or no sunshine on the solar panels as they faced in the opposite direction, so even on bright days the batteries didn't charge much, which meant that I rationed my music. After a few silent days I craved music so much that I turned *Dippers* to face the sunshine and sat with Bob out to hold our position so that I could charge the batteries and listen to just one album. Someone had asked a little while before what I found hardest on this trip and I think the enforced music-less days were up there with the boredom of a cabin stint.

My other big challenge was my dehydrated food, which I still struggled to eat because I didn't like it. Of course this meant I was missing out on valuable calories and protein which in turn meant that I was burning muscle instead of fat for the most part; not an ideal situation.

In a bid to combat negativity I often tried to make myself laugh when I was at a low point, literally forcing myself to smile and laugh out loud, maybe calling to mind a funny incident or story to distract myself. Pulling out the chart to see the distance we had already covered was also good, so long as I didn't focus too closely on the distance left to run. There was song and dance therapy, too, which involved singing at the top of my voice over the waves or listening to something through the speakers (ABBA is particularly good for this, if nothing else). My best trick was the Good Things About Today exercise, which kept me grounded firmly in the essentials and helped me to focus on positive things; a simple but crucial tool in keeping it together. All the same, it was sometimes easier said than done and actually a bit of screaming or shouting or a few tears did the job much better.

In spite of my keep-myself-smiling tricks, a week going backwards still felt like I was running up a descending conveyor belt, or a collapsing sand dune, and I found myself scooting back towards the Australian side of eighty-six degrees east. This would mark the loss of a whole degree of longitude; 60 miles lost to the west winds. While it was annoying, it was also rather funny in a way; the odd dope on my blog wondered if I was looping loops on purpose or if I was changing my course to some other island. I tried

221

to put an amusing twist on it by saying, 'I consider myself thrice lucky; not many people even get to see this 60-mile stretch of the ocean, let alone shuttle row across it. If ever there's anything you need to know about this little patch of blue, I am on my way to being an expert. Questions on a postcard.'

Andy and Guy had suffered the same sort of losses so we had a quick whinge together on the phone, swapping stories and comparing notes. I liked to wind them up by talking of chocolate too as they hadn't taken a single bar on board with them, stocking only ten bags of sweets for weekly treats. I found this idea completely absurd and so ribbed them about it each time I spoke to them, goading them to chase me down. The contact with the lads was invaluable, as they knew what I was going through more than anyone else. We were helping each other across with humour, a listening ear and practical advice – and I looked forward to sharing a pint with them in Mauritius. When we arrived would be anyone's guess, but I hoped that our landings would coincide. It was still too early to let Mum know when I might arrive, but I kept extrapolating, as did the boys. We all agreed that it would all come down to luck and weather.

I was all calm again by Day 70 and so didn't really care about my progress, miles or no miles. I had my Tweedles and sunsets, sunrises and moon bows, all the stars in the world, my deep blue swims. Resigned to mile loss until the new wind blew in, my main conundrum was what to do with my hair to prevent matting, potential birds nesting or major visual impairment. I had forgotten to pack a comb and so now looked like Robinson Crusoe or a hippy surfer. That day I spent a morning in the sunshine doing useful chores such as knife cleaning and sharpening, bracelet making, career planning and poetry reading, as well as a Tweedle observation and research session. It all felt very bohemian and was made all the more idyllic by finding a surprise can of fizzy drink nestled in the bows. I went to sleep looking forward to the arrival of the new Red Carpet, now due in very soon, and Bob's overdue banishment to the forward cabin.

CHAPTER 25

FIZZ # 3

'He who has gone abides with us, more potent,
nay, more present than the living man'
ANTOINE DE SAINT-EXUPÉRY

Now that I was closer to Australia than I had been a week before, every little metre rowed in the right direction felt sweet. With sunshine and blue skies overhead I took the opportunity to remove the barnacles from the hull. Knowing that it would make the boat go faster was satisfying, but I was still nervous about my overboard swims, attached to my tiny boat by a tiny line, thousands of miles from land and 4 miles above the sea floor with any manner of creatures waiting to nibble my toes. It was exhilarating, and the cool blue was a perfect tonic for my knotted shoulders. To be stretched out and floating was delicious and to look down into the unfathomable depth beneath was, well, unfathomable, as if I was suspended in time, all notion of the real world frozen, and no link to it but for my lifeline of webbing clipping me on to the boat. We bobbed along with the swell while I worked to scrape off the growth round the rudder and clean up the water maker inlet; it would be a mini disaster if that got fouled up. The Tweedles wiggled in close to check me out, chasing the evicted barnacles as they sunk into the murk. I was glad that no other creatures appeared, even though I was still hoping to see a shark before I reached land and a sea turtle, as I had never seen a swimming adult turtle, only hatchlings in the surf or nesting females on the beach. I lived in hope.

I was especially glad to be heading in the right direction on 13 June, Day 74. It was the three-year anniversary since Dad had died, and so dinner began with my third and final bottle of fizz. Though not chilled on ice it was a sumptuous treat, glugged out of my plastic Little Miss Giggles cup. I sat back against my cabin hatch, looking out to the sunset, enjoying the view as I savoured every mouthful, swilling it into my cheeks to explore the novel sensation of fizzing bubbles. The contrast of the tangy alcohol with the salty water and energy drinks I normally drank was very welcome. If only I had brought more – one a fortnight would have been perfect. I used the day to look back at the last three years for our family and to remember Dad's legacy and spirit. The one thing I didn't regret was that he would never hurt again. There was no pain any more. That was definitely worth toasting: 'So today, as every day, I salute you and thank you, Pops. We're still here, we're still laughing and we shall always remember you.' And with that I sipped back the bubbly and watched the sunset fade and the stars stand out on parade. I had a sudden urge to holler to the waves, empowered by the thought that I was carving this line across a massive chunk of the world.

Dad would have loved an adventure out here on the waves, free and close to nature. I felt so alive and so peaceful that I wanted everyone to taste it and feel it. I wished I could photograph all these things, particularly the stars on nights when they were so bright they cast beams on the water. I wanted to take all these stories home to people on shore, and to those who I knew would never feel life like this again, perhaps too old or with too many ties, or for those who would not have the chance, for whatever reason. I wondered what it would be like to meet people again and tell them what it was like out at sea. What would they think? Would they understand? I shivered as a wave splashed me and I realised that I had fallen asleep on the deck. The sky and sea were black now and it was time for bed. As I turned to go in I saw the words of the poem I had been learning, taped to the hatch door. It was W. H. Davies' 'Leisure', the opening line of which reads, 'What is this life if, full of care, we have no time to stand and stare?' I pulled off the sheet and grinned – this was exactly my life at the moment. I said good night to the stars and headed inside, warmed by the slightly squiffy-round-the-edges glow of my fizz. It had been a good day.

CHAPTER 26

HALFWAY IS NOT DOWNHILL

'Do what you can, with what you have, where you are'
T. ROOSEVELT

At the halfway point I had laughed at the suggestion from some of my blog followers that this meant that it would all be downhill from there on. I knew that I had probably not seen the worst the ocean could conjure up by way of storms and contrary weather; I knew there was more energy out there than I could ever comprehend. Fuelled by Red Carpet Weather I might be allowed to pass through safely and at relative speed, or I might be locked in battle with currents and westerly winds for a long while to come. For sure, to be the other side of the halfway line was a confidence boost, but it had already taken me a good while longer than I had expected to reach it. High hopes, low expectations – that was my maxim.

Ric's weather predictions were rolling in as fast as waves on a stormy day – everything seemed unstable in this final part of the middle sector so I shifted my maxim from low expectations to no expectations. He promised that the third sector would be better, though wetter and wilder; I might make more progress but the conditions would be rather more challenging than the weather I had experienced up to now. I had to try and keep grounded.

I just plugged on, rowing as much as I could to maximise the opportunities offered by half-decent weather, and bouncing back into rowing mode after each front passed through, often followed by another. My track now looked like a tumbleweed's path, twirling and looping around itself towards its goal. Zooming out from my GPS the wiggles didn't look too important – I was still closer to Mauritius than I was to Australia and generally headed in the right direction. The zoomed-in version was rather more frustrating and had already led various blog followers to question how on earth I intended to reach my destination. One had petitioned me to call it a day, a while ago, not long after my birthday, on the grounds that I must be lonely and had surely already given the ocean a good go. She didn't know me, clearly. There was no way that I was coming off that ocean before time unless my leg had fallen off or my appendix had put in its notice. In my head and in my heart there was only one way to finish this journey, and I hadn't considered any other option. Besides, how she thought I might get to land without rowing was beyond me.

I wasn't at all lonely and I still had more in the tank. Even though I was desperately tired at times, and at others frustrated and low, there were still more positives on the balance sheet than negatives. And while I could make myself laugh and find good things about each day and about the journey so far and ahead, then I knew that my next stop was Mauritius. That belief was rock solid – the moment I thought otherwise would be the moment I cracked. It wouldn't happen. These were only the final thousand miles of a three-year journey. It reminded me of my first two years of grieving and the long and lonely nights and empty days that I had spent in tears, exhausting myself. At the time I hadn't seen a way out other than to keep on trucking just a little at a time, making myself tiny goals and always looking for things to make me laugh. This stretch of the ocean was just the same. That's how I knew I would make it. I would always get back to the task in hand, sometimes after refreshing myself with a hair wash or taking a look at some of the messages from home. When the weather was so unpredictable and circumstances were changing so rapidly, I found that I had to take control of the things that I had the power to change. Attitude was the sole thing that I had control of each day.

Unfortunately, my dreams were not so easily reined in and I found myself waking up on many nights in a cold sweat, sometimes crying and often in a very agitated state. They were scaring me and stopping me from sleeping, something I couldn't afford to happen. After a week or two of this I emailed my psychotherapist friend Briony to get her perspective. My relationship with her was a little bit like that with Ricardo – I trusted her, in some respects more so than myself, and so felt relieved when she told me that the dreams were probably a subconscious reflection of my changing and uncontrollable situation. I encouraged myself to believe that they were Briony's problems now that I had told her about them, and it seemed to do the trick. My dreams were still a bit weird and at times disturbing, but at least I could sleep again.

By Day 76, the weather was getting wetter and wilder. Bob was in and out of the water so frequently that I had a finely tuned deployment drill and was confident that I could get him out in two minutes. Retrieving him was always trickier. Even when I collapsed the main chute, it was torturous dragging it back through the water and onto the boat in anything more than a slightly choppy sea. This meant that when the wind changed direction, I often had to wait a few hours until the seas died down sufficiently for me to bring him back on board, even while moving in the right direction; it was very frustrating, when I knew that if I hauled him in we could whizz along at over two knots, even without rowing if the wind was blowing towards Mauritius. I laugh now at the image of me standing out on deck, completely naked but for my lifeline, braced against the rail at the far end of the deck, heaving at the lines as the boat surged with each wave. After hours cooped up in the cabin it was liberating to be outside in the air, usually damp with salt spray and spume. I considered myself lucky if I didn't get soaked in the first two minutes, but I always anticipated returning to my cabin cold and wet from the combination of wind and waves. Each time I heard the hiss of a racing wave, I braced harder and held on to the rail. Sometimes it was fine and I could carry on pulling at the line; at others I had to let go for fear of rope burn. I was just glad to have decent calluses across my palms or I would have ripped them red raw. Even once I had Bob on board the drama wasn't over. My final (and perhaps most dangerous) task was to pack the 60 metres of soggy rope back into the bag and fold away the chute itself, then secure it down in the forward cabin. It was physically demanding, especially when the boat was surfing down waves or being knocked by slammers. The danger came in being surrounded by all the different lines on the lurching deck; it was my greatest fear that we should capsize at this moment and I would be trapped in a tangled mess during a frightening roll. I am glad it never happened. Neither did my other fear come true – that of pulling up some weird toothy beast from the deep. Instead, I often pulled bits of blue slime and tentacles of jellyfish from the rope and once I noticed a small remora fish stuck to the float with his little sucking mouth. I'm not sure which one of us was more surprised to see the other as he jumped ship as soon as he saw me.

Ric calculated a further fifty-four days to arrival, marking 12 August as The Day and bringing the total crossing time to 132 days. I had prepared myself for anything between a further forty and sixty days, but it still made me rant a bit, if only because I knew I would run out of chocolate before the end. I had already tried rationing myself to one bar a day and had even declared a complete amnesty for a day. I lasted until lunchtime when I gobbled down two at once and declared that Cadbury had never tasted so good. Another concern was how much it would cost to keep the satellite phone running that long and whether or not I would be back in time for various additional dates on which I had already been booked in for talks, including one at the Southampton Boat Show. Thankfully, my sensible head stepped in to remind me that I would get there when I got there, in true Winnie-the-Pooh style of thinking. I had plenty of food in the stores to keep going for a few more months because I hadn't eaten most of my dehydrated stuff as it tasted so vile, although I was running out of vitamin tablets, having apparently left out a full tub of them. Still, I was sure that scurvy took longer than that to set in and Mum had suggested I could brush my teeth with salt if it came to it, of which I had plenty. All of my clothes had white tidelines and felt sticky with salt and I had a permanent crust of it all over me unless I washed or baby-wiped it away.

All of my rubbish was rinsed and folded up into big bags, which I stored away in my cabin. As the weeks wore into months the bags grew bigger, surprising me with the volume of rubbish I could produce from such a limited stock of supplies. I had taken great effort to remove all surplus packaging before leaving but I had still clocked up nearly 80 litres of rubbish after three months. To my annoyance, I had also lost a few bits overboard to the deep, including a drinks bottle, a plastic bag and a sponge. As far as possible I tried to log all of the litter I spotted at sea, so that groups like the Royal Society for the Protection of Birds could use the information in their work on the distribution of litter in the world's seas. It is a sad fact that there is often more plastic in a plankton haul than organic matter, and my journey had shown me that there is masses out on the waves. I clocked a toilet seat, mugs, bottles and bags, various bits of polystyrene and lots of UFOs – unidentified floating objects, throughout my voyage. The scariest fact of all is that most of the plastic is beneath the surface, bejillions of tiny pieces slowly eroding and releasing toxins into the water. To think of my favourite wildlife being packed full of these chemicals was sickening, and to watch a mighty albatross soar past me and imagine his insides being clogged up with tampon applicators, lighters and other rubbish was upsetting. But there was nothing I could do but to stow away all of my rubbish as carefully as possible and to row on.

CHAPTER 27

WATER, WATER, EVERYWHERE

'And I have asked to be
Where no storms come,
Where the green swell is in the havens dumb
And out of the swing of the sea'

G. M. HOPKINS

I went to sleep on Day 79 sure we were about to take a beating, feeling dwarfed by mountains of cloud ahead. The sound of bullets woke me in the night, high speed rounds of raindrops eating into my cabin roof, shouting at me to wake up – sleeping was now impossible. It was exciting, though, and I snuggled down into my sleeping bag in the dark, waiting for it to stop and wondering what it would be like outside. I wriggled down into the lumpy beanbag, shifting to find a comfortable position and tucked my feet under the control panel. I was cosy inside and if it weren't for the noise I would have slept like a baby.

By morning it hadn't eased and I hadn't slept more than a few snatches either. The rain thumped on and the wind howled wild. Outside was a mix of greys and white, roughed up by crashing waves. Every so often it would hammer harder somehow, turning the surface of the water to a sort of spiky velvet as the sky emptied itself into the sea. This was my very first monsoon.

Needless to say, my enthusiasm faded after an hour of rowing in it and the novelty wore off abruptly. I had been soaked within half a second of stepping outside and well believe that I risked drowning just by breathing. To put it in perspective, I collected just over a centimetre of water in my bucket in just twenty minutes of being out on deck and filled a litre within an hour – it was awesome to be in the midst of so much water. I had never seen such intense rainfall – not even in Wales. Battered by high winds, 4-metre seas and a whole lot of rain, I rowed all morning in my swimming mask, eyes stinging, soaked and exhausted. I thought I loved rainstorms, but this was different.

I knew that my skin wouldn't be enjoying the enforced sogginess either, and by the end of the first day my feet and hands were a pulpy mess. I didn't dare look at my bottom with a mirror to get a full view; I knew it would be disgusting and that the greenish bits would be worse than the day before. Instead I just sluiced the lot with iodine, painting it red.

The monsoon lasted a fantastic thirty-six hours, a full day and a half of cloud dump. I realised that my love of rain on boats wasn't unconditional and I called on the weather gods to stop, offering up many songs and poems to the deep. I don't think it worked particularly as I was knocked off my seat too many times to remember and had bruised ribs after a wave threw an oar at full speed into my chest and winded me. It was so rough that I even rowed with my helmet on for the first time in the trip after taking a few slams broadside. It really did feel like I was rowing on the edge of my limits, battling with my fatigue and the conditions, and resting as infrequently as I could manage to keep the cabin dry. Bob went out again overnight and I spent another long twelve hours waiting for the dawn, nervous round the edges and trying to shout down the frustrated imp. We were being blown south faster than we could make west.

Day 81 started with a surprise can of Sprite, which I had found tucked away in one of the hatches. I loved how even after this long at sea I could still find gems like this in the stowage; as I knocked back the tiny can of fizz, I wondered what else I might find. I was spending so much of my sleep time dreaming of roast beef and fresh fruit. In between the rain, which was now trying to decide whether or not it would continue its relentless thrashing, I rowed as hard as I could, tending to my backside with talc and zinc cream as often as possible. It had rubbed red raw in places and was squealy sore, the sort that makes you wince each time you move. As I took my last strokes of the day, coaxing my body to pull just one last time, a Sooty albatross cruised by for a hello, calming me instantly. I sat still on my seat and watched as he patrolled up and down the lines of waves, disappearing as quickly as he had arrived. It was ethereal and I felt like time had stopped for a moment. Still thinking about this wonderful fly-by, I put Bob out as the grey day turned greyer, and whistled in the night. Just as I was putting the finishing touches to the rig I noticed a black shape sliding through the water towards us.

I was scared, my heart fluttering. It was enormous. Dark with a little patch of white. A huge black back rolled up and over the surface with a triumphant 'Phhhrrrff!'. Whale it is then. It was more than a tad scary as he circled us at close range, swimming right over all of Bob's lines, giving me visions of entanglement. I breathed a sigh of relief when I saw the glossy back arch again a few metres away from us. I think there were three of them in all, the biggest easily 15 metres long, a mighty giant from the deep. I had to reach down into my throat and push my heart back into its normal place once I had watched them surface and sail off south, blowing as they went.

I was buzzing after that, no longer bothered that I was going in exactly the direction Ric had told me to avoid or that my toes looked like shrivelled chipolata sausages and my hands like crêpe paper. Three giant mammals, an albatross and a surprise can of Sprite had made it all good again even if I was back out with Bob.

I employed the services of my Olympic hat to keep me in good spirits during my latest cabin stint, remembering the energy of Buffy Williams, a Canadian Olympic rower who had coached us and rowed with us at St Hugh's. She had a brilliant kick-ass attitude and a commitment to excellence I had never seen before, the sort of coach you always want to please and hang off their every word. I idolised her; I think we all did and so to have this hat of hers was very special. The wind eventually swung to a more productive direction and I kept Buffy's hat on for the next couple of days as the seas grew and grew. They were the most frenetic I had ever seen. As I picked my way through waves and lumps, I focused on being an Olympian. I still had it on one evening when I did another interview with Radcliffe and Maconie on Radio 2. They asked how things were going and, as I braced myself against the cabin to stop myself from getting thrown about with the waves, I told them that it was going well.

'Is it scary?' they asked.

'It is right now,' I replied.

They asked if I had capsized and I said that no, I hadn't. I didn't expect to either, having seen *Dippers* knocked down many times before, but always bounce up without rolling. I said cheerio as they played my chosen track and turned off my light looking forward to making new ground to the west the following day.

The winds were already gusting up to 30 knots when I stepped on deck in my waterproofs just after dawn on Day 83. It was scary out there, wild and white, and I had the impression that it was getting bigger all the time; the sea was so frothy that it looked like it had been snowing. I picked up the oars and started rowing, nervous but relaxing into it once I started pulling. I gritted my teeth and dug in hard with each stroke, easing her forward across the waves. It wasn't the perfect direction for surfing but it was pretty good, and I clocked my first decent mileage in days.

At lunch I stopped for a proper rest and a decent sleep but was rudely awoken when a wave crashed into the boat and threw us over. Having headbutted the cabin wall, and been squashed by my food bag, I was relieved to work out that we had just broached very violently. I was shaken up but amazed that we hadn't gone over. I wanted to get outside and carry on rowing – inside was scary. At least out there I could see what was about to bosh me and might have a little chance of avoiding a knock-down.

All I thought about was where to put the next stroke; monster waves made for a clarity of thought I had not had for a few weeks. I had to concentrate. This was not the time to make a mistake; discipline was everything and might mean the difference between life and death. It really was that simple.

There would soon be just thirteen more degrees of longitude until Mauritius; for now I had a mission from Ric. He had given me a target of rowing as far as I possibly could in the next few days, telling me, 'If ever there was a time to kick ass and row twenty hours a day then this is it. Row like a beast possessed!' I was perplexed and a little annoyed. Did he think that I wasn't even trying? I felt inadequate because I knew that twenty hours was impossible. It was a massive effort to row for ten hours each day and sixteen before had been my absolute limit and knocked me out the next day. After some grumbling and fruity language, I decided to go for it and clock as many hours as I possibly could. The opportunity to make miles before rude weather arrived was not one to be missed. It would take all the food I could physically stuff down to sustain a campaign long into the night, so I started Day 84 with an energy drink and a chocolate bar, before cooking up a deep pot of steaming porridge with extra fruit. I made sure to make it thick so that it wouldn't blow off my spoon in the wind – it was still my favourite meal of the day and I didn't want to waste any.

It turned out to be one hell of a day, long and exhausting as I rowed well into the night with the stars. I plopped onto my beanbag at 1 a.m. after sixteen hours of rowing, pleased but a little narked to have missed the big two zero. Still, there were plenty more miles left to row. Too tired to get changed, I slept for a couple of hours in all my clothes. When I woke up in the early grey morning, I discovered that no part of my body wanted to move. My hands were tight and clawed. My back was stiff and sore. My bottom stung and burned. I felt like I had been run over by a lorry. So I turned over and floated back into my contented slumber.

I made it back onto the oars a few hours later, again eating and rowing, eating and rowing my way through the increasing waves. Sloppy peaks blasted from the south, threatening to push me north. This was exactly where Ric had told me not to go; he wanted me to row as close to west as I possibly could. So did I. So did everyone. But that would be well-nigh impossible in these seas. I wrote in my blog on Day 85:

> 'Just to reassure you that I am actually trying my darndest to head to Mauritius. I've just spent nine hours rowing across a crazy wind hoofing up from the south and even some from the SW.'

Thankfully a Sooty albatross had also flown in that day.

> 'Imagine that you are walking along a hedgerow, minding your own business, and turn to find a sparrow flying low range right over your head, about a wing's length away. Bit of a surprise, eh? Heart might skip a beat. Now imagine the same again but a little bit bigger. An albatross at wing length away, low flying, straight at your head by the time you spot him. I laughed at how I had been spooked by one of the most majestic and peaceful birds to fly these seas, and watched him soaring over the waves, gently and smoothly, graceful and with no effort. There was a master mariner.'

Frustration at my limited progress gave way to concern when I had a new note from Ric, which read, 'It's about to get very interesting.'

With his track record of cryptic messages, I was worried. After the last storm he had said that it would all be OK because 'Sarah, you're a very brave woman'. 'Interesting' scared me.

He promised that new wind would arrive from the east in a few hours but twelve hours later I was still waiting, watching miles slip by to the north. It was a long night in the cabin, listening to the roar of waves outside. Eventually I slept, albeit fitfully, and on Day 86 I woke up to the wildest sea I had seen yet. Fluffy clouds raced across the sky and foam was being whipped up into a fury. My blood pressure had been sky high for days but I think this topped it. I was scared about going outside, intimidated by the sounds I could already hear from where I lay on my beanbag. My stomach lurched each time we dropped off the top of a wave and I giggled nervously. I was tired and not quite awake but had to tease my brain into thinking clearly about what I was going to do.

In my head, there were only two options. Number one was to sit inside all day. That would be horrendous and probably hurt as I was confident of a knock-down. Number two was to go outside and have a little go at rowing. That would be horrendous and probably hurt as I was confident of a knock-down. It was a rock and a hard place, and I didn't like to make the call. But being outside did have one thing over being inside: at least I could see what was coming our way. Sometimes, running at your monsters isn't as scary as you first think, and I knew that rowing would feel like a positive move towards progress.

So I slipped into my damp trousers, pulled on my jacket and rootled about for my neck warmers and headbands. I tied Buffy's hat onto my jacket and pulled it as far onto my head as I could, willing myself to believe that I still had the power of an Olympian within me. Gulp. *Come on Sarah, just believe*. Next I clipped on my safety line, giving it an extra tug to check it was on correctly, before pasting my face with zinc. There was an element of foreboding about today's preparation ritual – I was not in the least bit excited about going outside, even though the cabin was now like a sauna. I reached for my sunglasses and seat pad and then peered out across the deck. It was lovely and sunny out there, on top of the waves at least. Water crashed overboard from time to time, occasionally filling the deck completely before draining slowly away. I knew that I would be drenched in an instant. My first task would be to empty the footwell. To do that I would need to get out on deck, clip on, close the door and shimmy to the forward cabin. The bilge pump was in there. It was always precarious when we were running in big seas as my back would be to the waves as I walked forward and reached inside for the pump; I wouldn't be able to see what was coming. Each time we dropped into a trough we fell into the shade and I felt cool for a moment. But this was no matter because I was soon sluiced when an incoming wave flooded the deck.

I looked at the footwell, the water level with the deck and rolling over the sides. I knew that it would be filled up immediately with a single wave dump but decided to empty it anyway. At least I would start the day with a clear rowing space. It was all about good admin, maintaining standards and all that.

Even though I hadn't been excited about it before, now I was out I was glad to be in the fresh air, busying myself with little tasks. Once I sat down to the oars I felt ever so slightly calmer, too. I was taking control of the boat and I found I could pick my way through the waves, as though tiptoeing around sleeping giants. That felt good.

Over and over I repeated out loud, 'Every stroke we take, takes us nearer and nearer; every stroke we take, takes us nearer to home.'

I had Buffy's hat on, so even though I was scared I was coping. I was learning the power of make believe, forcing myself to believe that everything would be OK. I just had to keep rowing, focussing on one stroke at a time. Just one little stroke. Again and again. It had got me this far so it would get me to the end, too. 'Come on Sarah, just one stroke. Keep it together now,' I kept telling myself.

After four hours I stopped rowing. I needed food and a rest, and I also needed to empty the footwell, which had been full since my third stroke of the morning. We had taken waves over the side regularly, and on a few occasions I had been hurled into the safety rails with a face full of salt. It hadn't been fun but I had made it to lunchtime and I was proud. We were doing it, *Dippers* and I. And we were even headed west, a real smile-maker.

I let out a squeal of laughter and shouted at the waves; I was soaked, cold and still nervous but I felt well and truly alive. I sang as I bent down to empty out the footwell, pumping hard. I was leaning forward with my shoulder on the bulkhead and had one leg on the side of the boat as I worked. Lunch and sleep were just around the corner.

CHAPTER 28

THE FULL 360

'No mercy, no power but its own controls it. Panting and snorting like a mad battle steed that has lost its rider; the masterless ocean overruns the globe'

HERMAN MELVILLE

I heard the wave rush at us and I felt it hit. Before when this had happened the boat might slam over on her side but we always jerked back to the upright in a moment. This time we went right over. We capsized and tumbled down the side of a massive wall of a wave.

I was terrified that I might hit my head and I hoped that I could hold my breath. Everything was white because of the foam, yet dark because I was under the water. It was also the loudest thing I had ever heard in my life. Time seemed to stop still and I felt like I was suspended in a waterfall. I suppose I was.

My lungs started to burn and I clamped my mouth shut, gritting my teeth. I hadn't had a chance to take a breath before the wave hit so I didn't know how long I would last.

I felt saltwater invading my body and rushing past me in all directions. My lungs burned on.

'Just hold on, Sarah. Just. Hold. On,' I told myself as we rolled on, unaware of which way up I was. There was nothing I could do but hold my breath and hope that air would arrive before death, that *Dippers* would roll round and that my lifeline hadn't detached. I was like a rag doll, passively rolling through the surf, not sure if I would see tomorrow.

I was resigned to my fate but equally determined to hold on as long as I could; I was not going to take a mouthful of water until my lungs imploded. They burned some more and I gritted my teeth even harder, grinding them together until I took the sweetest breath of my life.

We had rolled the whole way round and I broke the surface of the water as I came up from under the hull. I gulped lungfuls of air, coughing to clear the salt while I looked round to work out my next move, screaming hoarsely to nobody. Clinging to the grab line with both hands I kicked my legs to drive me up higher so I could climb back on the boat. I was still attached by my lifeline, so I still had a chance. But no matter how hard I kicked and pulled, I couldn't get up over the side deck. I cursed and sank back into the water to catch my breath, looking over my shoulder at the grey monsters still charging my way. The water around me was white and fizzing with bubbles. I tried sinking into the water and then pushing up on my arms to create some momentum to climb back in but again I failed.

I felt very isolated. No one could hear me scream and no one could help me back on board. 'Come on, Sarah,' I growled at myself, talking myself through the steps I needed to make. I noticed that my lifeline was caught around the metal gate which holds the oar in place and saw that in this tangled state the line wasn't long enough to let me back on board. Frustratingly, I couldn't reach it to untangle it either; I would need to undo the clip to climb back on board. Simple but scary and I would need to do it as quickly as possible. Having just seen my seat pad whipped away by the waves, never to be seen again, I knew I would have no chance if I got it wrong. I felt even smaller and even more alone.

The moment of unclipping was difficult – the line was pulled taut and my fingers fumbled with the safety clip. My other hand tightened around the grab line on the boat; I was literally holding on for my life. If we capsized again now only my hand would connect me, a sobering thought. I managed to scramble back on board under the safety rail on my third attempt, so excited to be alive. I wasn't out of danger; I needed to clip back on and check *Dippers* for damage. Once we were connected again, I let out a huge shriek, a combination of happiness and fear. I was half drowned, maybe, but I was well and truly alive. I patted *Dippers*' cabin and thanked her for looking after me; she had just given me my ticket to another day. Turning to face the waves again, I stood on my tiptoes, trying to spot any big ones rolling in from the south. They all looked big but as there were things to do I just resolved that if I was outside I would always be facing the waves.

Desperate for anything resembling human contact I did a piece to camera immediately, whimpering my way through the recording. My voice shook and I shivered as

I tried to maintain some sort of composure. Then I went about sorting the boat, assessing the damage and re-stowing strewn gear. Everything in the forward cabin was where it shouldn't have been and my own cabin looked like a field raided by elephants – a complete disaster zone. The thought of pumping out the footwell again didn't exactly fill me with excitement, but it had to be done. Standards again.

Thankfully, the damage list wasn't too bad. My wrist felt bruised and my toes felt sore, but I declared myself OK, albeit a bit shocked. When you are both medic and rower you sometimes have to force yourself into believing that all is rosy if there isn't time or scope to rest up. I would be OK. I had to be; there was no one else to row us home.

It did worry me that an oar had broken, the blade snapped in two, of which the outer portion now hung limply, attached only by threads of carbon. It looked repairable but for now I stowed it away and let it be, swapping it for one of the spares.

That said, I was nervous of going inside the cabin now. But I had a pre-scheduled radio interview with ABC Perth in Australia for lunchtime. I was worried that if I capsized inside it would be more painful than it had been outside, yet if I didn't answer the phone at the appointed time they would worry. And I was worrying enough people already.

So I took a deep breath and went for it, reaching for my helmet as soon as I had closed the hatch behind me. I don't think the interviewer quite realised the significance of the capsize until I talked him through how I had nearly drowned. Poor bloke, he seemed quite shaken by it. Next I made a call to Mum to let her know what had happened and left a voicemail for Ricardo telling him that, yes, it had been very interesting. No ham and cheese in my roll at lunch, just a whole lot of sea salt.

Even a couple of hours afterwards, my heart still boomed and I was concerned that I might go into shock. I decided that the best thing I could do to avoid this was to keep eating and rowing as much as I could. Comfortable inside the cabin after my interview, I was afraid of going out again. I had to rationalise it and tell myself to get back out on the oars. How the hell did I think I would row to Mauritius if I was too scared to go out on deck? The decision was made for me. And so onwards I rowed into the sunset, repeating my mantra out loud, 'Every stroke we take, takes us nearer and nearer; every stroke we take, takes us nearer to home.'

Every single stroke. Every single minute. Every single day. It was all in the right direction, even if it wasn't. Even if we had somersaulted, we had still chalked another line onto my wall chart and moved a day across to the other side of the balance sheet. That felt good.

Ric's response to my capsize made me chuckle. He said that I obviously needed refreshing. Refreshing? It had nearly drowned me! Still, we had survived sporting only minor war wounds. Importantly, Ric said that all was OK and so I believed him. He obviously felt that what didn't kill me made me stronger and that he wasn't too worried about what lay ahead. The crazy seas were the result of two mighty weather systems crashing into each other a few hundred miles beneath me, creating some very messy stuff (as if I hadn't noticed!). With fewer than 1,300 miles to run until Mauritius and news that the south-east winds were due again soon, I was buoyant, if a little more cautious than I had been the day before.

To make Mauritius in one piece, I knew that I would have to put today's episode aside. On the one hand I could use it as a confidence boost that both boat and rower were resilient and floated in all the right places, and on the other it reminded me just how powerful the ocean can be and how little we are in the face of it. Capsizing had been a cold, sharp slap in the face, a sort of wake-up call, and I had to fully expect that another might follow before I was safe and dry. I had to expect the unexpected.

Capsizing an ocean rowing boat must be like crashing a car, because on the morning of Day 87 I felt like I had been through a high-speed wash, battered and bruised and then dragged through a hedge backwards for dessert. My chest muscles and upper arms screamed before I had even thought about lifting them up; they were tired and weary after hauling myself back on board the day before. I was so exhausted that I went back to sleep until midday, trusting that the wind had shifted enough to blow us west without me feeling guilty. Overnight we had added another 16 juicy miles to the campaign and the same again lay between us and the much anticipated seventy degrees. I had been in the eighties for way too long now with all my toing and froing about the ocean and I was ready for the next run. Frankly, I was absolutely zonked and in need of a decent rest, mentally and physically.

My nutrition was suffering a bit with the all-too-bouncy weather – I hadn't cooked for a few days, instead living off chocolate, snacks and nibbles. As much as I didn't enjoy 99.9 per cent of the mush meals, I did enjoy the warmth and the savoury flavours. This section was proving to be the most challenging rowing of the journey, too, so the added energy and bulk would have been well received. Picking my way up and down mountains of confused surf beneath sunshine and squalls, I gritted my teeth as I pushed on. I had always been very alert and very cautious, but the rolling had cranked it up a gear – I now felt like a meerkat on sentry duty, always watching, listening and anticipating danger. There were a few moments where we took waves side on or broached on a downhill surf, but we managed to avoid a full capsize. Thank goodness – I was terrified of the same thing happening again, even though I knew that I could hold my breath and that she rolled very quickly. I had confidence in myself and in *Dippers*, but still the thought was there. I would hold my breath in anticipation of the slam each time a big one came or we lurched violently, often throwing back the oars and hurling myself over to the windward side to counteract the weight. Of course, if a wave wanted to roll us, we would roll – hurling or no. With a good few hundred thousand tonnes of water in a wave, my shrinking frame wouldn't add much ballast to the counterbalance. Still, instinct had me leap up from my seat like that every single time. Although I was tired, I was still full of fight.

The wild stuff was worse at night. I would lie in my cabin, legs and arms braced out against the walls, sweating in my helmet and imagining what *Dippers* must look like from above. It was a sobering thought; she would be a little cork in the surf. Gulp. A bit of fear was good; it helped keep me on my toes but I had learned to be rational about it and keep it in boxes I could handle. There was no room for panic attacks or freaking out. It all had to be maintained within sensible limits and I had learned some tactics along the way. I hugged my albatross Alberto every night as I went to sleep, and spent many hours thumbing a rose quartz crystal that Mum had given me. It was cool and smooth, exactly the right size for my hand. I don't believe in the powers some folks claim that crystals hold, but I found that the very action of rubbing it concentrated my mind and kept me calm. Mums can make things better even when they're not there in person; it's just one of those magic mum powers that they have, isn't it?

Despite the freaky bits, the wind did have some east in it for a while and allowed a decent couple of days progress before it veered to the south and brought with it some terrifying monsters. Rolling up from Antarctica, these waves had been gaining energy and growing in height for thousands of miles. The meeting of giants like this was always messy, the two wave sets mixing themselves into confusion and kicking up lumps and foam and general havoc.

The waves thrown up by the wild weather often meant that I was soaking within a second of stepping outside the door, my cabin was always full of wet clothes, which then meant (and I don't recommend that you imagine this) that Eau de Cabin wafted out whenever you opened the hatch, and threatened to choke you when inside for too long in one sitting. Talking of sitting, my bottom took a beating in the wet weather, and I played host to an array of raw and peaky saltwater boils and sores, pointed reminders from my behind that it was really ready for a rest and looking forward to the sunshine. It was like a small child repeatedly asking 'Are we nearly there yet?' all the way to the end of a car journey, annoying and painful, and well-nigh impossible to placate.

Soothing came in the form of sunny weather and an easing swell. After all the mad dropping off the backs of giants into the troughs below, the gentle swell made for a happier rower all round. I celebrated in my usual fashion by eating four days' rations of Mars bars in one sitting – absolutely delicious, even if it was a dangerous plunder of dwindling stocks. I washed my hair and made water, dancing in the luscious sunshine and singing the happiest of songs. I was glad that life could still be made gloriously rosy again by the simplest of pleasures. Hanging my clothes out to dry was brilliant for morale and the air quality in the cabin; and cooking food for the first time in a week felt like a novelty. Re-stowing my clutter and tidying away the rubbish was the final piece of the treat and made me feel like I was back on top of everything again. Everything apart from the water maker, which was leaking. The seal was obviously disintegrating but without being able to take the whole thing apart I hadn't been able to replace it, and so had innovated. Gaffa tape and petroleum jelly had saved the day and I now just topped it up, hoping that it would last until the other side.

Andy and Guy on board *Flying Ferkins* had recently overtaken me and were jostling with the other pair's boat for pole position. It was interesting to see the effect of competition on their morale, something I didn't have or need to be worried about. Having been behind the other boat, *Southern Cross*, for so long, the boys were now in contention for victory and became addicted to the thought. They had been through the crazy weather, just as I had, and were now putting in all the hours they could, just as I was. Unlike me, they were clean out of goodies by this stage, and I pitied them for it, albeit with a lot of bantering and teasing. It had long been a joke between us that they would chase me down and steal my chocolate supply. Having made friends with Andy and Guy, I wanted them to win their race now. Over the next few weeks I received regular updates from home about who had looped the loop, run south, pushed north or gone backwards or broken their toilet bucket. My blog followers joined theirs and vice versa, and they had their own little dialogues across cyberspace. Guy's mum and family even called in to visit my mum at home one day and they emailed each other often, supporting each other and swapping stories from the ocean. I still thought that it was harder for everyone at home; while I might be scared at times, tired and broken, at least I knew what was going on, understood it, and could deal with it. At home, all the trials and storms of the sea were left to their imaginations, helped or hindered by our emails and little snatches of phone conversation from time to time. My poor mum. I salute her, nonetheless, especially on those phone calls when she knew I was frightened or hurt, yet still managed to make me smile. I know that she did sometimes get twitchy about it all and stay up late worrying or wondering, but for the most part I think she was so used to me being away for long periods of time that it wasn't really any different from usual. I knew that she wanted me home now, however, and the more I wrote back with tales of heavy seas, the more she longed for that first hug.

I was surfing towards the '1,000 miles to go' sign and Ric was excited to point out that on my web track at home, Australia had disappeared off the page and Mauritius was creeping into view quite nicely. 'My little English rowing girl is coming home,' he signed off one day, promptly causing me to burst into tears. They were the proud, happy, sad, exhausted tears of one very content rower. I was excited about finishing, but I was already sad about the prospect of leaving my little bubble of ocean life to go back to shore.

Two whales popping by for a hello on Day 90 confirmed this feeling of being at home on the waves, and as I watched them slide beneath the boat and investigate, I knew that I would be back. It was bewitching to be so close to such huge and gentle creatures, wondering what they might do next, guessing at where they might have come from and where they were headed. A purple sunset made for a serene backdrop, and I leaned back on the hatch and smiled back the tears at how wonderful my world was after three months at sea. One quarter of a year, alone and rowing. I was still chuffed to note that I had managed three months at sea without a face-to-face slapping by a flying fish. While I loved the little fellas, I preferred to watch them sprinting over the waves from afar and was less keen on finding them splatted onto the deck of the boat. The learners lost a few in the aerial displays and I generally provided burial services to one or more each day. Lucky, then, for the little dude who leapt out of the water onto my lap, from where I swept him back over the side and onwards to safety and new life. Or perhaps the jaws of a bigger fish. It was all part of life and death on the high seas and after three months out there, I was getting the hang of it all.

So I signed out from June, and rowed on towards my first hundred days at sea, the final 1,000 miles to run. Tired, but still fighting. Scared, but still smiling.

CHAPTER 29

THE 100 CLUB

*'When alone and out in nature, time does not exist.
Nor does the future'*

THOR HEYERDAHL

Before the ocean I didn't count days; I don't think that many of us do, unless of course you're six years old and counting the sleeps until Christmas. After Dad died I counted weeks and then months in my bid to claw my way towards healing. I counted terms at school and university, but never had I been so fixated on days. At sea I chalked off each one with a marker pen on my cabin wall and scribbled mementoes of important days or sights. Day numbers were my reference. Not because I wanted to get them out of the way necessarily, but because I needed to know how much food I had as I progressed across the ocean and as a record. Mostly I had no idea whether it was Monday or Saturday – my days had quickly become one and the same and names had no relevance. But the numbers were important. They were badges of honour and checkpoints of the journey, and afterwards would be anecdotes in themselves.

Day 100 was a pinnacle I had thought about for a long while, and as I rowed closer and closer it rose up in the foreground, like the summit of a mountain coming in to view, teasing me and congratulating me in equal measure. To join The 100 Club was just as momentous as I had expected in all of my wondering and anticipating. I had set aside a bag of Minstrels for the occasion and had repeatedly battled with myself to save them; you know by now how useless I am at saving chocolate. Several of my blog followers knew also and promised me lots on my return. They understood that this was a big deal for me; saving chocolate just wasn't a done thing on board *Dippers*. The day turned out to be full of treats, some edible and others not.

I started the morning off with my usual breakfast and dose of rowing, before turning my attention to the Minstrels. I am proud to say that the blog inspired a global chocolate fest; Mum posted descriptions of Minstrels for foreign readers and even tracked down a website where you could order them for international delivery. As I sat reading my emails that morning, I ate the whole bag, by the handful, all in one sitting.

I also interviewed with BBC *East Midlands Today*, in a live session where Mum and Matthew were filmed at home. Staged and a bit stilted it might have been, as you can imagine, but it was great to touch base as always, and to pick Mum's brains about painkillers. After a tough week of rowing mostly with just my left arm and the rudder hard over (which slows the boat down), my back was not enjoying life. In fact, I was in agony and finding it difficult to row at all. I was debating whether or not to take painkillers to silence it. I decided not to – I didn't want to risk clouding my judgement.

The expedition website also received a hit of comments that day, a reminder that this was more than just my journey; this was a huge team effort. Without them, there would have been no growing total for Arthritis Care, now nearly £10,000, and I wouldn't have had the moral support I did. The messages meant a lot to me and often made me laugh. I knew I could rely on people to provide answers to questions or conundrums on all sorts of subjects. One chap from across the Atlantic, Barry, copied and pasted scores of poems for Mum to forward on for me to learn and another, Robert, had volunteered various brilliant and nerdy services to the website maintenance. This was pure, glowing kindness and it was becoming clear that there really wasn't a lot of room on the boat any more, for I was surrounded by so many souls across the planet, all living and breathing the adventure. It was a privilege to share and an honour to have them on board.

> Hello Sarah, I've been following your epic voyage across the high seas over the last 100 days. What an achievement. You really are amazing; so strong, so courageous, so determined. I often think of you and remember sitting together on the bow of *Silurian*. It was a beautiful Hebridean summer evening, glassy calm seas, porpoises for company and the overwhelming mountains of

Skye towering above, glowing pink as the sun set behind us. I knew there was nothing I could say or do to help the pain of losing your dad. But I knew that you would succeed in turning this bitter experience into something positive and full of energy. Thanks for taking us all with you. My warmest regards and respect, Laura.

One of my most supportive and interactive sponsors, Susie Hewson of Natracare, also put up a lovely note:

I bet there are few of us without a teardrop after Ricardo's amazing tribute to you, Sarah. What a truly wonderful memorial from a daughter to her father this challenge is. We have all sat in that boat with you emotionally over the journey thanks to your blogs and phone calls and I for one want to thank you for that opportunity. I look forward to the next instalments, Susie

And here is that very blog from Ric, written especially for the occasion. It made me cry and it made me smile, and here's why:

On my side of the world the voyage clock has just reached the almost surreal 100 day mark. Wow. I mean, seriously wow! What were you doing 100 days ago? What have you done since? How my times have you gone shopping, walked in the park or enjoyed a bike ride through town without a care in the world? How many miles have you driven or flown? Isn't it just great to put your feet up with the weekend paper, and just sit back and switch off for a while? Cup of tea anyone? Or a cool fresh orange juice from the fridge? Hmmm… delicious.

Bed perhaps instead; you've had a tough, long day. Maybe just catch a quick hot shower first though. You feel the endless supply of water caress your clean hair and skin as you unwind with your eyes closed, enjoying the easy therapy. You lean with one hand against the wall and exhale. The tapping sound of water falling off your tired shoulders adds to the moment and you simply go with it, relaxing every muscle of your body. You long for the warm, soft bed that awaits and dry off with a new towel, smiling at the flowery smell of clean linen. You feel as good as new. Well, almost. A few hours' sleep will fix that and you know it, too. As the bed embraces your shell, your soul becomes lighter and you let yourself fall into a deep, restoring sleep. Everything around you is still. Silence is a luxury you take for granted. Your day has come to an end now and you take only a few seconds to look within, perhaps in prayer, before you are absorbed into the magic world of dreams and free emotions. Hours of sleep await; safe, dry, comfortable. This is you; your life. Probably every day, including the past 100 days, whilst Sarah Outen was at sea. Rowing. Rowing. Rowing…

Sarah, my little English rowing girl, I am so incredibly proud of you, as are all your friends, family and global fans. You are reaching many with your beautiful life journey and marine adventure. You are a sea animal now, a real beast of the oceans just like I said you would be. I know you are not really counting the days any more. You haven't been for weeks and weeks. Time doesn't really matter where you are. It's all about progress, effort, survival, harmony. One stroke at a time. What a lesson; one that we will never forget.

You've had it tough girl. The weather was not kind to you for more days than you deserve. But this is the home run now. You are in the final weather sector of your voyage and this high pressure system is set to look after you until your proud bow pushes into the soft white sands of the paradise island. Thanks for your fantastic effort, especially in the last month. You have been consistent with your discipline and you have made such good progress, even with far from ideal weather. The last few days have been particularly hard. I don't know how you managed to keep that boat moving so close to west with the wind not quite right. But you did it and you are now in the right place to eat up some good miles.

I believe the next challenge will soon be in your

heart, as you begin to realise that this amazing blue world will be left behind. You will have to find a new strength to face the real world again and so many new and overwhelming emotions. We are all here for you, Sarah. Ready to welcome you home with a big loving hug.

See you soon, OK?

Your mate,
Ricardo

He had become an indispensable friend, helping me with more than just the weather across the ocean. He understood what it meant to me to be out there at one with the wild, making such an intense journey. He knew that part of me didn't want to come home and that stepping off *Dippers* would be the end of an era. I would miss him too; we were mates now and had crossed that ocean together.

We still had some way to go, however, and I knew that the final run in to Mauritius would be challenging, dangerous and probably more than a little bit scary. When it came to the route, Ric was my navigator and right-hand man. He had my life in his hands.

CHAPTER 30

KEEP IT TOGETHER

'When you have completed 95 per cent of the journey, you are only halfway there'

JAPANESE PROVERB

Pain is an interesting concept. It is universally experienced, but it is relative to each of us and, emotionally and physically, has the capacity to break us and ruin lives. I had seen it with Dad. Out on the ocean my experience of it took on a whole new meaning and I was hurting in ways that you can never understand until you have been there and forced your body into such physical endurance. My body didn't always want to do what I told it, and for weeks up to this point I had aches and pains and sores from top to toe. Even breathing hurt me now, having somehow strained the muscles in my chest while pulling Bob in a few days before. My back was a wasteland of solid knots, while my hands groaned constantly for rest and an ice bath, neither of which I could supply. Their default position was clawed and increasingly swollen, making rowing hugely uncomfortable at times. Once again, I saluted my Dad for his stoicism over all those years, coping with pain 24/7. Mine wasn't a patch on his and the other millions of arthritis sufferers around the world. So I just gritted my teeth and cracked on.

I had to – there were still 700 miles between Mauritius and me on the chart, and I was already 60 miles north of the island's latitude. With the prevailing wind a south-easterly, there was a very real worry that I might get blown too far north and not make it back down again. This would mean flying straight past Mauritius and into the open ocean to the north. It had happened to two previous solo crews to row the Indian, who had both gone too far north and were towed in to the island of Rodrigues a few hundred miles to the east of Mauritius. When Ric told me that he was worried about this happening to me, my heart sank at the thought of a bill and the collapse of my bank account. I whipped back an email immediately asking him if he was serious; I knew him well enough by now to know he sometimes said things for effect. Thankfully, this was one of those times, and he had been joking. While it had been a concern previously, he was now confident that if the weather did what he predicted and I was able to push south 20 miles in the next six days to make the most of the wind below me, then we could make it and row into that white sandy beach as planned.

We called it a beach but it was more of a jetty, apparently, with a bit of sand off to one side. Not that I had seen it or indeed any photographs of it. A recce trip to the island beforehand would have been way out of my budget. I had only my laminated chart of the island to peruse, which up until now had been stored under my beanbag, collecting crumbs. Often in storms, when I was bored or scared and in need of distraction, I had slipped it out to study my approach and dream of the finish, wondering at what point I might see my first bit of green and spot the faint shadow of land tickling the horizon. Now that there was more of the journey behind me than ahead, my tummy leaped in excited anticipation each time I thought of it. There was a bit of fear leaping in there, too, as Mauritius is surrounded by a coral reef, with limited options for getting through it. Ric and I had decided that the east coast would provide the best chance of me making it in under my own power. The west coast might be calmer, but to swing underneath the island and then row back into it would be tough and dangerous, and if I skirted up north then I risked missing the island completely by being blown out to sea and needing a tow. It was a tough call, but we decided that Mahébourg Bay on the east coat would be my best chance of a safe landing.

One of my regular email correspondents and advisers in all of this was Marcel, a Mauritian chap linked to the government, who had offered his services many months before, promising hospitality and support. Escort boats, welcoming parties, helicopters for the media, accommodation and all sorts – there wasn't anything he couldn't sort out and I was grateful and relieved to have his enthusiasm at our disposal.

I wasn't counting my chickens, though; the sea was still feisty. As if to remind me of this, a huge wind system blew up from the south and pushed me into the cabin for two days, as I deployed Bob to hold our ground while the waves grew and grew to monster heights, making rowing impossible and unsafe. The rest probably did my battered body some good, although I always found it frustrating not to be out rowing. Sally Kettle aptly commented that the only thing worse than rowing is not rowing and she was right. The second day of my incarceration was hot and stuffy as the sun had shone down all day and I had rarely been outside. My body ached after spending most of it braced across the cabin and my head throbbed after twenty-four hours wearing my helmet. I had dozed in and out of fitful sleep for hours and, as it grew dark I took it off, believing the seas were settling a little bit and telling myself that I didn't need it on anyway. Sleep came again and carried me off gently to somewhere much calmer. The next thing I knew, I was lying on the roof of the cabin, where I had been thrown with a thud a moment earlier. I yelped as we rested the wrong way up for a second and then again as I landed back on my bed, underneath a bag of food, my foot walloped by the mini-suitcase which housed all of my camera gear. The realisation that we had just rolled was perhaps even worse than the rolling itself and I whimpered out loud, shocked that it had happened, scared that it would happen again and suddenly feeling very tiny and insignificant, humbled by the might of the sea.

Still rubbing my head, I blogged: 'The past forty hours have reminded me of how far we have to go still. It's not the "home strait" until I see my landing spot on the jetty – it's just closer to Mauritius than it is to Australia.'

Time ticked by very slowly that night – my heart racing, my body shaking and my mind willing the wind to drop off and calm down.

The wind shifted on Day 103 to something more rowable, although the waves were still imposing. With the boat plunging into huge hills of water and waves crashing into her, it took me over an hour to heave Bob out of the water, pack him away and tidy *Dippers* again. The salt stung my sores as I worked and I sang and whooped, straining at the effort, keen to get back to the oars. After all, I had an island waiting for me.

We surfed on under a dazzling sky, me with the biggest smile I'd had on my face for a long time. It was wet and wild but heaps of fun; I felt deeply content, but with twinges of sadness around the edges at the thought of renouncing my sea creature habits and saying cheerio to my faithful Tweedles in the not too distant future. To think of life without *Dippers* was unthinkable; we were a team now and had kept each other safe through the highs and lows of the ocean. With debt to clear I knew I couldn't keep her, but I promised that I would find her another loving, singing and dancing fruit loop to take her adventuring again.

Most people probably think that one day on the ocean is indistinguishable from the next, but for me they weren't. My days became significant for various things: milestones, losses to the deep, phone calls home, albatross visits. The morning of Day 111, I remember clearly. I was up and rowing before the sun had even contemplated its arrival. Cloud fairies had been out decorating the sky with fleece the night before and so as the colours worked their magic across the fluffy weft and warp, I was treated to a gorgeous display above and below as the sea turned through shades of pink grapefruit, rose and orange. Radio 4 out-of-date podcasts from Melvyn Bragg and Sandi Toksvig alongside too-thick porridge under a burnished sky made for a very contented, if surreal, start to the morning.

With each day that passed I felt more and more like a runner striding out towards the bell which would signal the remaining loop of the track. For me, it was about to herald in the final 500 miles to the island. Ric prophesised a week of perfect, idyllic weather ahead, and I just hoped that he was right and there were no more funny tricks waiting to blow us off course. While I loved dear ole Bob, it would be nice if he stayed put until the end now. I felt I was well on the way to earning my first salty stripe of an ocean crossing and further complications wouldn't be missed too sorely. The same can be said for the Unchocolate Age – I knew it was coming but hoped that it wasn't going to happen too soon. From now on, any chocolate was a clinger-on from a doomed species, and would soon be condemned to memory as the stores were nearly empty.

I was sorry to note a dwindling of my fishycade as we approached the island. I was hopeful that the shallower waters and island topography would kick up some interesting wildlife as I still needed to see a shark and a turtle before I landed. They had been up in the top five of my wish list alongside the albatrosses and the whales since the start. Unlike the latter, they still had no tallies beside them.

I decided to surf under the stars again that night. Luminescent plankton swirled in the black water like a child with sparklers and the Milky Way stretched above in a curving white bow. I swear you could get tipsy on such a delicious, awesome sight.

In spite of the wiggles, wobbles and frustrations, I was madly in love with the ocean and all that it offered me. Apart from cargo ships, that is, because they represented my best chance of an early end to my journey and my life. During the voyage I had spent many a night up in the wee hours putting calls out on the VHF, urging captains not to squash me, and trying to figure out their direction and course. A few hundred miles out of Mauritius on Day 118, as I was doing my washing, I noticed a ship rising and falling across the horizon towards the open ocean. Excitement! It looked like we might be close enough to talk. Hoping for a friendly chat, I put out a couple of calls over the VHF and was very pleased when the captain replied to say that yes, he could see me and no, he wouldn't squash me. I told him that he was the first ship I had spoken to in months but as soon as I had finished my sentence he told me that he was en route to China and went silent, as if it was a completely normal thing to speak to lone women out at sea in small rowing boats. I was taken aback and inwardly disappointed – I had a whole stream of questions to fire at him and things to find out, and he had just cut off my only opportunity for a social chat. Nonetheless, I stared after him as he powered off to the east, grinning inanely at the radio chat with only my second ship since leaving Australia – the rest either hadn't heard me, hadn't seen me or couldn't be bothered.

With land just around the corner, the shipping traffic was increasing. So, too, were the birds – each morning a variety of terns would fly out to sea, off fishing for the day, before squawking home at sundown. Sadly, there was more litter about as well. I had seen at least one piece of litter for every day that I was at sea – it made me feel quite sick and sad to scale it up and imagine the enormity of the problem. People say we should call our world Planet Ocean, not Planet Earth, because it is 70 per cent water and only a smattering of land. But in the not too distant future, I reckon we might want to rethink and call it Planet Plastic, such is the volume of plastic in our oceans.

CHAPTER 31

THE FINAL COUNTDOWN

*'The port, well worth the cruise, is near;
and every wave is charmed'*

RALPH WALDO EMERSON

As the miles dwindled, my excitement levels rose and rose while the Tweedle count got lower and lower. For a few days I tried to coax the final solitary stripy follower with bits of food, until the morning of Day 118 I found that he, too, had deserted. Whether he had succumbed to the food chain or joined another caravan of fish or boat on some other journey I didn't know, though I was glad to have had his and the other Tweedles' company. It was another reminder that land was about to become a reality, and the Tweedles had obviously picked up on the signals and headed back out to sea.

There were now just 300 miles stood between Mauritius and me. This was great for my morale, until I found out that Mum could only arrive into Mauritius on 8 August at the earliest and so at my current rate would miss my arrival, estimated at 3 August. To put out to sea and worry her senseless for all those months, just to land up ashore before she had even left the UK was just not cricket, was it? I thought about deploying Bob to slow down and wait around a while, though thankfully I was talked out of it by Adrian and various others with ocean rowing experience – they all just wanted me in safe and sound now.

Not least Ric. At 250 miles to go, he was convinced that the wind was going to pick up and turbo me in, threatening to whisk me north of the island. 'Let's land this baby!' he wrote, the perfect catalyst for a quick cry on my part. I was swinging between excitement, satisfaction, surprise and sadness at the approaching finish, now just five to seven days away. One minute I would be laughing and the next I would be crying, but either way I was smiling inside, even if I couldn't quite comprehend all that I had come through and all that lay ahead. The distance and dimensions alone still baffled me.

With such a short distance left to row I had cut my rest and sleep time down to the bare minimum. That line from Kipling's poem 'If' about pushing your heart and nerve and sinew to serve their turn long after they are gone was a squeaty reality now. I was more worn out than I had ever been, muscles weary and sores stinging; I was running on adrenaline. Meanwhile I dreamed of roast beef and knew it wasn't too far away. The British Ambassador to Mauritius had already offered to cook me a meal of my choice when I arrived, and even said there was horseradish to be found from secret supplies.

Ric was still nervous about the final stage, with winds forecast to blow in and blast me to the very end. Under his instructions to 'defend my course' I dived south of west so as to drop beneath the island. I was so close but there was still a lot that could happen, which is why I was so keen that Ric should be in Mauritius to help with the landing. He had to be there. So I was gutted to take the phone call saying that he wouldn't be able to make it because the flights were too expensive at this late stage. My bank account had already been emptied by other costs so I couldn't help out either. We agreed it would be impossible. I returned dejectedly to my oars to vent some rage.

Then I had an idea. My blog followers loved Ricardo and had been so supportive up to now. I figured that it would be worth a shot, to ask if they might be willing to help fly him out to me. I posted a quick blog and went back to the oars. When I nipped inside to check the sat phone shortly after I saw a note from Adrian: 'JIM FROM MACTRA SPONSORED £300 FOR RICS FLIGHT.' Susie from Natracare was next, confirming her brilliance as my top sponsor, and my friend Geoff Holt came in too with a really generous gift as I knew he was saving towards his own big expedition. Within the hour we had cleared the sum we needed and even had a bit extra. Once again, I was dumbfounded and humbled by everyone's generosity; it was as much as I could do to stop myself from crying as I rang Ricardo back with the news. The contrast between that and our last call was massive; this time he squawked with delight. A day later he would be on the paradise island, welcomed into a beautiful luxury apartment on the Anahita resort that a friend of a friend had offered.

Through the help and support of all these wonderful folk from around the world, it was all coming together.

I was so relieved to read that Mum had finally managed to change her flights and was also really touched that my cousin Jeremy planned to be there, too. We had only really got to know each other after Dad died, and he and his wife George had become special friends and real supporters over the last two years. Guy and Andy would also be on the island as they had landed after their 102-day crossing, nipping in a day ahead of *Southern Cross*, elated to have won their race. With news of their landing and more than a touch of fried breakfast envy, I was getting more stoked with each stroke. Physically, I was getting more tired, pushing out fifteen to sixteen hours rowing a day as I skipped over the imaginary line into the fifties towards the final 100 miles to go, mind-boggled but ultra-focused.

On Day 123 a strong wind blew me further north than I had hoped during my snatched few hours of sleep. I was finding it tricky to hold course and so got back to the oars at 3 a.m. and pulled like a beast possessed under a starry sky while facing off some big waves. There were shooting stars everywhere, a big yellow moon and I think some 'land glow' too. By now I was increasingly focussed on the end, very aware that this was the last of those times to kick ass and row for twenty hours a day. 'Only a couple more days, so we can do it. Have to. You only get one shot.'

In fact, this was about to be the most stressful and challenging point in the whole expedition.

Ric's first blog from Mauritius read as follows, although I wouldn't see it until I landed:

Hello Everyone; exciting times, eh?

Just when it was looking easy and smooth, about a week ago I told Sarah that her last few days would be anything but romantic. She has built a unique relationship with the Ocean and with Nature, a love affair if you will, with all the emotions, fears and thrills of teenage love. Amazing highs and devastating lows.

As she approaches this Paradise Island she will be thinking of family, friends, crunchy lettuce and soapy bath tubs. These final eighty miles are, in my mind, the most stressful of all. I expect Sarah will be feeling the same. Arrivals can be tough on spirit as you go from solo mode to crowds and TV reporters.

Sarah, however, has Nature playing its last dose of intensity, as if saying her final goodbyes to one of its conquered children. As a solo sailor I have learned that I only make it because the ocean lets me through.

I am concerned about Sarah; I won't hide it. The wind was strong all night with huge heavy rain clouds, gusts of more knots of wind than we need right now. I haven't really slept since Thursday morning and I don't really think I can unplug until I see Sarah eating a salad, safely ashore. I can see the white sandy beach and the outer reef with big waves breaking. I know those waves will increase further in the next few hours. Nature is alive and putting on her best for the grand finale. But Sarah could do without it. She is not comfortable any more and fear is settling in again. I can tell by the tone of her messages. 'Crap' is her nice way of saying that she is frightened and her emails in the past 24 hours have contained a lot of 'crap'.

Once she closes in on the final ten miles to go, the waves will get bigger, steeper and closer together. This is what happens when a charging ocean swell goes from 4,500 metres depth to 200 metres in only a few miles.

For now all she can do is rest and row. It will take so much energy and commitment to row the right course. If she were to row with the elements she would be blown out to the open ocean again. She must row with the waves at an awkward angle, meaning that with these big seas her oars will miss the water enough times to hurt her body and her soul. She must give it her best in every swing anyway, as each time she does catch some water she must pull, and pull hard. That simple gesture, one after another, is what will bring her in.

Now would be a good time to light a candle and say a little prayer. I know many of you already have.

Ricardo

His prediction was right – out at sea I was being tested in some very steep seas. It was so draining that I even started hallucinating, imagining that I could hear people. Who they were or what they were up to, I don't know. That hadn't happened since the very early days so I knew I needed to get some more food and water in me and rest a tiny while inside the boat. I felt better after a little snooze and prepared to row again, pulling on my soggy waterproofs and pasting my face in another layer of suncream. As I looked through the door, the afternoon sun was still quite high in the sky, and I noticed a green shape surfing in the water ahead of us, and headed straight for us. Nervous but intrigued, I hopped out through the door, simultaneously clipping on and shutting the hatch behind me. The green shape grew bigger and bigger and darker and darker until it divided into two and turned into black whales, fins slicing the surface towards us and sliding under the hull at the very last moment. It was absolutely breathtaking and I screeched with joy; if ever there was a cure for hallucinations then two massive whales did the job perfectly. Once again I was left guessing as to whether it was a fin, a sei or a Bryde's whale as they had disappeared as quickly as they arrived. Nonetheless, it was a beautiful moment. That evening marked the start of the final countdown, the night before the big day, 3 August, with just 55 miles left to run. Mum and Matthew were due in that morning and I was set to follow a wee while afterwards.

Ric had been monitoring conditions from the shore and it didn't sound good. Wind had been hoofing in to the island hard and steady all day. The poor boy hadn't thought to bring any warm clothes with him and so had been enjoying the Mauritian winter from under the snuggle of a blanket while he discussed landing options with me. There were all sorts of questions and debates, but with a record mileage of 64 nauties in the last twenty-four hours, we decided that there was only one option: to row like I had never rowed before and head straight in. We were in the perfect position now, having lined up to approach from the south-east for the last two weeks. A coastguard boat had been arranged by Marcel to guide me in from a few miles out and the helicopter was on alert as well. Ric closed his final blog of the day promising full pictures and news of my arrival for the next evening. I couldn't quite believe it.

As I lay down on my beanbag late that night, I looked up at the stars through my hatch, jolting in and out of view as *Dippers* raced down waves. This was my last night on the ocean, my last sleep in *Dippers*. I was nervous about the finish, especially as Ric had promised me that it would be a dramatic landing through that reef entrance. With Mum and Matthew in the air, I was looking forward to those hugs, too. It was strange to think that I was only 60 miles from Ric, looking at the same stars and the same sea, yet feeling as isolated as I had ever done out there. For one final night I was alone and doing my thing. For one last day I would row. Then tomorrow it would all be over. I would be going to sleep in a real bed, soft and cosy. Clean. I liked that idea as my beanbag stank and was sticking to me. My tummy grumbled too – I had been hungry for weeks but it had got worse a few days before when my stove had finally broken, the burner succumbing to corrosion and resigning from service. Not wanting to brave cold rehydrated meals, I opted for cold porridge instead and had eaten nothing but this and a few little snack bars for the last two days. I was hungry for land food and wondered what I might have eaten for dinner by this time tomorrow. Giggling at the thought of it, I snuggled down to sleep for a few hours. It was going to take all I had to row this baby home.

CHAPTER 32

DON'T STOP ME NOW

'Courage is being scared to death, but saddling up anyway'

JOHN WAYNE

'Sailing and ocean rowing can be like a chess game. For weeks Sarah has played ahead and now she is about to win the game.' So wrote Ric on my blog on the morning of 3 August, Day 124.

I had been rowing since before dawn, singing my way through the waves and swinging between fear and deep nervous joy. The waves were getting steeper and there were a few moments when I thought we might capsize. Once *Dippers* broached as she raced down a wave, knocking me off the seat and pinning me to the deck with the oar. Had we gone over at that point I would have been in serious trouble, trapped under the water by the oar during the capsize melee. It didn't bear thinking about so I put it to one side and rowed on. The morning was misty and grey, so when I first spotted a faint whispery smudge on the horizon I couldn't quite believe that it could be Mauritius. I stood out on the length of my lifeline, craning for a better view as we ran up and over the waves. It was. It bloody was! 'LAND AHOOOOYYYYYY!' I screamed over and over again, jumping up and down and laughing and crying at the arrival of this new blur in the distance. I was 25 miles out and it was just after breakfast, at 8.40.

It was the first land that I had seen for months since the other side of this ocean and I was addicted to the view, keen to watch it emerge as we rowed closer. I winged off a message to Ric to tell him and one to my best friend Roostie, too, as I knew she would be at work busily doing nothing except watching for tracker updates. Ric had coordinated a live feed to the website meaning that he and a colleague in Portugal would update on everything as and when it happened. And it was happening fast. Adrian and Amy, my PR team in the UK, had arranged various interviews, and ITV wanted me to land in time for a lunchtime broadcast – but after two calls we decided that rowing and rowing alone was the priority now. With a window of just three hours of daylight to get in through one of the reef entrances, the narrowest of which was less than half a mile wide, I had no time to spare. To hit it in the dark just wasn't an option; I would be fish food.

Mum and Matt had landed and were preparing to come out to meet me on a boat in the early afternoon. I imagined what it might be like to see everyone again. What would they be wearing? Who would cry first? I kept turning round to scan the horizon for the first sighting and to absorb all the information from land as it became more defined in shape, colour and textures. Greys became greens and lumps turned into towns. When the sun came out and started bathing various peaks in shafts of bright light, it looked stunning, but somehow intimidating after all these months at sea. The volcanic peaks cut up into the air. Commuter planes en route to Rodrigues buzzed overhead from time to time, though I wasn't sure if they could see me. Container ships ploughed up and down the coast and I occasionally heard a crackle over the radio from them, but none directed at me. So I rowed on. Ric had asked me for an update on how I was feeling so he could relay it to the blog crowd. 'HUNGRY. EXCITED. TIRED. EMOTIONAL. SUPER HAPPY!'

All our estimates of timings had been made on the basis that I would cruise in at 3 knots or more with the following wind and seas, with the understanding that I would be escorted in by a coastguard boat, removing some of the difficulty from the navigation. Finding your way at these small coastal scales is tricky for any boat, but particularly for me in *Dippers*, rowing backwards and so low off the water – the steepening seas dwarfed us easily. Pointing and shooting at a tiny reef entrance was tricky as hell. So when I took a call from Ric that afternoon to say that they had arrived at Bois des Amourettes and discovered that the coastguard boat was just a glorified rubber dinghy and therefore not allowed outside the reef, there was serious concern all round. I was annoyed for a few minutes, angry at the situation, and then got to the task of rowing in by myself. Ric detailed the plan, which involved me rowing to the reef entrance where the boat would meet me. I had to drop south of one island and make sure I didn't hit another.

'How big are the waves where you are?' I asked.

'You'll be OK,' said Ric, 'One or two metres high, I reckon. It will be scary but you'll cope.'

Madman. The waves were much bigger where I was and I didn't think they were going to get smaller.

I put the phone down and swallowed back the tears; an answer like that meant that he was scared and didn't want to tell me. We knew each other well enough now to know what the other was thinking without even talking. And I knew that he would know that I knew.

In true British fashion I tried to put it to one side and carry on. I kept getting interrupted by the coastguard, however, calling me up on the radio to confirm my position. If I ignored them, I could row on in peace, but if then they would have no information on me; Ric didn't have Internet access with him so only had tracker reports messaged back from Portugal. The communications loop was already widening and ironically I felt more and more isolated, especially when I found out that the coastguard wouldn't let Ric use the VHF radios, so we had to do everything by phone.

Earlier that day, Ric had advised me to alter my course and point to the south of the reef entrance. Until then I had been aiming straight for the middle of it. I obeyed him and inched my way south. By now I could make out trees, cars and fields on the island – it was coming to life. The haze which I had spotted curtaining the length of the coast became whiter and whiter, until I realised it must be the fizz from the reef. At a few miles out the water suddenly changed colour and became a bright turquoise as the water went from ocean deep to coastal shallow. The waves changed too – becoming steeper, less rolling and closer together. I didn't feel comfortable any more and bordered on feeling out of control. Ric must have heard it in my voice when we spoke to confirm final details but was too kind to point it out. He advised me to get a throw line ready, so that if anything happened in the reef entrance then their boat could pick up the line and help me. I cut Bob's retrieval line and pick-up buoy and coiled it ready on deck, hoping we wouldn't have to use it.

Lining up with the compass and looking at the chart, I could see where I needed to be. Unfortunately, it involved rowing across the waves, always the most dangerous and difficult thing to do, especially as some of them were starting to curl and roll, curving into beautiful glassy crescent tops. Soon they would turn into breakers, crashing into the white curtain over the reef. All this slowed my progress considerably and meant that I was pushing further and further into the final hours of daylight, with everyone on shore waiting for my arrival and expecting me around 5 p.m. I was torn between rowing and ringing in to let them know my position, but decided that rowing was more critical so rowed on in, the reef now roaring behind me. *Dippers* was rising to the top of the waves and then falling into the troughs quite violently, sometimes broaching down the side of the turquoise hills, making me throw down the oars and hold on tight.

At 5.41 I tried ringing Ricardo. I was terrified and confused, not knowing what to do. I couldn't see any clear water – it was all white behind me and more waves were breaking. I felt a cold numbing fear that I was about to be obliterated. I had just enough time to shove the phone in the cabin and lock the door before throwing myself to the deck, holding on tight to the safety rails.

As I screamed, a bomb of a wave exploded over the boat and my world went white. But it was dark somehow, beneath the water, it was loud and I could taste salt everywhere. I was a rag doll, somersaulting through the surf which was now rushing us along the reef, growing louder and louder. And then I breathed a sweet breath – we must have come back around. I had floated off *Dippers* on my line and was surrounded by fizzing water while the wave receded. I looked round and saw no one and nothing but surf. I screamed again, and even I struggled to hear it over the sound of crashing waves. *Dippers* tilted over to one side with the water on deck but I scrambled on board, heaving myself through the safety rails. An oar was broken and the throw line was tangled, but there was no time to do anything but hold on; another wave was on its way. I knew that the reef must only be metres below now and with it certain annihilation.

As we rolled through the next wave and my lungs burned some more, I thought of the irony, cruel as it was, that having survived the open ocean for all those thousands of miles, now I was about to die. What made it even worse was that my family was right there, too. I didn't know if they could see it and I didn't know if that was good or bad. There was nothing I could do anyway. Despite the lack of air and the fact I was about to die, it was strangely peaceful beneath the water. When there is nothing you can do but hold your breath, time slows right down to a standstill. It must have looked like a killer whale boshing a seal pup – you know the seal pup doesn't stand a chance. I think we surfed upside down again before finally slowing in another patch of fizzing water, while the wave tracked back out to sea. My foot stung as though it had been cut and I spluttered to catch my breath. The water was so shallow now that I knew that with the next roll we would be mullered; boats and reefs do not mix. Having scrambled aboard once more and seeing the next wave thunder towards me, I knew I had to be inside. This is where I would die – at least in there, there was more chance of finding my body. I whipped open the handles on the hatch and undid my line, leaping in as fast as I could. I wasn't fast enough and as I sat down to close the door, the wave roared into us, white water pouring in through the door. I yelled as I tried to close it, my voice filling the tiny cabin, but still being drowned out by the raging water. We rolled and I hit my head before *Dippers* was rushed forward at speed, lurching left and right on her side. It went quiet as the wave went back to sea and I braced myself across the cabin for another hit. It came and we were forced forwards again, this time the sound of the hull ripping across the reef filling me with terror. At any moment I expected to see reef and rock coming through the cabin. Luckily it didn't; or at least I couldn't see it. Everything went quiet as we came to a halt. There was water and stuff everywhere; it looked like chaos and it was. But peering out through the back hatch I saw that we were now grounded on the reef but far away enough from the surf to be safe. Out of the front hatch I could see clear water. It was dusk and I was late – everyone on shore would be worried. I still didn't know if they had seen me.

I put out a Mayday call on the VHF and turned up the volume to listen for an answer. None came and I was left with the crackling squelch ringing in my ears. I cursed the coastguard for their silence – having pestered me all day, where the hell were they now that I needed them? Nowhere. I rummaged about through the mess and found my satellite phone in a pool of water. While it was splash proof I didn't think it was pool-of-water proof. And I was right; it didn't even switch on. I couldn't even find the spare one – the hatches were in complete disarray after the rolling, everything in the wrong place. Next, I reached for the EPIRB – a nifty satellite transponder 'only to be used in situations of grave and imminent danger'. Well if this wasn't imminently bloody dangerous then I didn't know what was. So I pulled the pin and put it to one side, flashing and beeping. Falmouth Coastguard back in the UK would pick up my signal sooner or later and coordinate a rescue. Finally, someone knew that I needed a hand out of this.

There was only one thing left for me to do, and that was to let Ric know where I was and that I was alive and in need of some help. I had to put up a fireworks display of flares. I remember it being exciting when we did this in training. Now it was anything but; for the first time in my voyage I felt truly lonely. It was after half past six and almost black with night as I ripped off the cap and pulled the cord of the first one, shooting a burning red parachute up into the air, filling the sky above me with glowing trails. I willed it to burn on, looking down at the water to protect my eyes and noticing various fish going about their business on the reef as though nothing had happened. I guess it hadn't for them. Everything went black again as the flare burned out and grey swirls of smoke drifted downwind towards the lights sparkling on shore. Surely someone must have seen it – it seemed like a mini atom bomb to me. My eyes were fixed in the direction of the island, where I knew everyone was waiting, no doubt also worried sick. I hollered with glee when I saw three white flashes, followed by another three. In maritime code this means 'Help is on its way'. I was being rescued! Wahooooo! Then came a crushing low with the realisation that it might have been simply a branch swinging in front of a street light and maybe there was no rescue coming. Maybe I would be all alone out there all night.

I had already dismissed the daft idea of swimming over the reef and ashore – at least *Dippers* and I were bigger together and therefore easier to spot, even if we were only a mile out. I thought about floating her off the reef and paddling her out. To do this I would need to release the rudder, which I was sure was now digging into the reef. I clipped on my safety line and put my knife in my teeth so that I could climb over the back cabin to reach the rudder. Hanging at arm's length above the water, gripping with my toes, I couldn't actually reach the rudder so had to undo my safety line to wriggle forward. I was relieved to see that the rudder was floating, just held by its steering lines, which I sawed through with my knife before manoeuvring back onto the deck. I was amazed that the rudder was barely scratched, with only a few broken fittings; Jamie was one maestro boat builder and our reef meeting had proved it.

After trying and failing to float her off the reef by pushing and punting with my oar, I realised these were not viable options as she had sunk into the coral enough to make it impossible. I put up another flare and a smoke signal, then set about making the boat as safe as I could and preparing for a rescue.

Next came dry clothes and more lights – I needed to keep warm and make *Dippers* look like a Christmas tree, which I did with those funky snapping glow sticks and a strobe light attached to my broken oar, hoisted as high as I could get it. Then I filled my big dry bag with all my precious things as I figured I would only be lifted out by chopper and would therefore have to leave *Dippers* behind. As I stepped back out onto the deck dragging my huge bag after me, I spotted a helicopter flying out of the airport, its search light down on the water. Someone was coming to rescue me. Relief and joy surged through me as I swung the oar in the air, strobe light flashing so that they could see me. The ordeal would soon be over.

CHAPTER 33

MUM, I JUST ROWED FROM AUSTRALIA

'The journey is the reward'

CHINESE PROVERB

I could still hear the bee-like drone of the helicopter, and watched in disbelief as it flew in completely the opposite direction. Was another person being rescued in Mauritius tonight? I stood on deck waving the oar madly. Then I let off an air horn, the bone-rattling roar deafening me.

The chopper banked round and started towards me. I waved on and then screamed as he flew straight over the top of me, apparently oblivious, despite the fact we were the only illuminated thing in a sea of black. I held up a smoke flare and shone the beam of my head torch on the torrent of thick red smoke that bubbled out of the tube and floated downwind, towards shore. I hoped that the searchlight on the chopper would pick it up and follow it back to me, though with his recent performance I wasn't very hopeful, convinced that it was being flown by a twelve year-old.

It reached the shore and turned again to me, tracking low with its light down. This time there was no way that it could miss me and I put everything in to my waving, hoping he would see me. It hovered above me and jiggled left and right, fixing me in his tube of light. There was no answer when I tried asking him what he wanted me to do on the VHF, so I just stood with my arms outstretched in a V, the international 'Get me out of here now' sign. The hatch opened and I expected to see a smiling young rescuer appear and swing down to me on a winch. Instead, the winch swung down to me by itself, the rescue sling swinging in front of my face like a pendulum. I waited and waited, but it was clear that we hadn't done the same training. In mine, I had been distinctly told not to touch the winch until it had been in the water, or you will get a fully charged zap from the static electricity that builds on the wire. Goodness only knows what this maverick had been taught in his training, or indeed if he had ever done any.

With no other solution jumping out at me, I decided to carry on my V-shaped vigil and wait. Thankfully, I didn't have to wait long because I noticed some shadows and noises with a light moving towards me from a few hundred metres away, coming at me from across the reef. Blinded somewhat, I couldn't make out who they were until I was hugged from behind by a Mauritian who, after kissing me, explained that he was Yan and that I wasn't to worry about a thing. I was already whimpering and apologising for causing so much hassle, a barrage of questions streaming out. I was interrupted by another hugger from behind and felt the prickles of Ric's stubble on my face; he gripped me tightly, also telling me not to worry and asking me if I was OK. I pulled back from him and asked if it counted, if the row was official after my reef landing.

His smile widened into a huge grin as he laughed. 'Of course it does. You said you would hit Mauritius, and you did!'

With Ric and a few other local guys, we heaved and pulled *Dippers* off the reef, waving the chopper back to base once we had her floating. It was just a little way to their boat on the clear water side and then another short tow to the pontoon where Mum and Matt were waiting. I was lifted up into their boat and hugged from all sides by Mauritians who spoke very fast French which I didn't understand – but their smiles said it all. As I shivered on deck under a towel, Ric handed me bits of food and water, the first I had touched in hours. On the one hand I could relax, but internally I had fireworks going off and my heart was charging along to a rapid beat, singing and dancing and screaming alternately as I struggled to comprehend everything that had happened and was about to happen. We rang everyone to say that I was safe and on my way in, and then Ric turned to me and asked what had happened. He fell silent as I told him and then apologised for having made me change my course. I assured him that I didn't blame anyone but myself. Shit happens. I should have insisted on knowing the name and details of the captain of the escort boat and confirming all details directly, rather than taking Marcel's word for it. At least then we could have looked for an alternative when it turned out to be wholly inadequate. I was just chuffed to have come out of it in one piece. Once again, I felt that alive was such a good thing to be.

Worried that the shore party might have gone home for tea, I had one last question for Ric, 'Are they still waiting for me?'

He grinned again. 'Of course they are, my little English rowing girl. There were about twenty people there when I left.'

My heart skipped a beat; twenty people was a crowd after all that time by myself and I was nervous. I hoped I wouldn't faint or do anything silly. So, bearing in mind I was already nervous about the thought of twenty people, imagine what I felt when we neared the jetty to see a crowd of about two hundred people waiting for me, all clapping and cheering and shouting. Someone held up a flare and lit the place up, to the sound of more cheering and clapping. I was half crying, half laughing and absolutely speechless, gripping the boat.

A microphone was pushed in front of my face briefly before I heard Mum's voice and turned to see her. Matt appeared and the three of us went in for one of the best hugs I had ever felt. He was the first to cry and then Mum as we gripped each other tightly. I kept reassuring them that I was OK and we didn't need to worry any more. I pulled out of it and asked her with a smile to guess what.

'What?' she said.

'I've just rowed from Australia!' I shrieked and went back in for another hug. I could feel the tension and angst melting away, our bodies relaxing into each other, acknowledging the journeys we had all made and the trials we had each faced with that ocean. I also liked to think that Dad was there, too, wrapping his arms around us.

I jumped back on to *Dippers* for one last goodbye, sorry to be leaving her even though I was glad to have arrived. I patted her bulkhead and turned off the electrics, and closed the hatch tight before being hauled up onto the pontoon by the arms hanging down towards me. My wobbly legs managed to stand without too much effort and various people hurled themselves at me for hugs or asking me to sign their arms or shake their hands. Guy's mum, Christina, was wrapped in a Union Jack and handed me a box of chocolates before giving me a huge hug. She had rowed that ocean too, just like my mum. Her boys from *Flying Ferkins* were there, as well as the *Southern Cross* lads, James and James, all with huge beards and shaggy hair. Looking round at them, it was crazy to think that we had all just rowed from Australia – but how different our journeys had been. Each had tested their respective rowers to their darkest depths and shown them some beautiful highs, and I suspected it would have changed each of us forever. We each of us had a mutual, deep respect – we were part of the club now.

Someone then held out a box of pizza and asked if I would like it. Of course I would! Who wouldn't after four months? I stepped forward and then fell backwards into the arms of those behind me, my land legs clearly still in the boat. When I did finally make it to the pizza, it was every bit as delicious as I had hoped, even if I did only manage one piece – my shrunken stomach and nerves prevented me doing much at all apart from grinning.

After a while of answering questions and signing bits of paper and various bits of people's bodies, I was helped to the car and land life beyond, my body aching with every step – not just with the effort of walking again, but with the pain of finishing the greatest journey of my life. Three years and over 4,000 miles in the log. As I turned my back on the ocean, I was finishing a story – one of the happiest and saddest and most challenging and rewarding of my life. I had been through the best of times and the worst of times, hurt and healed, and grown up. It had been an incredible journey and I was proud to have made it, grateful to have survived and humbled by the power and beauty of all that I had seen out there and all the wonderful warmth and support I had experienced from around the world, from my team and others. Without them it would have been a very different story and I wouldn't have made it; it had taught me that no woman (or rower) is an island, not even way out to sea in a boat by themselves.

In my time at sea I had tasted something so pure and refreshing, addictive and mind-bogglingly brilliant that I knew that one day, somewhere, I would go back for some more, in spite of the frustrations and fear and monotony. It is magic out there – like nothing else in the world. Although I didn't know where or how or when or who with, I just knew that I would.

CHAPTER 34

THE AFTERLIFE

'The adventure is over. Everything gets over, and nothing is ever enough. Except the part you carry with you'

E. L. KONIGSBURG

My first days on land were very surreal. Everything was a first. The first sleep in a proper bed. Taps. Cupboards. Rooms. Cold drinks. Cars. Money. Shops. Clean clothes. Choice.

I woke early on 4 August in the hotel after just a few hours of fitful sleep and I showered briefly, still keenly aware of saving water, while enjoying the sensation of warm water running over my tired body. Then I stood open mouthed at the wardrobe where Mum had laid out all my clothes, not quite knowing what to do. The array of clean, fresh clothes was a bit confusing and it took me a while to choose. I then slid on my flip-flops for the first time in four months, slipped out of the room and hobbled down the stairs as carefully as I could towards the beach to walk on the grass.

Walking is a bit of an overstatement – it definitely needed some work to pass for that, but one foot moved in front of the other and conveyed me forward with a vague semblance of an upright mammal – I must have looked a sight. Either very damaged or very drunk, I suppose. The wind swished through the palm leaves and was kicking up the sea into a field of white horses beyond the reef. It was lovely and I sat quietly in the morning sun, ruffling my fingers in the grass as I shuffled to find a comfortable position for the sores. I sat there with my legs outstretched, leaning on my elbows, soaking in the sight of the ocean from this side of the beach, my nose twitching at all the new smells and my eyes drinking up all the different colours. I breathed deep and relaxed into the space and the quiet – it felt like my very own piece of paradise. Breakfast was just as novel, both for me and for Mum. I wanted to try some of everything on offer and it seemed Mum couldn't stop smiling at me and photographing me with Matthew, who really just wanted to get on and have a good feed, like any young lad.

We drove to Ric's apartment along roads with sugar cane fields on either side, and I spent the rest of the day in phone calls to journalists, stretched out on a sofa. I enjoyed the interviews for the fact that I was speaking to more people than I had spoken to in the last four months, and I laughed each time they asked if I was OK to wait for a moment. Having just rowed the Indian, I was Queen of Waiting. The most common question was 'How does it feel to have broken all these world records?' I was the first woman and youngest person ever to solo the Indian, as well as the youngest woman to row solo across any ocean. My answer every time was that I was just so happy to be alive, that the records didn't really matter. Maybe one day they would, but mostly I was relieved to have survived. I felt like I had been through the mill, physically and emotionally bruised and a bit battered, so I knew that simply being alive would feel exhilarating for a while to come yet. I had some coral reef in my foot and it was starting to swell up into an ugly red mess, throbbing as the hours went on and causing my hobbly gait to become even more hobbly and ridiculous.

The following ten days in Mauritius provided many highs and many lows as my emotions freewheeled crazily. It was great seeing Matthew chilling out and enjoying himself, and likewise to see my cousin Jeremy again, who flew out for a few days. We were being hosted by a wonderful Mauritian man, Nicolas Vaudin, and his crew at the luxury resort of Anahita, who had offered their full services to us. Meanwhile I was running on overdrive, incapable of making much sense when I spoke (all at 100 miles an hour) and crying at the weirdest of moments. Some of the simplest tasks seemed to freak me out – partly because I was so used to living in my tiny 6-metre capsule and partly because I was so used to doing it alone. I found it hard to delegate and let other people take control. It was all very strange and I imagine not just for me either.

The evening I landed we had left *Dippers* down on the beach in Mahébourg, from where she had been towed round to the little coastguard depot just at the end of the bay. One afternoon, we all set out with a couple of the resort staff to go and collect her. I was eager to see her again and bring her home and sort her out; I had missed her. I wasn't quite prepared for the emotion it would stir up as we headed back out there. As our speedboat bounced over the waves I was stopped in my tracks by the sight and sound of the reef, breakers thundering into white surf. It chilled me and I shivered to think what we had been through. As our boat slowed through the shallows and into the little cove where *Dippers* was moored, I went silent and felt a lump in my throat, threatening to make me cry. Poor little *Dippers* looked a right state; the ensign cut, the light broken off and the oar hanging limply. Even from the outside, it was clear that we had run the gauntlet. Thoughts of what might have been flashed vivid and clear and everyone else stood quietly and watched me. I got out and walked towards the coastguards, standing on the bank smiling at me. I tried to smile back but the lump was really big by now and I couldn't see for tears in my eyes. I climbed on board my favourite friend reluctantly and stood still, silent and sorry and sad. The coastguards were adamant that I should open the doors and check that everything was in order, but I didn't want to; it would hurt too much. It felt like I was visiting a teammate in hospital after an accident and I was sorry that she looked so forlorn. I tried getting off the boat without looking but the coastguards insisted I check, so I opened the main cabin hatches. Both stank of stale water and were in complete disorder. My spent flare cases sat on my beanbag in my cabin alongside the EPIRB and I could see only empty spaces where my photos had been stuck to the wall – I had torn them down into my dry bag when I was waiting to be picked up.

After signing the release documents and posing for some photographs, we towed her back to base behind the speedboat. I burst into tears as I watched her planing up, a tiny speck bouncing along like a cork, the blue grey of the sea lying huge and imposing behind, now framed by a mantle of ominous rain cloud. Now I understood why everyone had worried – *Dippers* and I had been nothing on that ocean and seeing her from that angle had given me a whole new perspective.

Marcel's promise of organising officials to visit us didn't materialise, so Mum and I spent half a day chasing round Port Louis trying to sort out immigration requirements, waving bits of the local paper to get me through. It is amazing how officials change their tune when they think they are having their photo taken with a celebrity. Misguided souls, I was still the same old me. We had coffee with the British Ambassador, a chirpy chap with Mr Happy cufflinks, though unfortunately both of our schedules were too full to allow for *le rosbif*. I would have to wait until England for that.

Annoyingly, I had started to swell up and felt like I was on my way to resembling a puffer fish – something to do with my protein intake now I was back on land causing water retention. It may have had something to do with the coral in my foot, too, which I had scraped and scrubbed out rather ruthlessly on the first morning, although it was still inflamed. Besides that and a few other scratches, on the face of it I looked very healthy, tanned golden with a mop of silky sun-bleached hair. My bottom was sore for many weeks afterwards, though enjoyed the break from continual sogginess, as did my hands and feet, which had dried out to near normal within a few days. Apart from the aches and bruises I felt very healthy too, though it took three days for me to be able to walk in a straight line and it was a further two weeks before I walked without any pain.

Hugging Ric goodbye as we dropped him off at the airport in Mauritius was a big moment – he had been such an integral part of my life for the past four months that I knew life post-Ric would be strange. It was the same with the ocean – I was sad to be leaving and disappointed to have to leave Mauritius just at the point I was settling into something resembling a holiday mode, after twelve days on the island. However when we landed at Heathrow, I was delighted to be greeted by friends and family and an Arthritis Care contingent. My friends were dressed up in all sorts of interesting nautical outfits and came bearing goodies of champagne and cake and balloons. It was such a lovely surprise and I couldn't stop grinning – or eating the delicious cake.

After this initial joy, my emotional state took a while to settle. Around eight months, in fact. I threw myself straight back into the action with interviews, visits to friends, a few talks and the vague idea of book writing. My first day back in England was spent driving for six hours to collect Bonnie, our dog, followed by a train trip to London ready for the national BBC *Breakfast* the next morning, before coming back home and being whisked off to Nottingham for BBC *East Midlands Today*. I pretended to sleep all the way there and all the way back, so that I didn't have to answer the taxi driver's questions. All I had done since landing was answer questions and I just needed a little bit of peace and quiet. I was empty of energy and with my sleep patterns all askew and a huge list of things to do, I didn't feel I could relax, even though I wanted to. I was due down at the Southampton Boat Show a few days later, then up to Manchester for a show with Radcliffe and Maconie, after which I was scheduled to shoot straight out to Portugal to announce my entry in Ricardo's round-the-world yacht race. Yes, a round-the-world yacht race. I had said yes on a whim because it sounded fun, before realising a few days later that I had only said yes because it was Ricardo who had asked me. In reality, I knew that it wouldn't be a sensible move to jump straight into a project not of my own making and while I still wasn't sure where my life would take me. In a tearful phone call I told him that I had been mistaken – I wouldn't be in his race after all.

In terms of the charities, I was over the moon with the totals we pulled in after I returned home. Cheques and letters waited for me on the doormat at home, and through various other fundraisers and donations, the final total for the three-year project clocked a very satisfying £31,000 for my two supported charities – a third over my original target.

The contrast between my simple life at sea – where my big decisions of the day were limited to debates about the number of chocolate bars I should eat for breakfast and which pair of shorts was smelliest – and the frenetic life on land was huge. Things seemed so trivial in some ways but so confusing that I got freaked out easily by crowds and clutter and decisions. At home I cleared out bags of stuff I didn't think I needed any more and on my first trip to London a few days after landing I wanted to scream and run away. I escaped as often as I could to the fields behind our town with Bonnie for long walks, desperate to be outside again. After a while I learned to sleep properly, allowing me to at least start recharging my batteries and processing all that had been on the waves.

Soon after I returned home, I drove to Wales to visit my Taid. As I pulled up outside his little bungalow, I saw balloons hanging in the sunshine and a sign in the window proudly telling the world that his granddaughter was the first woman to row the Indian Ocean solo. My stomach was in knots and I told myself not to cry – this would be an emotional reunion. My Taid was one wide smile all day and when he hugged me I thought he would never let go – we were both so happy to see each other again. On the drive back I let the tears run free – a blend of happy, sad, nostalgic, relieved tears. Before I went to sea, I wasn't sure that he would be around to see me home, for he was frail and tired of life. Just days after that return visit, he had a major stroke and died. It felt as though he had waited to see me home and now, content that I was safe, had signed out from this world. At his funeral, I read 'Sea Fever' by John Masefield – one of our favourite poems that we had recited to each other during my row. The final line was particularly poignant as it asks for sweet and gentle sleep after a long and wearisome journey.

And what of the lovely *Dippers*? She went on to pastures new, after much love from Jamie and Emily, who refitted her and spruced her up for her new owner – a kindly seafarer from America who bought her for an ocean-rowing trip. It felt good to know she would soon be back to doing what she was made for.

I MUST GO DOWN TO THE SEAS AGAIN

'The sea, once it casts its spell, holds one
in its net of wonder forever'

JACQUES YVES COUSTEAU

My months of feeling like a hormonal teenager passed and I ploughed on with speaking events, which were growing in number by the day, dabbled in book writing until we found a publisher keen to take on my story, and planned another expedition.

That's right, another expedition. Even though I had vowed on the reef never to put my family through that sort of hell again, I still yearned for the ocean and for another adventure. It would be global and based on an idea I had started to cook while out at sea – a human-powered loop of the planet. I love maps and journeys across them and I thought that to trace an expedition right over the surface of the globe would be a fitting next step and one heck of an adventure.

I found that once I had started talking about the notion of it, people wanted to know all the details. So I was forced into announcing a date at a dinner at Windsor Castle in November 2009. I was speaking to a hall of diners at a fundraising event for the Duke of Edinburgh's Award and had been asked by HRH Prince Edward to tell the audience when I might be leaving. Put on the spot, I said 2011. Gulp. I was committed now. And so I conceived 'London2London: Via the World', a journey to loop the planet under my own power, rowing the Pacific and Atlantic Oceans, cycling across Europe, Asia and the USA and Canada, and kayaking all the bits in between, while telling stories and sharing the adventures on the way. For I had discovered that one of the best bits about adventuring is being able to involve as many people as possible in the journeys – especially youngsters.

So as I sit here at my desk in Autumn 2010, finishing off this book, I am firmly looking ahead. 'Why?' I hear you whisper, looking at me a little confusedly, remembering that I nearly died out on the Indian. To answer that, just remember how alive I felt, too.

I have given over a hundred talks and presentations since returning to shore to an audience as broad as the ocean. From boardrooms in Europe and seminars at some of the world's leading brands to classrooms of inner city schools, I have shared some of the tales and passed on some of the lessons I learned on my journey. I see it as a privilege and enjoy it as much as I did the ocean, just in a different way. My work with youngsters is my favourite and the most rewarding, particularly where I am working with children who, through no fault of their own, have had limited opportunity to explore and engage with the wider world. One school I have worked with on a few occasions is in Coventry, and many of the children haven't ever been outside of the city before, let alone seen the sea. So my message to them is that the world out there is theirs if they want it and are willing to work for it – whatever it is they want in life is within their reach if they believe it and strive for it. Others are rather more worldly wise and often make me smile with their ideas and comments. One girl sticks in my mind particularly. Aged about eight, she asked me if I signed autographs. Yes I could, and I worked my way around the thirty or so children in the classroom. I arrived at her desk and she asked if she could have three autographs. Surprised, I asked, 'Why three?' Straight-faced, she said, 'This one's for me; this one's for my brother; and this one's to sell on eBay!'

Priceless moments like this have confirmed my love of working with young people and each talk or day of workshops with schools drives me on to carry on, even if it means recounting ocean tales over and over. If it inspires just one person to make a change in their lives or set themselves a goal, then it is worth it. I receive so many letters from people telling me how they have given up smoking, started triathlons, confronted their suppressed grief or similar after hearing my story, and that is humbling, touching and motivating.

Therefore, it is my plan to make this next expedition a

shared adventure, one that is live with lots of online content and opportunities for others to get involved with questions, following and perhaps even joining me on the ride. I go out on adventures to feel alive and to find stories, to challenge myself and live in nature, to get away from the clutter and pressure of our man-made world and experience life in its rawest forms, where the boundaries between life and death and success and failure both terrify me and excite me and I can never be sure just how things will turn out. Whether it will satisfy my appetite for solo adventuring I cannot tell; people already ask me about my plans for afterwards and I laugh. I don't need to know yet. Does anyone know their plan for three years down the line and really believe it? I am confident that serendipity and hard work will lead me to the right course, whatever that may be. They usually do.

These journeys, both across the ocean and through grief, taught me a lot of things – namely that to survive anything you have to believe good times will come again, for nothing lasts forever. When you're blue there is always an albatross of some sort to make you smile, you just have to keep looking and focus on the good bits. The ocean taught me that fear is healthy and that if you let go of all else in the storms, then tenacity is everything – we never get anywhere by giving up. My row also crystallised the need to seize every opportunity by the scruff of its neck and shake out all the great things, chasing dreams and making them happen – life is too short not to.

Most of all, perhaps, these journeys have taught me about courage – everyday courage. A child recently asked me how brave I thought I was before I rowed the ocean. I thought about it and said that I didn't really know, but that I had learned we are all much braver than we think we are. At my talks, when I ask the audience the question 'Who thinks they are brave?', only young children put their hands up and above about eleven years old no one does. If I ask the same audience the question 'Who has been scared before and had to do something anyway?' then most people put their hands up. Why is this? Where does the bravery go? The answer is nowhere – we just somehow don't believe it. Without belief, then we go nowhere; with it, we can go anywhere.

I pledged to solo the Indian at a time in my life when I didn't feel at all brave. I was broken, empty and lost. But I made it. Just like my dad's battles with arthritis, the ocean had taught me that we win by having the balls to keep going and the courage to get up each morning and have another go, even after warm-up laps, capsizes, boshings and bruises. Seeing the map of the world with my wiggly route traced across it, I have seen that anything is possible, that the adventures are more than worth the risk and that the reward is all in the journey.

ACKNOWLEDGEMENTS

'I can no other answer make, but thanks, and thanks'

WILLIAM SHAKESPEARE

Writing this book has been as much of a challenge as rowing the ocean, with some exciting highs, frustrating lows and everything in between. Writing my thank yous now is even harder – there are so many wonderful people who have helped me on all these journeys – at home and abroad, family, friends, sponsors, followers, welcomers, strangers, and my team et al, et al, et al.

There are a lot of et als who I cannot mention for lack of space – but please know that your efforts, your support, your sponsorship, your kindness, your wisdom, your beers or breakfasts, your boat or your hugs – or whatever it is that you did for me, the project, the charity, my family and so on, are all gratefully felt.

Mum: I apologise for worrying you but thank you forever for your unwavering support, happy socks, porridge packing, transcribing, banking and baking – everything and all that you have ever done and do for me.

Michael & Matthew: I might not always say it, but I appreciate your support, banter and belief and I love you both to bits. Thank you.

Cousin J & George: I am so glad you wrote that letter. Thanks for believing in me, for letting me stay, for the gin, for the music, for Mauritius.

Uncle David: Thank you for understanding.

Aunty Joyce: Thank you always, and for helping Taid share the journey.

Sara: You are one in a million. So grateful for all you do for me and happy to call you my friend.

Jamie & Emily: Proud to be a Global boatie – there is no one else I would rather have build my boats. Cordial beverage?

Roostie: (Forever chuffed you didn't choose pharmaceuticology), Jonesy, BPC, Siena, Em, Lou, Ras, Vix, Spickett, Rosie, Anna, Flick, Amy, Tova, Nicole, Hibbert – before, during, after, forever – you're all bloody brilliant and have helped me to get across that ocean in ways that only mates can.

Spal: What a journey. Thank you for standing by.

Jimbo C: Super kind, super appreciated.

ACKNOWLEDGEMENTS

Dave Cornthwaite: allsorts and everything. Here's to more adventures.

Adrian Bell, Amy & Laura at Whisper for all your efforts on the PR front.

Lumpy Lemon for all things web and design.

Ric: An ocean of thanks. What an adventure. Proud to be a Sea Ani.

Roz Savage: Thanks for the chat, the advice, the gin.

Sally: My first ocean rower – thanks for everything – advice, support, banter.

Michael Morpurgo: Here's to Kitty IV and the albatrosses. Thank you for everything.

Richard Dawkins: May the Force be with you ☺

Ellen: Thank you for the foreword and inspiring me all those years ago, now and into the future. Massive respect.

Susie Hewson: You are one in a million. Proud to be a SISTER.

Geoffers: For jumping in and helping out, the log book, the summer of '07.

Jim from MactraMarine: for jumping in and helping out.

Anj Jowitt: Long live Rad & Mac! You're a star.

Expert Geoff, Jamie Dunross & Janet, Clem TMWC, Sally, Margot and the mice, Hilary & Patrick, Roger & Caroline Winwood, Craig Rourke, the Commodore of the Royal Perth Yacht Club, Rob, Norman, the boys of Hale, the guys of Fremantle Sea Rescue, Lina & Gerard: Grateful thanks for everything down under. See you sometime.

Nicholas Vaudin and your wonderful team at Anahitas; René Soobaroyen for the photos; Marcel; John Murton. One day I'll come back.

Anita & Lars, Stuart & Elaine & the boys, Tricia & Winston, Tim & Kitty, Mr & Mrs Benge, Julia Howes, Andy & Guy, Xtina & Nigel, Tom & Correne from Exweb, Ian Clover, Libby, Mel Dulling, Richard Butchins, Briony Nicholls for the brain training and support, Phil Morrison, Pete Litton, Barry for the poems, Robert for the podcasts, the staff and girls of Stamford High School and staff and children of Stamford Junior School; The Sands in Exmouth; The Hudsons in the North; The Carters in the North; Sarah Teale; Radcliffe & Maconie; Tatyana and Kenneth of ORS; Brian Tustain; Sam Hale; Adrian Moss; Mrs S and your stories; Peter Walker; Termec; George Butcombe; Anita Corbin; Nigel Millard; Jude Edginton; Jim Shannon; David Yiend; Bob Caren; Ashika & Sam; Mike Mason; Sue Jackson; Sarah Black & the Green Blue; the RSPB; Arthritis Care, the Arthritis Research Campaign; Mark Beaumont; Rebecca Stephens, Christine Foley; Tony Hanley, Tim & Sheila Haldane, Jamie Combs.

ACKNOWLEDGEMENTS

Sponsors: Natracare, Anglian Water staff, Buff, Brian Tustain, OzSale Jamie Jackson, Cactus, AB Agri, Biojoule, Gill, Buff, Aquapac, Whisper, Advance Performance, Greens Café, The Whipper Inn Hotel, National Boat Shows, Marine Track, Natural Balance Foods, Dave Widdicombe Training, Dr Briony Nicolls, Precision Stitching, Urban Wholefoods, B Well, Vinnie's signs, GreenPeople, Berghaus, Glanford, Titan Fire, Rutland Worldwide Freight, Maersk, Starlift, Sea anchors Australia, Kelvin Hughes, Walmsley Chartered Surveyors, gp3, Roffe Swayne, Hay Hampers, Force4, Jimmy Green Marine, Anahitas Mauritius, Fitness Fanatics, AB SportsMassage.

All the sponsors of miles, donors to the charity and anyone who followed the journey and wished me well.

Peter Buckman: You were right. Trust your instinct.

Stewart Ferris: I am glad you kept pestering me to carry on writing.

My editor, Jen Barclay: I'm glad you came to the Pecha Kucha. I envy your tenacity in guiding me through the bookish waves. Fancy another?!

Thanks to everyone at Summersdale for their hard work, patience and encouragement in making this book a reality.

Charity: If you would like to find out more about arthritis and the charities I raised money for, then please see www.arthritiscare.org.uk and www.arthritisresearchcampaign.org.uk.

I mentioned albatrosses a few times in my book. If you ever get a chance to visit albie territories, then take it – these birds are beautiful and, sadly, threatened. Check out the work of my friends at the Royal Society for the Protection of Birds www.rspb.org.uk for more information on the threats and the solutions.

Ocean Rowing: If you are interested in rowing oceans see the Ocean Rowing Society at www.oceanrowing.com or the Association of Ocean Rowers at www.oceanrowers.com.

FELICITY ASTON

CALL OF THE
WHITE

TAKING THE WORLD TO THE SOUTH POLE

EIGHT WOMEN
ONE UNIQUE EXPEDITION

CALL OF THE WHITE

Felicity Aston

ISBN: 978 1 84953 134 4   Paperback   £8.99

COULD YOU SKI TO THE SOUTH POLE?

That was the challenge that British adventurer Felicity Aston put to women from around the Commonwealth, as she set out to create the most international all-female expedition ever to the Pole. The team would not be experienced explorers but 'ordinary' women who wanted to inspire others to follow their dreams or make a change for the better in their lives. She received more than 800 applications. 'What is skiing?' asked someone in Ghana.

At the close of 2009, Felicity led a team from places as diverse as Jamaica, India, Singapore and Cyprus on one of the toughest journeys on the planet. Eighty-mile-an-hour winds ripped through base camp and deadly crevasses cracked beneath their feet. But along the way they also shared beliefs, ideas, philosophies – and laughter.

Have you enjoyed this book?
If so, why not write a review
on your favourite website?

Thanks very much for buying
this Summersdale book.

www.summersdale.com